D0903108

IMAGES OF LAW

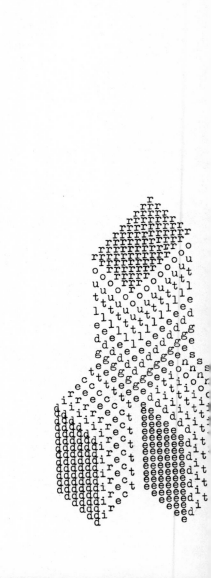

IMAGES OF LAW

ZENON BANKOWSKI
Department of Public Law
University of Edinburgh

and

GEOFF MUNGHAM
Department of Sociology
University College, Cardiff

PB 406

/ |

ROUTLEDGE DIRECT EDITIONS

ROUTLEDGE & KEGAN PAUL
London, Henley and Boston

First published in 1976
by Routledge & Kegan Paul Ltd
39 Store Street,
London WC1E 7DD,
Broadway House,
Newtown Road,
Henley-on-Thames,
Oxon RG9 1EN and
9 Park Street,
Boston, Mass. 02108, USA
Reprinted in 1977
Printed in Great Britain
by Unwin Brothers Limited,
The Gresham Press, Old Woking, Surrey
A member of the Staples Printing Group
© Zenon Bankowski and Geoff Mungham 1976

ISBN 0 7100 8339 4

6/17/80 *Becker & Taylor* 9·95

To our parents:
Zbigniew and Danuta Bankowski
Tom and Marie Mungham

CONTENTS

ACKNOWLEDGMENTS

In producing this book, we have received help from various friends and colleagues and here, though we cannot name them all, we would like to acknowledge some of them.

Our main debt is to Phil Thomas. He was responsible for the collection and collation of the interview material used in chapter 3 - part of a larger study at present being undertaken by him and one of the authors on duty solicitor schemes. We also thank him for his collaboration and help with the rest of the book and for his support during the writing of it.

Second, we acknowledge the help, given in various ways, of the following: Maggie Bluck; Colin Campbell; Kit Carson; Patrick Lefevre; Stuart Midgley; Ann Murcott; Isabel Roberts; Joan Ryan; Ian Taylor; Peter Young. Also we would like to thank Peter Hopkins of RKP for his help in the publishing of the book.

We are grateful for permission to quote from 'The Tales of Hoffman', edited from the official transcript by Mark L. Levine, George C. McNamee, and Daniel Greenburg; Introduction by Dwight Macdonald Copyright (c) 1970 by Bantam Books, Inc. Reprinted by permission of Bantam Books, Inc; and to reproduce our article 'Warwick University Ltd continued' which appeared in 'British Journal of Law and Society' in 1974.

INTRODUCTION

> The law is the fox, poor men are the geese: he pulls off their
> feathers and feeds upon them. (Gerrard Winstanley)

The message of this book is simple: law, in the forms that it is
practised and taught, means domination, oppression and desolation.
Law does not help but rather hinders people on the way to free
society. In this book we concentrate upon a particular brand of
law and a particular way of teaching law. What we have in mind
here are movements to liberalize law; to give it a 'human face'.
We claim that this liberalization and the concomitant idea that
law can be used to transform society by alleviating its problems,
cannot work; that there is no difference in form from this sort
of law and the traditional 'rich man's' law.

Our main theme is the two factors which we use to explain the
rise in the 'law for the poor' movement. They are:

(a) The economic and material forces within society. Thus the
     movement is a reflection of the changing market situation
     that lawyers find themselves in. It is a new and welcome
     addition to their income when traditional areas of business
     are drying up: 'helping people' pays.

(b) The efforts of lawyers and law teachers to make sense of
     their worlds by trying to show how law can help: have 'nice'
     law and you have 'nice' society. This reflects the assump-
     tion that it is the content of our society and so of laws
     that needs changing and not the form. The radical trans-
     formation of society, we will argue, implies the abolition
     of law or at least a radical change in its form.

The book aims at (i) providing an analysis of this liberal
moment in law and especially in the English legal system by looking
at the whole enterprise of socio-legal studies; (ii) providing an
introduction to students of the law, be they social scientists or
lawyers, of the relationships of law and a capitalist political
economy.

The book is political. It is a dispassionate look at law from
a Marxist point of view. We claim that you cannot understand law
except in the context of some theory about society and we make no
attempt to hide our theory. We do not believe that domination is
a simple notion; nor that law is the only agency of domination in

an authoritarian capitalist society.   Domination is a complex
phenomenon which appears at all levels and in all the structures of
this society.   For lawyers, however, law is at the centre of things.
Their image of the world is one that is overshadowed by law and so
when trying to save the world they set to work upon one that they
have created in their own image: a world dominated by law.   But
trying to save such a world means concentrating upon law to the
exclusion of other and greater modes of domination especially the
social formations that produce the law we have.   Our book concentrates on the law because we want to analyse how, for lawyers and
others, this assumption of centrality marks a deflection from
radical politics.

This book is polemical;   we want society to be transformed and
the socio-legal enterprise prevents this.   We want to get across
what trying to solve the problems of the world with the help of
law and men with 'lawyer-like' skills really means.   We do not
want to create 'radical law' for law is locked in the interstices
of social structure.   We want a society where men can freely come
together and decide how to run their lives.

We call this book 'Images of Law' because we counterpoint the
images of freedom that the law raises with their reality, enslave-
ment.

First, we see how the liberal answer - 'bringing the law to the
people' - is but a way of ameliorating the harshness of an authoritarian society.   But that society still remains.   Second, we go
on to show how law-centred the lawyer's world is and how he can
only describe it and history in terms of solution to 'legal
problems'.   Third, we show the practical effects of these sorts
of views by studying various schemes to help people through law, in
particular duty solicitor and neighbourhood law schemes.   Fourth,
we show the practical effects among lawyers and law teachers by
looking at how they practise teaching and how they practise law.
We finish by considering, in the context of the political trial,
the sorts of theories needed for men to break loose from the abstract
ideology of capitalist society and construct their own law and their
own world.

We write polemically because that is the only way we can express
what we think and feel.   We want to leave a positive message;   we
do not want it lost in a tangle of qualifications and consideration
of opposing theories.   The message must remain clear and the text
unbroken.   The form of the book must be different as well as its
contents.   The book is the statement of a position and not its
detailed working out.

Throughout the book we sketch in alternative forms of action but
we do not do this to any great extent - we concentrate on what is
wrong.   This is for two reasons:

1 The book is in the nature of a prolegomenon and is pointing
   the way in which theory and practice should follow.   We are
   pointing a way and not describing, in heavy detail, the great
   leap forward.

2 'the alternative is the unfinished' - we do not give a description of what is to be, for that denies what this book affirms,
   that men create their own future.   Our first step must be the
   abolition of what is wrong.   What is important is an analysis
   at the present and not a reification of the future.

But one thing that we know is this: law is an imperial code, it emasculates man by offering the solution of his problems to 'experts'; it reflects the professionalized society.   The only way out is for men to seize their lives and transform themselves and the world.

Chapter 1

IMAGES OF LAW

'LAW IS THE LAW'

We start with the story of a failure.   When the student movement
was in full flood, the cry was the universities and their courses
should be 'relevant' and not confined to 'ivory towers'.   The
idea was to go to the people and give back something to the community.   In this way the universities were to be more in touch with
'social reality' and being so would have a useful function to play
in society.   But the movement was initiated and carried through
without any clear theory as to what social reality is and what
part it plays in society as a whole.   The answer to this came in
the form of a rude shock to the student radicals when they realized
that one of the best examples of their future universities was
'Warwick University Ltd'. (1)   Through its connections with finance
and industry the university was heavily committed to the new
capitalism and it soon became clear that other universities were
committed to a similar reality.   The mistake that the student
radicals had made was that they had not thought about the notion
of 'relevance'.   They had taken it to mean that the university and
its courses must in any way be in the world and it was with some
dismay that they found out that this was not enough.
   We argue that, as in the case of this ill-fated radicalism, many
of the recent developments in legal education lack any explicit
theory about the nature of law and the effect of the connection of
law with the world.   We take two examples of recent developments
in legal education and show that, though they can partly be
explained by a growing social conscience and political enthusiasm,
they are also heavily influenced by redefinitions forced upon them
by the changing economic market.   This quest for property takes
two forms: that of the average lawyer for greater profit and that
of the law teachers for intellectual property.   Just as the
changing market situation forces lawyers to redefine their traditional markets and so finally influence legal education, the
changing market in intellectual property forces teachers to
redefine their market in research and so directly influence legal
education. (2)   But this still involves the acceptance of the
notion of control and the faith that law can do something for

people.   The two examples that we take are curriculum reform and
clinical legal education.
     Curriculum reform is cast by arguing for more 'relevant' curricula
and for 'socially useful' courses.   What are more 'relevant'
curricula?   First we look more closely at the aims of this movement,
for this gives an idea of the type of reforms that are demanded and
of where exactly the movement is heading.   The aim of the movement
is to provide a cohort of 'liberal' lawyers, not stuck in the
confines of 'black letter' law, who will be more involved in aiding
the community as a whole rather than being so concerned with perform-
ing the traditional lawyers' role of working for the rich. (3) For
a law school curriculum this means that subjects which are seen as
relevant to the needs of poor people are introduced, that subjects
are taught with great emphasis on social reform and social policy
and that the more traditional legal subjects are discarded or at
least changed so that they have more to do with 'social reality'.
Thus, courses in land law concentrate upon landlord and tenant and
courses in common law are transubstantiated into consumer protection.
In general the emphasis is upon the problems of the poor rather than
those of the rich and upon law as affecting social policy changes
rather than as acting as a conservative force.   Further, this
involves a denigration of the theory that the law is the law, but
instead a celebration of its links, through the 'social context',
with reality.   That this movement draws support from law teachers
and from some of the profession can be seen in the growth of 'liberal'
law schools and the interest of bodies like the Law Society in
neighbourhood law centres, legal advice schemes and the like.
     Two reasons, altruism and economism, are connected with this
movement and clearly affect lawyers' and law teachers' behaviour in
this context.   Altruism affects both groups, in that it arouses
liberal consciences, outraged at the money that is made from law and
prompts a desire to repay this debt by 'putting something back into
the community'.   The important reason, among lawyers, why this
movement is gaining support in the establishment and among the
established is linked with the market situation in which the legal
profession finds itself.   The interest in what can broadly be
called welfare law must be seen in the context of an increase in the
number of solicitors and a decline in certain traditional areas of
their business; this creates a situation where there are too many
solicitors chasing too little business and hence profits will go
down unless new markets are found and traditional areas of income
supplemented.   This is where 'law for the poor' emerges.   It
enables lawyers to compensate for their curtailed and threatened
markets and move the legal enterprise into new fields, to tap the
hitherto unexplored markets among the poor.
     Economism plays its part in the redefinition of the market for
law teachers.   This means not simply the market in academic jobs,
but rather the market in intellectual property in those areas of
legal knowledge and legal scholarship not already appropriated by
others to which a teacher can legitimately lay claim, and thus,
amassing his property he can climb the ladder of academic success.
In the realms of legal scholarship the traditional areas have been
over-researched and have declined; the market is saturated and
careers less easy to make.   This means that new markets have to be

created for legal research so that there are more ladders and stepping stones on the routes to success. So 'socio-legal' studies, 'law for the poor' and 'welfare law' are enjoying a boom creating a vast new market for the legal academic. The change in the content of the curriculum does not make much difference to the purpose of the curriculum for it is a move to more lucrative areas. It is the search by people who are primarily legal academics for new ways to survive in an increasingly competitive market-place.

It is of central importance for such lawyers to place at the centre of legal education these 'discovered' subjects, which are at present placed by their traditional brethren at its periphery. (4) This has to be done to legitimize them as lawyers and in order that the property they amass can be seen as truly legal property. This is achieved in analogous manner to the redefinition of the professional lawyer's market. Traditional 'black letter' subjects are seen and designated as peripheral while the new subjects now occupy the central core of what legal education should be. This produces the strange situation in which the traditional subjects, many of which tell us more about the underlying structure of capitalist society than those like social security legislation or welfare law, are forgotten. Work in this area concentrates upon the marginalia of capitalism: how many poor do not get benefits? how many truncheons break how many heads? So subjects such as land law and commercial law are by-passed, yet these are the ones which tell us for whose benefit and how society really operates. By concentrating upon these new subjects, legal study reflects the actual power relations in society and indicates the true nature of society. The new field has produced many would-be social reformers, but no new Renners. (5) This activity leaves these areas of study to those who have far more commitment to the system than the liberal reformers, for theirs is the ideology of doing and they forget that before you can change the world you have to understand it. They see the need for change, but desert the critical study of it to those who do not.

The curriculum is supposed to move in relevance for both altruistic and economic reasons, but what effect has been achieved and what has been changed? Broadly speaking, nothing at all, for altruism sees the changing of curricula as a relevant act in itself and economism is concerned with new markets; the world is seen from those perspectives. Both groups take social reality for granted, the one because it cannot see the need for analysis and the other because it is satisfied with the existing society. All that has been done is to produce changes in curricula which might or might not touch more people, but are unlikely to produce a new type of lawyer. The fact that poverty law and the like is taught is no guarantee that anything will change. It might provide lawyers with a social conscience, but only in the sense that they will be working in non-traditional areas. They learn nothing more about social reality than what they have been told before. They learn to impose their definition of social problems on people who cannot fight back. They see themselves as agencies of groups in society that can help but do not ask themselves if their 'help' is actually a hindrance. They also learn that the use of the law is acceptable if it helps the socially disadvantaged, but understand

nothing new about the social context within which the law operates,
nor develop a critical theory of law in society.   They learn a
different set of rules, it is true, but in the same way as before,
with all the fundamental assumptions unaltered.   It is redundant
to say that we must teach 'law in society' for all law of necessity
operates in society, trusts and succession as well as consumer
protection and landlord-and-tenant.   Concentrating upon more
'relevant' subjects, or teaching in a more 'relevant' style means
nothing unless you have a clear understanding of 'relevant'.   Law
schools and lawyers will not be changed by such reforms for they
will not change the social formation of the law school, nor will
they give a better idea of what the law actually does.   But it
will, however, give lawyers opportunities to make money in different markets and enable them to feel the warm glow of having 'put
something back into the community'.

We now turn to 'clinical legal education'.   Here, though the
emphasis is on style, it is also a reflection of the changing
curriculum interests.   'Liberal' content paves the way for liberal
ways of teaching.   And so this movement is also based in the
redefinitions of the market and the need for better and more
efficient lawyers.   We discuss it because it shows admirably the
lawyer's notion of control.

The image in clinical legal education is of the lawyer and the
law student as social worker, as one who helps.   We see how this
helping ideology masks, as it does in the case of the social worker,
the undercurrents of professionalization and the distance and
control that go with it.   Clinical legal education has developed
extensively in American law schools in the last fifty years and it
is now beginning to appear in the curricula of some law schools in
the United Kingdom.   It seems clear that the trend will continue
to develop for the reasons that we have already mentioned and also
because of the increasing popularity and use of the McKenzie (6)
case ruling.

The model for clinical teaching is borrowed from social work
and medicine, professions where trainee practitioners have long
been required to do 'on the job' training.   We can best show the
aims and methods of clinical law teaching programmes in the United
Kingdom by looking at the statements of the vanguard movement.

The object of the involvement of students in activities in legal
clinics is to bring them into contact with practical problems
which illuminate their study of law and make it, in that over-
worked word, relevant.   Additional advantages are the increase
in contact and communication between practitioners, intending
lawyers, and academics, and increases in collaboration which
could lead to research on the legal profession and the problems
encountered in practice.... (7)

The definition has three principal aspects: the emphasis on
solving 'practical problems', the rather self-conscious claim to
'relevance' coupled with a concern for a smoother running profession, the 'increase in contact and communication';   and for
research into 'the problems encountered in practice'.   More can
be found in a similar vein.   Clinical legal education is seen as
'helping to integrate...the law as taught and the law as practised'.
Specific parts of the clinical teaching effort, such as allowing

law students to engage in McKenzie-man work are similarly justified.
McKenzie opens a door which allows law students...to undertake
a limited practising role before the lower courts, at least, as
an integral part of their legal education. ('Praxis 2')
The theory of society and community underlying these new developments
is seldom made explicit by the harbingers of clinical training, nor
are the consequences for the client-consumer of implementing the
new concerns discussed in depth, except to confirm the ancient
polarity between the givers (the law expert) and the receiver (the
client or 'community').   Indeed, it sometimes appears heretical to
raise any doubts about the efficacy of the new education.   The
critical question invokes only the arch reply: 'What are you doing?'
'How are the people to be helped if not in this way?' or 'We
acknowledge the shortcomings of our methods but at least we're trying
to do something.'
   We spell out now some of the assumptions that are buried by the
cry 'at least do something'.   First, advancing the cause of
clinical education under the banner of 'relevance' without questioning the relevance of these innovations to people themselves, helps
only to perpetuate the dominance of the lawyer's notion of social
justice and social need.   Second, clinical training is, in part,
intended to teach people how to gain access to legal services.   The
problems attendant upon this approach have been succinctly summarized by Morris (1973, pp.7-8).
   Giving access to the legal system in ways which ignore the
   conflicting values in society serves an extremely important
   function which many lawyers active in reformist movements fail
   to recognise, or alternatively see as 'acceptable'.   I refer
   to the imposition of social order - the law as a means of social
   control.
Again (1973, p.11):
   Access to what?   To a traditional form of legal service which,
   in the context of social welfare becomes a form of social
   control.   To whom is this access given?   To those who are
   defined by the profession as being in need.   The profession
   control through (a) their definition of the situation, (b) the
   kinds of services set up, (c) their financing control.
As we suggested earlier, some of the most strongly articulated
demands for more relevant courses in the law schools come from
radical students.   But the fact that in law at least, their
demands are being met does not herald the increasing 'radicalization' of the law but rather its increasing professionalization.
This means that those who have as their aim radicalization are,
paradoxically, at one with the most austerely professional lawyers,
whose orientation is anything but radical. (8)   The interests of
the two groups neatly converge, both wanting a strategy for a more
'professional' and 'efficient' legal service, one which the place
of law and lawyers in society goes by without fundamental scrutiny.
Clinical legal education is about extending the hegemony of the
law and legal institutions.   It does not help to change relationships or manufacture new knowledge through which changes and fresh
ways of acting in and on the world would be opened up.   Nor does
it force a redefinition of power and resources, but merely adds to
the problems of the poor.   Previously they were oppressed by their

poverty, by the state, by landlords, by employers, but now they have
to carry a powerful new burden on their already straining backs,
that of law, lawyers and all the attendant paraphernalia.   But that
is not all, they also have to be grateful for being 'helped' and to
recognize the lawyer as friend.   The movement can never hope to
achieve the things that it claims as its objectives;   as Meszaros
observes (1972, p.189):

> In formalized institutional change there is no guarantee
> whatsoever against the reproduction, in new form, of the contra-
> dictions of the old institutions.

Both these examples show that what is being achieved is the training
of better technicians for capitalist society.   Their relationship
to the people they help and the effect of that help is taken for
granted.   The developments we have discussed assume you can teach
students how to make more money and be better managers of an unjust
society and then expect them to have a critical theory of that
society.

'LAW IS OUR STATE'

We want, then to concentrate upon the socio-legal enterprise and
our aim is a theoretical substantiation of the polemic with which
we started this chapter.   There, our aim was a polemical attack
on the political practices of those in the 'liberal law' movement.
We want now to discuss some of the issues raised by that section
and explain why it is that nothing changes.   In this chapter we
are going to concentrate upon the notion of control.   One of the
reasons that the lawyer's notion of control is perpetuated is
because of an atheoretical conception of society and this occurs
because of the concentration upon purposes as an epistemological
base.   Thus it is seen as sufficient for changing society to have
the right moral purpose;   that purpose being, 'bringing law to the
people'.   It is this that is supposed to make law better and to
justify clinical legal education and the concentration on fields
like poverty law.

In opposition to this we contend that what is important are the
objects of study and that it is in this way that we can find out
both the nature of oppression and domination in our society and the
steps that have to be taken in order to free people from such a
society.   The objects of our study then are concerned with the
material base of the society;   its production relations; and in
particular, as our book is concerned with the law, the role of law
in relation to this society.   Because of this we come to differing
conclusions as to which legal subjects are worthy of close scrutiny
and the role of law in affecting change.   Since, for us, the law
is something that is subordinate to the material base of society
it follows that our concrete practice for change is not something
that is self-reflexive and legal but something where the law plays
a minor role indeed.

We will deal with this in the last section of this chapter but
we now want to concentrate upon notions of control and the way that
liberal ideology in this respect shows no radical difference from
the notions that they implicitly criticize.   This is because,

though the liberal view is one which recognizes that the law has
something to do with society - hence the insistence on 'relevance' -
it can only locate the connection in terms of people's purposes.
The law becomes a 'technical-rational' means of achieving certain
ideological ends and, as a means, is once again separated from
society and given an autonomy of its own. From this perspective
what matters is the purpose that that law is used for rather than
the political economy of a society; what is emphasized is substance -
poverty law - rather than form-control.
    This view of the autonomy of the law is a liberal development
from one that was far more austere. Here the law was seen as the
guardian of freedom in a society in standing above and beyond that
society; concerned with society only in so far as it guaranteed
certain 'legal' values. The assumption, shared by many lawyers,
is while politics is always potentially oppressive because it is
seen as essentially 'ideological' the law, by definition immune to
ideological influence, is not.
    Liberal lawyers tend to oppose this view on the grounds that
they see, in this idea of law standing above the society, a failure
to supply the 'freedom', which is precisely that feature central
to the ideology of English law. Their solution is to bring the
law in to closer touch with the needs and desires of 'real' people.
Thus instead of men coming to the law, as under the old dispensa-
tion, the law comes with its gifts and mingles with the people.
This change is well illustrated by the latest Hamlyn Lectures -
a series dedicated to upholding the virtues of law and especially
English law. In these Scarman (1974, p.29) said:
    Undoubtedly a more positive approach is now called for from the
    law to the problems of daily life, if only because a more
    positive contribution in terms of money and administrative help
    is called for from the government. It is no longer sufficient
    for the law to provide a framework of freedom in which men,
    women and children may work out their own destinies: social
    justice, as our society now understands the term, requires the
    law to be loaded in favour of the weak and the exposed, to
    provide them with financial and other support, and with access
    to courts, tribunals, and other administrative agencies where
    their rights can be enforced.
In this and the succeeding section we will look more closely at
the autonomy of law and its relation to social structure. From
this we will look at an important ideological role of the law in
capitalist society, that of legitimation. We will argue that it
is only by considering the law seen as, in some sense, standing
apart from social structure that this can be done at all. Our
starting point in this examination will be a statement by the
former president of the National Industrial Relations Court (NIRC),
Sir John Donaldson (1972):
    Some commentators say that the Industrial Court is a political
    court and that I am a political judge - that is not true and
    never has been - I look upon politics as a monk looks upon sex,
    with nostalgia.
Let us now see what different interpretations can be given to this
statement. First of all it can be seen as a contingent statement
about the non-involvement of the British judiciary in what is known

as the political life of the country.   Thus they are supposed to be
rigidly neutral with respect to their involvement in party politics;
they are to remain unbiased with respect to the political views of
those who appear before them in the courts.   They are then, as the
British Civil Service is supposed to be, political castrati.
Whether or not such impartiality indeed exists can be shown empirically.   At the same time this is to define politics in a narrow
sense and to attempt no analysis of politics as a way of organising
society and of its connection to the law. (9)
    Second, the statement could mean that the NIRC is not specific-
ally political.   For if we take politics to be the political
economy of a society - the way that society is organized - then
everything that has to do with that organization is political.
Thus the sort of laws that a society has are connected to the
organization of that society in terms of its productive mode.   As
Eldridge Cleaver (1970, pp.121-2) said:

> Which laws get enforced depends on who is in power.   If the
> capitalists are in power, they enforce laws designed to protect
> their system, their way of life.   They have a particular abhor-
> rence for crimes against property, but are prepared to be
> liberal and show a modicum of compassion for crimes against the
> person - unless, of course, an instance of the latter is
> combined with an instance of the former.   In such cases,
> nothing can stop them from throwing the whole book at the
> offender.   For instance, armed robbery with violence, to a
> capitalist, is the very epitome of evil. Ask any banker what
> he thinks of it.
>
> If Communists are in power, they enforce laws designed to
> protect their system, their way of life.   To them the horror
> of horrors is the speculator, that man of magic who has mastered
> the art of getting something with nothing and who in America
> would be a member in good standing of his local Chamber of
> Commerce.

Thus the law is the distilled essence of a society; 'your jurisprudence is but the will of your class made into law for all'
(Marx, 1848).   But, though it is this signature of a society, you
cannot know a society merely by looking at its law.   For that gives
undue importance to the law, in that it assumes that law can be an
object of study unconstituted by any theory.   For us, however, law
is an object of study only in so far as it is constituted by Marxist
theory.   Thus law is dependent upon the forces of production and
can only be understood in the context of their specification.   As
Marx in the Cologne trial of 1849 said:

> Society is not based on law, that is a legal fiction, rather law
> must be based on society;   it must be the expression of society's
> common interests and needs, as they arise from the various
> material methods of production, against the arbitrariness of the
> single individual.   The 'Code Napoleon', which I have in my hand,
> did not produce modern bourgeois society.   Bourgeois society,
> as it arose in the eighteenth century and developed in the
> nineteenth, merely finds its legal expression in that Code.   As
> soon as it no longer corresponds to social relationships, it is
> worth no more than the paper it is written on (Marx: 'Speech
> in His Defence' in McLellan 1973, pp.215-16).

Thus law is analytically connected to the mode of production and
so, in capitalist society, oppresses in the way that that society
oppresses.   Thus the activities of the lawyers described in 'Law
is the law', can be understood in terms of a model which sees
capitalism, in the search for profit, creating new markets to take
the place of declining ones.   The whole socio-legal enterprise
can be seen, on this model, as a new market. (10)

We have noted so far that the system might be non-political in
that it is impartial and fair, in that no man's political beliefs
will be taken into account when he is brought before the court.
But we insist that although the system might administer justice
impartially, justice itself is partial in the sense that it is
part of a particular way of organizing a society. (11)   If this
exhausts the significance of Donaldson's statement then the cry
that the law is political could be the cry of those, caught in the
net of a capitalist society, who realize that the law is one of
its meshes.   The importance of Donaldson's statement, however,
lies in a third meaning that it could have: that the law guarantees
freedom, by transcending social structure and having an autonomy of
its own.   For it is this meaning that can and does neutralize the
ever growing realization that law is an arm of capitalist society.

We will now examine aspects of the bourgeois theoretical base
for this.   As we have hinted, the basis for this sort of notion
comes from slogans such as 'the rule of law', 'government of laws
and not men', 'freedom under the law'.   The law is seen as a
framework within which we live out our lives and which sets the
parameters for freedom.   This creates an image of the law as
something that gives a sense of order to our lives;   something that
becomes the most important thing in the world;   it regulates our
being and gives it meaning;   life without it becomes inconceivable
because it acts as a backdrop to our lives circumscribing them and
giving them fulfilment.   Thus for the gardener law is the sun
because that to him is the most important single thing in his
existence.   It defines his working life as he grows his crops
according to its inflexible routine.   As Auden (1966) puts it:

Law, say the gardeners, is the sun,
Law is the one all gardeners obey
Tomorrow, yesterday, today.

Law is seen as of paramount importance;   it alone by its inflexible
routine, can define our working lives.   This image again appears
in novels and films of the small town American country lawyer who
dedicates his life to the 'Law' - with a capital L - and so
implicitly to peace and prosperity.   The best example of this part
of the American dream coming to life is Senator Sam Ervin, the
chairman of the Senate Watergate committee. (12)   But, as we saw
when we went through the different interpretations of Donaldson's
statement, the law never totally divorces itself from social
structure and there is a tension between the law, seen as a transcendental force, and the law seen as an agent of the society.   Thus
the law becomes both eternal and concrete.

D'Entreves (1970) alludes to the distinction between the 'verum'
and the 'certo' of a law i.e. that part of the law that embodies
eternal norms and that part that is used to manage a particular
social structure. (13)   And so we can see the beginnings of a

tension between the societal aspects of law and those aspects of
law that stand outside of it.   It is this tension that prevents
the rule of law from devolving into nothing more than mere rule
following.   In this version of the rule of law even countries
like South Africa can be deemed law-abiding, as long as they follow
their substantively unjust rules.   Discussing criticisms of this
kind, Lon Fuller (1969), asks whether the Nazi legal system could
be called a legal system at all.   He asks what sort of things does
'the enterprise of putting ourself under the governance of rules'
entail.   That question is - what is the point of law?   And he
answers this by showing eight ways in which law making can fail
(1969, p.39):

> there are in this enterprise, if you will, eight distinct routes
> to disaster.   The first and most obvious lies in a failure to
> achieve rules at all, so that every issue must be decided on an
> ah hoc basis.   The other routes are: (2) a failure to publicize,
> or at least to make available to the affected party, the rules
> he is expected to observe;   (3) the abuse of retroactive legis-
> lation, which not only cannot itself guide action, but under-
> cuts the integrity of rules prospective in effect, since it puts
> them under the threat of retrospective change;   (4) a failure to
> make rules understandable;   (5) the enactment of contradictory
> rules or (6) rules that require conduct beyond the powers of the
> affected party;   (7) introducing such frequent changes in the
> rules that the subject cannot orient his action by them;   and,
> finally, (8) failure of congruence between the rules as announced
> and their actual administration.

He claims that it is these that make up what he calls 'the inner
morality' of the law and that making 'law' is a struggle to achieve
these aims.   Thus though the law is neutral with respect to substantive aims, the fact that 'the governance of rules' logically
implies these eight parameters does have some effect upon the
substantive aims of the law.   You cannot coherently, within this
framework, set up a system which is substantively evil;   for systems
such as Nazi Germany and (presumably) South Africa would tend to
break the eight points outlined above.   Even Hart (1961) who
attacks Fuller from a positivistic standpoint makes the same sort of
points.   Though he sees law as a formal framework, neutral with
respect to substantive aims, and so in its form outside the context
of the society, the tension between the societal substantive, and
asocietal formal aspects of law is maintained.   In his discussion
of 'the minimum content of natural law' he says (1961, p.188):

> Reflection on some very obvious generalizations - indeed truisms -
> concerning human nature and the world in which men live, show
> that as long as these hold good, there are certain rules of
> conduct which any social organization must contain if it is to be
> viable.   Such rules do in fact constitute a common element in
> the law and conventional morality of all societies which have
> progressed to the point where these are distinguished as different
> forms of social control.   With them are found, both in law and
> morals, much that is peculiar to a particular society and much
> that may seem arbitrary or a mere matter of choice.   Such
> universally recognized principles of conduct which have a basis
> in elementary truths concerning human beings, their natural

environment, and aims, may be considered the minimum content
of Natural Law, in contrast with the more grandiose and more
challengable constructions which have often been proffered
under that name.
However much Hart talks of them as 'contingent' they act in the
same ideological way as Fuller's 'inner morality' and give law
both a foothold in the realm of society and in some sort of eternity.
What is important is the formal structure of the law which, standing
outside our lives, enables us to run them within a society.   But
that formal structure has some substantive content which is reflected
in the 'simple truisms about man'.   As Selznick in an essay aiming
to extend Fuller's theory with some sort of sociological perspective
says (1963, p.171):

> In framing a general concept of law it is indeed difficult to
> avoid terms that suggest normative standards.   This is so because
> the phenomenon itself is defined by - it does not exist apart
> from - values to be realized.   The name for these values is
> 'legality'. Sometimes this is spoken of as 'the rule of law' or,
> simply, 'the legal order'.   Legality is a complex ideal embracing
> standards for assessing and criticizing decisions that purport
> to be legal, whether made by a legislature or a court, whether
> elaborating a rule or applying it to specific cases.
>
> The essential element in legality, or the rule of law, is the
> governance of official power by rational principles of civic
> order.   Official action, even at the highest levels of authority,
> is enmeshed in and restrained by a web of accepted general rules.
> Where this ideal exists, no power is immune from criticism nor
> completely free to follow its own bent, however well intentioned
> it may be.   Legality imposes an objective environment of
> constraint, of tests to be met, of standards to be observed, and,
> not less important, of ideals to be fulfilled.

Thus legality, the formal structure of the law, is not totally
divorced from the substantive content of the law and the way that
it directly organizes a society.   For as we see, the formal
structure is supposed to have some effect on the substantive content.
Thus law is one in its 'political' and 'apolitical' parts, though
they co-exist somewhat uneasily.   However legality, that part of
the law which is seen as autonomous and astructural takes on the
most important role and it is within that framework that all aspects
of the law come to be seen.   The aim then, is to haul the positive
law, the 'political' part of the law up to the transcendental realm.
The society has to be in the image of the eternal form of law.   This
again is seen in Selznick (1963, p.179):

> Plainly, positive law includes an arbitrary element.   For him
> who must obey it, it is to some extent brute fact and brute
> command.   But this arbitrary element, while necessary and
> inevitable, is repugnant to the ideal of legality.   Therefore
> the proper aim of the legal order, and the special contribution
> of legal scholarship, is progressively to reduce the degree of
> arbitrariness in the positive law.

It is because of this the bourgeois law and the bourgeois state get
their 'natural' right to exist.   They become invested with the
eternal form of legality and the role of law.   And so Lukacs (1971)
can write:

Even in the midst of the death throes of capitalism, broad
sections of the proletarian masses still feel that the state,
the laws and the economy of the bourgeoisie are the only
possible environment for them to exist in.   In their eyes many
improvements would be desirable (organization of production),
but nevertheless it remains the 'natural' basis of society.
This is the ideological foundation of legality.   It does not
always entail a conscious betrayal or even conscious compromise.
It is rather the natural and instinctive attitude towards the
state, which appears to the man of action as the only fixed
point in a chaotic world.

And it is this elision between the formal and the concrete, between
law as a liberating force (in the sense of Cicero's aphorism 'We
are slaves of the law, in order that we might be free') and as a
force that organizes society that enables it to be used to legitimate social structures.

'LAW IS THE WISDOM OF THE OLD'

Though it is our contention that both these aspects of law are
rooted in the material base of a society, we will now examine what
happens (a) when this is denied and both aspects are elevated to
the transcendental realm, and (b) when the tension between the two
aspects is used by those who oppose capitalist society.   In the
former case, capitalist society is legitimated and in the latter
an attempt is made to de-legitimate that society.

Let us start with legitimation first.   Legality then, becomes
something to be achieved.   In situations of chaos and tension what
is striven for is the return of 'legality' and 'normality'.   Then
everything is seen as safe again.   What is truly disastrous is the
breakdown of law and order.   That takes precedence over the fact
that corrupt regimes are entering their death throes. (14)   Questions
of legality then, take precedence over social, moral and political
questions and these questions become transmuted into whether one can
attach the label 'legal' or 'illegal'.   It becomes important in our
everyday life to say something was done legally even when there was
no point in doing so.   Let us look at some examples.   In the First
World War the Germans ridiculed Britain for going to war 'over a
scrap of paper':   the treaty obligations over the neutrality of
Belgium.   But it was important for the British to be supported by
law because it could transform an essentially imperialist war into
one where 'good' clashed with 'the filthy hun'.   After the Second
World War, the treatment of the Jews and other races was not only
castigated as immoral but the full horror of it was that it was
seen as in some way 'a crime against humanity' i.e. illegal.   In
Rhodesia Ian Smith has concerned himself with the problem of
legitimacy even through his party is in complete and effective
control of the country.   Such was that concern that the issue was
argued in the Rhodesian High Court. (15)   Although the arguments
could have no immediate effect on the regime they were important
for, if won, and the regime declared 'legal' then both the Prime
Minister and his government would be legitimized.   Finally, to
take an example nearer home, the allegations about the methods used

in interrogating those detained by the British army in Northern
Ireland were seen in terms of whether the methods were legal or
illegal. (16)   Little space was devoted to questioning the morality
of what were virtually disorientation techniques.   If it could be
shown that it was legal, then it was beyond question.   In this way
political questions are not only deflected but are made to seem
entirely inappropriate.   As long as the given social order is said
to be legal then the world is all right.   It is good because it is
'legal' and 'legal' stands outside the social structure and so
guarantees it.   What happens is that the courts and similar agencies
of law enforcement are seen as standing outside of a society and so
subsume the political questions.   Thus Honore (1967) sees the
courts as important guarantors of 'legality' - for which read civil
society - during a revolutionary period. (17)

This then, is the way that the law legitimates social order;
let us now turn to the attempts of radicals to de-legitimate it.
Here the attempt is to characterize the law as illegal.   This is
done by taking at face value the bourgeois theory;   by assuming
that the law does provide justice and a framework of freedom and by
going on to show that in this particular instance it manifestly
does not.   So the law and the society is illegal and therefore
wrong because it fails to deliver justice.   The substantive
'political' part of law has not fully been taken up into the
'eternal' apolitical part.   A vivid example of this could be seen
in the defence speech of Fidel Castro.   He was tried for organizing a coup at the Moncada Barracks against the Cuban dictator,
Batista.   He claimed that it was not his coup but the Batista
regime that was illegal and that the courts should be trying
Batista and not himself.   Though Castro was basing this claim on
the fact that Batista had himself overthrown the constitution of
1944 which he, Castro, was now accused of attempting to topple, he
could also be understood as asking the court to judge between the
purities of his intentions and the savage realities of the Batista
regime.   He was, in effect, saying to the court, if you are
independent of the state and are the guardians of eternal justice
as you would have us believe, then prove it by finding me innocent:
by not siding with depravity and corruption and by denouncing the
tyrant Batista (Castro, 1968, p.161).

How can Batista's presence in power be justified, when he gained
it against the will of the people and by violating the laws of
the republic through the use of treachery and force?   How can
anyone call legitimate a regime of blood, repression and ignominy?
How can anyone call revolutionary a regime which has gathered
the most backward men, methods and ideas of public life?   How
can anyone consider legally valid the high treason of a court
whose duty was to defend the constitution?   With what right do
the courts send to prison citizens who have tried to redeem
their country by giving their blood, their lives?   All this is
monstrous to the eyes of the nation and the principles of true
justice.

Logic tells me that if there exist courts in Cuba Batista
should be punished, and if Batista is not punished and continues
as master of the state, president, Prime Minister, Major General,
civil and military chief, executive power and legislative power,

owner of lives and farms, then there do not exist courts, they
have been suppressed.   Terrible reality?   If that is not so,
say so as soon as possible, hang up your robes, resign your
posts. (18)

This sort of tactic can only succeed when people have a clear and
agreed conception of what the 'eternal justice' is to be.   When
people are by and large convinced that the defendants are standing
on the side of justice and freedom.   This, of course, does not
normally work for radical groups and paradoxically it works best
for liberal and 'highly moral' groups.   So the tendency is to
defuse protest, by continuing it within the parameters of liberal
society.   The only way in which you can use de-legitimation as a
tactic is by assuming bourgeois justice.   A recent example of
this was in Wales in 1972.   A justice of the peace, Mrs Davies,
was forced to resign because of her publicly stated sympathy with
the Welsh language movement and for paying the fines of some of
those convicted of demonstrating under its aegis.   Her resignation
statements resembled, in principle, those of Castro.   She had
always understood law to be a provider of justice and, in this
case, justice was clearly on the side of the Welsh language movement.   If anyone should have been convicted it should have been
the law;   it stood at the door of eternal justice and was found
guilty (Davies, 1972, pp.56-7):

The counsel regarding one's duty to enforce and obey bad laws,
which you gave in a recent speech and is implicit in your
letter, is far too simplistic.   We have here an abiding dilemma
which has tormented the spirit of man from time immemorial and,
as you well know, there have been judges throughout the ages
who have stretched and bent bad laws to breaking point in an
endeavour to do justice despite them.   Furthermore you
insinuate that I consider people free to pick and choose the
laws they obey, or free to disregard laws in order to draw
attention to 'what they conceive to be' unjust - all this is
travesty of what I have said to you.

Your argument is made plausible at the cost of divorcing law
from principle with the result that the meaning of 'good' and
'bad' becomes no more than a matter of personal choice, and in
the end there is no justice beyond 'conceptions' which can
legitimately vary from one person to the next.   As a Christian,
you must surely recognise that Justice is an external principle
against which human laws should always be measured.   By that
'yardstick', to deny to others fundamental human rights which
the group to which you belong enjoys, is not just a form of
'badness' about the magnitude of which people are free to argue,
it is not a 'grievance' which one 'chooses' or does not choose
to deem 'substantial'.

Here we can see that a conception of law as autonomous, which is,
by and large, a formal rational structure, takes on the substantive
content of the society in which it is located.   Thus 'freedom
under the law' takes on the aspect of freedom of a western liberal
democracy.   The 'rule of law' works as a standard of criticism by
assuming that western liberal democracy is the 'eternal' law.   But
as the value goes into this transcendental (i.e. the eternal) law
then it loses its identity as a value and becomes the 'natural
appearance of law' and a criterion for de-legitimation.

The problem with de-legitimation as a tactic for radicals is that it is idealist and the only ideals that have any common currency are those which support a bourgeois society.   Values do not exist in a vacuum, but in the material practices of people fighting for liberation from this society.   Why then are these values accepted? For some this is because the law and the society that it represents is freedom.   For them it is fair and just.   It supports their interests and is something that they understand.   For them the policeman is someone who tells them the way home when they are lost and not someone who locks them up.   Thus Engels (1920, p.227) says:

> True the law is sacred to the bourgeoisie, for it is his own composition enacted with his consent, and for his benefit and his protection.   He knows that if an individual law should injure him, the whole fabric protects his interests;   and more than all, the sanctity of the law, the sacredness of order as established by the active will of one part of society, and the passive acceptance of the other, is the strongest support of his social position.   Because the English bourgeoisie finds himself reproduced in his law, as he does in his God, the policeman's truncheon which, in a certain measure is his own club, has for him a wonderfully soothing power.
> But for the working man it is otherwise!   The working man knows too well, has learnt from too-oft repeated experience, that the law is a rod which the bourgeois has prepared for him; and when he is not compelled to do so, he never appeals to the law.

Thus de-legitimation is a way of changing law for those who are fundamentally in favour of the society.   Thus when the Schwendingers (1975) seek to do this, they are already in some way presupposing the definitions that have been prescribed by capitalist society:

> Is there wonder why we have raised questions about the legalistic definitions of crime when the magnitude of 'social injury' caused by imperialism, racism, sexism and poverty is compared to that wrought by individual acts which the State legally defines as crimes?   Isn't it time to raise serious questions about the assumptions underlying the definition of the field of criminology, when a man who steals a paltry sum can be called a criminal while agents of the State can, with impunity, legally reward men who destroy food so that price levels can be maintained whilst a sizable portion of the population suffers from malnutrition. The USA is confronted with a grave moral crisis which is reflected above all in the technocratic 'benign neglect' shown in the unwillingness to recognize the criminal character of great social injuries inflicted on heretofore powerless people, merely because these injuries are not defined in the legal codes (p.137).

Radical tactics have to be able to transcend bourgeois society and build the foundations for something different.

What is important is to attack and develop ways of fighting the way that social control confines the majority in our society.   This is well summarized by Young (1975, pp.82-3):

> The control system in such societies works not through beatings of paddy wagons (though these are always present as an ultimate arsenal, at the terminus of social control), nor indeed by

beliefs and ideologies marketed as natural and uncontestable, but by a judicial distribution of rewards tied into a thousand pinpricks of punishment in the workplace that is society.   These pinpricks act on the personality structure set up in childhood. The family itself is the product of such personality constructions, and is in turn geared to producing more children to undergo such character-training.   Thus, a certain personality set is main- tained throughout life in aspic.   Both the individual, and the working-class culture of which he is a member, are dominated by memories of the costs to be paid for deviation and dissent. Such a culture contains and relays knowledge of the inhumanity of unemployment, the gross stigma of prison (and its real social consequences - in terms of job chances and personal isolation), and is acquainted with the poverty and despair of the lumpen- proletariat.   At the same time, it has knowledge of the contemporary and continuing mechanisms of the soft machine of control: the perks of conformity, the incessant minutiae of punishment for rebellion in the job situation.   Cudgels and baton charges are unnecessary in the maintenance of this aspect of control.   The real locus of social control is in the work situation.

'LAW IS OUR FATE'

So far, we have seen how de-legitimation, in order to work, has to accept the substantive values of a western liberal democracy.   But the form of law in a bourgeois society also has to be accepted. Because those like the Schwendingers posit some form of idealist model of the law in their attack on capitalist society, their criterion of de-legitimation takes on the form of the bourgeois legality that we discussed earlier.   Thus their 'ideal' law takes on the transcendental form supplied by bourgeois society and begins to look like a plea for the return to a law, which is really autonomous and thus freedom-giving.   This then takes on a transcen- dental aspect and it is forgotten that this aspect of the law also reflects the material base of a society.   And so the form of the law is taken for granted.   It is assumed that 'bourgeois legality' can really work in a socialist society;   that what is needed is a change in the content of the law and not the way that it is produced.

Let us now look at what bourgeois legality does reflect. Bourgeois legality reflects subtly, what the more substantive versions of law reflect clearly, that is control in a society.   This takes the form of there being a class of 'order givers' who make and administer the society and a class of 'order takers' who do what they are told.   'Bourgeois legality' then is based on a society where a certain class (the propertyless) do not understand and are seen as not being fit to have anything to do with the running of their lives.   The running of the society must be left to the experts: those who know.

How would the perfect society look in terms of this model?   We focus upon the slogan 'the rule of law'. (19)   Primarily this supports the system of 'constitutionalism', that is to say 'the government of law and not men'.   What is the purpose of such a

system and what assumptions does it make about man and society?
In its eyes societies are akin to 'states of nature' where man
fights against man, with the inevitable result that pyramid social
structures are set up.   Therefore, a system is needed that will
prevent the abuse of the power that some men 'naturally' have over
others.   Authority then, exists and is a natural fact about the
world.   It is the job of constitutionalism to curb some of that
power by legitimating it and investing it with the authority of
the law. (20) 'This is done by providing a framework of laws
around the society which regulate this natural power and prevent
it from being abused.   Law will be necessary to control this flow
of natural power and to do this properly it will have to be above
and beyond society, unconnected with the day to day running of its
affairs.

This is the only form of law because the society that it serves
is the only possible form of society.   Models that rely on notions
of mass democracy do not work because they will be inevitably broken
down by abuses of power; the only effective safeguard being the
law that is above all that. (21) Thus when, after the Russian Revolution, the USSR tried to organize on this mass democratic model,
failure was seen as inevitable because of the inextricable linking
of the law with the running of the society.

There was not the transcendental aspect of law which would solve
the problem of power abuses.   This does not take into account the
historical circumstances of the time (22) but attributes failure
to the lack of 'bourgeois legality'.   And so these failures 'prove'
the need for an authoritarian society and for bourgeois legality.
This is also seen in the way that some Soviet dissidents are treated
like a Solzhenitsyn, fighting for a return to legality.   The views
of those dissidents who are trying to bring the material base of
Soviet society back to a mass democratic model are underplayed. (23)

Consider again the Watergate crisis: this has been seen as the
great success for constitutionalism in that it prevented - finally -
the dictatorship of Richard Nixon who was seen as taking too much
of the law and the running of the country into his own hands.   The
emphasis here is on 'too much', for what is at stake is the juggling
around of the various relationships between Congress, the Supreme
Court and the President.   What is not questioned is the 'natural
fact' that society should be organized upon a liberal democratic
model - with power going not to everyone but the few.   Watergate
then, is taken as a critical demonstration that the machinery works.
But the machinery that bourgeois society sets up to counter situations like Watergate - 'bourgeois legality' - is at the same time
the sort of machinery that sanctions the sort of society that
produces Watergate. (24)   In other words, what is ignored is that
this is inevitable in a society which puts some men in positions of
power over others.

How do lawyers fit into these notions of control?   They are
those who service this distant and austere law;   they are skilled
in its manipulation for the benefit of society.   They are seen, by
themselves at least, as priests at the shrine of freedom, having
nothing to do with the dirty business of running a society.   But
the law is based in the structure of the society and so lawyers take
their place as agents of that society's system of control.   In

their case they strive to make the society fulfil the transcendental
ideology of the law.   They care that the content of the law be
good.   They desire that all should receive equitable treatment
under the law and so they labour to make law good and soothe society.
In so doing they take upon themselves the mantles of gods for they
and the state that run the society become those who know best, whose
job it is to direct others.   But this image is not something
that is alone the property of those who benefit by it.   It is also
taken up by those who are commanded, who give up part of themselves
to the law, for that is the only way in which they can conceive of
being able to attain freedom.   Thus, they mirror Feuerbach's (1841)
characterization of religion as something that emasculates man.
Man creates an entity and transfers his powers to it.   Therefore
things that I can do I can no longer do because I have given my
power up to a non-existent god.   I pray to the god for victory and
success etc. instead of acting and achieving.   I abdicate to him
my powers.   Thus I accept the idea of someone above me who has
control over my life because he has powers that I have not.   The
same thing happens in the law.   We allot our powers to the controllers who determine the content of the just law (if they are good
men) and we do this because we assume that we do not have their
talents and capabilities.   We give them our power and they control
us.   We, and they, accept implicitly and without question the
truth of Cicero's aphorism: 'We are slaves of the law, in order
that we might be free.'
    The lawyer then, takes on the mantle of the law.   The image of
control is one of distance.   The law and so also the governing of
the society becomes distanced and inaccessible.

'LAW IS WE'

We want now to look at some of the ways in which this distance has
been neutralized.   For this is the way that the liberal lawyers
that we discussed in section one operate.   The image that
we have discussed above is still attractive to its many adherents
(25) - especially among more conservative lawyers.   But, in the
context of the declining political economy of western capitalism
this image begins to lose its attractive qualities and the distance
that it projects becomes more closely associated with control.   The
law must modify itself in order to exert its controls in a more
liberal form.   This move takes place, as we have seen, in 'bringing
the law to the people';   in taking the law to 'where the action is'.
We saw this clearly stated in the quotation from Scarman (1974)
(p.7 above). (26)
    This move, and the effect that it has on lawyers' notions of
control, has to be seen in the context of a general ideological move
in western capitalist society to identify structural crises in that
society with 'crises of communication'.   This outlook implicitly
accepts that control is to be equated with distance and that the
solutions are to be more 'open' government;   to let people know and
to participate more.   Thus the solution to the industrial crises
in Britain is sometimes seen as a matter of granting workers knowledge of the financial affairs of the companies that they work for

and some degree of participation in the running of them.   These
policies, and the debates associated with them, always take place
within a structural framework which assumes that the employers have,
in the final analysis, a right to own and so control.   Consequently
all discussions try and fix the relationships between the workforce,
the owners, and sometimes the state, within those parameters. (27)

   It is this ideological process at work in the law that we will
now examine.   One of the ways in which this is realized in the
sociology of law is through studies of the knowledge and opinion of
law (KOL).   Such research is, in the main, a continental phenomenon
but its import is spreading to Britain as the sociology of law
expands. (28)   Its thrust is one of liberal social engineering and
a desire to find out what is 'really' happening.   This fits in very
well with the political practices and the theoretical thrust of the
liberal law movement.   These sort of lawyers want to be 'where the
action is' and the studies show them how. (29)

   The scenario for this sort of research is set in the introduction
to Podgorecki et al. (1973, p.8) where the editors state:

   The orientation set out is one which a sociology of law purporting
   to embrace not just the rules of law but the rule of law cannot
   afford to ignore...

and so we have the move to a new 'framework of freedom', one which
is more in touch with reality.   Thus Vinke (1970, p.5) says:

   It is especially here, that research may help to provide information on the importance of legal sociological factors in determining judicial opinions and usages so that the manner of
   wielding legal rules may be more in keeping with the legal
   reality than is often the case at present.

This is important because Vinke and also Van Houtte (1973) claim to
have verified two hypotheses, confounding some of the underlying
assumptions that writers on legal philosophy make: First, that
with respect to various rules of law in the collective sphere the
population have highly divergent attitudes;   second, that the
difference in attitude to various types of legal rules is related
to socio-structural, socio-cultural and psychological factors.
These results might not seem to be startling, perhaps even considered
a sociological commonplace.   But when they are applied to theories
that try to legitimate the action of law in society, then if they
rely upon such notions as 'the sense of justice', 'the moral
attitudes of the community', etc. they may tread upon dangerous
ground for they seem to make certain unjustified empirical observations (1973, p.16):

   Our times demand that jurisprudence should have the sociological
   imagination to realize the extent to which social changes in
   tempo and in values, in the groups involved, have fundamentally
   changed the social milieu of our law.   Investigation into
   attitudes towards legislation can contribute towards a clearer
   understanding of that milieu.   This understanding becomes
   increasingly important, when, for the ultimate legitimation of
   legal rules in a society, it becomes less and less possible to
   resort to the teachings of philosophy and theology.   Philosophy
   of law must become more and more modest in its claims, just as
   religion now tends to shrink back from many subjects about which
   it would have pronounced decisive judgments.

The key notion here is that of legitimation.   As bourgeois legality goes into crisis and shows what it really is, then the need arises to bring the law down to earth and to legitimate it with science. Concepts like 'the sense of justice' and 'moral solidarity' must be verified by seeing what people actually think and not through arm-chair hypothesis.   This 'scientization' of the world and the appearance of neutrality that supposed 'objective' scientific work brings will be looked at in more detail in chapter 5.

We cannot then, according to Vinke and Van Houtte assume that a society and its laws are working all right.   We must find out (1973, pp.16-17):

> But in the long run this kind of research can supply information
> about a series of facts relevant for jurisprudence, facts which
> might seem to indicate that a law should be considered obsolete,
> that submissive compliance is involved, that a law is not
> comprehended, and that informal codes underlie a formal rule.

In this way law is brought to the people because it is put in touch with their needs and feelings.   The 'communication gap' begins to be broken because the law comes from 'out there' to the world. This is necessary because in a period of restriction of choices, when behaviour controls are increasingly tightened as crisis situations multiply, it becomes important to look to the acceptance of legal rules.   This will become one of the primary tasks of a sociology of law.   As society becomes more complex and further divorced from people then it is increasingly important to do work that will ground that society in the reality of the people's attitudes to its rules.   They quote Shonfield (1965, p.67) with approval:

> How much of the original objective of government by popular
> consent can be sustained in a system in which the sphere of
> active government has been greatly enlarged and is likely to
> become more so.

The KOL work rests on a profound belief in social democracy and the use of the law to accommodate its crises by a continually more and more efficacious social engineering.   The crisis then is one of knowledge and opinion.   Democracy is achieved when people know the rules and see them as good.   KOL is useful because it helps to gauge the extent of public feeling on a subject and so help to democratize the society's institutions.   Its mission then is to make the sociology of law 'serve the people'.   It 'serves the people' in the context of a theory which implies that the law and its institutions are and should be entities which are entirely separate from the people - but that individuals should have more access, more knowledge and perhaps some degree of participation in them.   Fundamentally the law remains an arcane institution and whilst the object of the exercise is to make the knowledge more easily available, it does not include the examination of the essential power relations implied behind this democratic theory. The 'access theory' is that the law and its institutions tell people what to do.   They can be more democratic or less so by the degree of knowledge made available to people.   However, people simply relate to the law and its institutions but they do not control them. As Kaupen (1973, p.43) puts it:

The question of the public's relation to law and its institutions has not so far been recognized as a relevant problem for jurisprudence.

This assumes that there are to be separate institutions and so one has always to study the relationship between them.   The fact that mass democracy, for example, would do away with this by dissolving the separateness is never taken into consideration.

KOL studies, then, become vast public opinion polls to test the extent to which the message is getting through to the governed and to see what adjustments have to be made.   In a sense they are marketing a product and, as with all marketing of this type, the relationship is not one-way.   The question is not just to see whether or not the public likes the product - in this case capitalist law - but also, in the event of the public's not liking it, to change public opinion so that they do.   The product is not to be radically changed.

This is done first by setting up the studies in particular ways. Though the KOL researchers have an interest in morality, the morality is one that is reflected through legal categories.   For what they are looking at is morality viewed through existing categories of legal offences;   that is to say how far can morality justify the law as it is.   Law and the legal category of offences are viewed as essentially non-problematic alternatives that spring up from the natural social structure.   These are the natural facts with which the researcher can play.   They seem to be generated in an almost laissez-faire manner and the prime research task is to fit them into some form of empirically grounded moral consciousness.

Let us look more closely at Kaupen's (1971) study of the relationship of the West German people to law and the institutions of law. In this study one of the things that is done is to take fifteen specifically defined bits of behaviour.   All but two (albeit in four cases problematically) are actually against the law. Respondents are then asked to say whether or not the behaviour is illegal (they are not told its legal status) and then morally to evaluate that behaviour.   The result is that (Kaupen, 1970, p.1):

> The attitudes towards legal rules are - independent of the
> punishment that the law calls for - closely tied to moral
> valuation.   Penal laws that cannot rely on the moral disapproval
> of the people are ineffectual.

This can only tell the society how it should frame its laws.   It cannot tell anything about the status of the legal system as an instrument for maintaining that society.   The whole emphasis here is on the relationship between what are seen as legal offences and what people think of them.   What is omitted is the question: what laws do they want to have?

It might be argued that they could go on to ask about the moral status of other behaviour which is obviously socially injurious and outside of the legal category of offences.   But this would miss the point of our criticism, for within these studies it is impossible to put the question in that way.   If 'socially injurious' behaviour, of the kind that the Schwendingers (1975) talk about, was introduced, then it could only be seen as a way of finding out how law followed morality or vice versa.   The actual status of the behaviour would not be questioned.   The way these studies are done assumes a

defusing of its actual moral status by giving it a moral status
relative to law.   Again there is something absurd about assuming
that these surveys could be used to support radical attacks on the
social system by showing that people may not like it. (30)   The
point of radical politics is to build material practices that enable
people to transform society.   There is no need to run surveys to
find out what people think of capitalism.   There is support for
capitalism because the system is still standing.   People's false
consciousness can be overcome by describing clearly what the system
is and does, and not by finding out what people think of it.   KOL
studies can never be anything more than ways of co-opting moral
feelings into the social order by a spurious participation of people
in the law.

The moral feelings themselves, to continue our study of the
marketing of the product, do not count as unproblematic arbiters of
the law.   For the point of these studies is, as Podgorecki says,
'diagnostic'.   It enables the state to enforce certain laws and,
perhaps, to influence moral feelings.

If the legislature enacts a bill which does not coincide with
the prevailing legal feelings of society, it must expect resistance promoted by those feelings.   The greater the conflict
between such feelings and the proposed law, the more difficult
will be its enforcement.   The legislature may force such a bill
through, but then the social costs will increase accordingly.
Laws which are compatible with social sentiment do not face such
obstacles and hardly need enforcement.   Such kinds of legal
measures may be said to be cheap.   Sometimes, however, a
legislature may be aware that a bill is incompatible with some
social sentiment or other and it will consequently be prepared
to resort to more drastic measures of enforcement.   But such
a decision should rest upon what are thought to be particularly
important political or social principles (1973, pp.65-6).

Here then the message is clear: these surveys can only be taken
internal to a particular social system since the only type of
information that they can provide is how to accommodate people to
that system.   Thus when Podgorecki investigates the general
prestige of the law and finds that people who are better socially
situation respect it more than those who are not, his most favoured
explanation is the psychologistic one of under-socialization.   In
this way then, the moral feelings that are important are those of
the rational, well situated, fully socialized man.   And so the law
and the people move some way to accommodate each other but the
framework remains the same.

To finish this discussion of the KOL studies we will look at the
conflation of law with laws.   These works tend to assume that when
people's attitudes to various laws have been studied what will
emerge is their attitude to law as a whole.   And so again we see
an aspect of law divorced from society; a watered down version of
the legality that we have discussed above.   Podgorecki (1973) talks
of the 'legal sentiments' of a society.   This becomes an entity
which should control the use, in some cases at least, of the state's
use of law and order to achieve certain ends.   The two aspects of
law of our earlier sections appear again and they also exhibit the
same tension between being both inside and outside of society at the

same time.   Though it is used here as a 'technical-rational'
(i.e. neutral) means to achieve certain ends, it is still to some
extent part of and controlled by the 'legal sentiments' of society
which themselves, as we have seen, take on the values of the society
itself.   And so it is in this way that 'bourgeois legality' comes
down to earth, and thus society/law is justified by the one-to-one
correlation of laws and people's knowledge and opinion of them.
There is the 'legal-sentiment', the form of a 'technical-rational'
law standing above society, and there is the substantive content
of the law that organizes the society.   The aim of the legal
sentiment is to provide a 'framework of freedom' nearer to society
than the ideals of the old role of law.   Thus the substantive
content of the law should gradually become one with the 'legal
sentiments' of a society.   But we saw how, though that is supposed
to pay some respect to people's views, these are found in a context
where those views are already pre-determined.

Thus law is no longer a distant and aloof institution.   The
people have some knowledge and some control in so far as their
opinions and their feelings will be taken into account.   The whole
thrust of these studies is to emphasize the content of the law
rather than its form.   The vital question is the amount of knowledge that is to be disseminated about law;   it is assumed that
there is no problem about who is to construct that knowledge.   This,
then, is the meaning of Kutchinsky's phrase (1973, p.134):

> The functioning of law in society cannot be properly studied
> without continuing research into the public image of law, the
> legal conceptions, the knowledge and opinion of those who are
> not only being controlled by the law, but who should also be the
> controllers of law.

It becomes clearer still that the fundamental questions on control
are not asked directly when we analyse their work on legal institutions.   Here again the focus is upon consumerism;   to see whether
the official image of the lawcourt matches up with popular images.
In Kaupen's (1971) survey it was found that familiarity with the
court system by no means produced confidence in it.   This was
explained by assuming that the public had too 'idealistic' an image
of the courts and the court structure and that coming in contact
with the reality of the courts tended to shatter that image.   The
answer to this was obvious: make the courts in the 'image' of the
people.   Make them friendly, informal and able to give 'satisfying
solutions'.   Kaupen concentrates upon the paraphernalia of the
court;   the dress, the location and, to an extent, the composition.
But the structure of the court, however 'informal' it becomes, is
still assumed to be above and beyond the community.   Law is not
something that comes from people but something that comes to them.
Bourgeois legality is rescued from its aloofness and comes down to
the people.   It is that that enables it to remain a guarantor of
freedom.   But the lawyer's notion of control has only been slightly
modified by this knowledge and participation.   The law still
belongs to him and to the society that controls it.   It still
reflects a society divided into those who own and give orders and
those who are propertyless and take orders.

'LAW IS THE CLOTHES MEN WEAR'

So far we have shown the ideology involved in the move from the 'framework of freedom' to 'active involvement with the poor'.   In the law control has been seen as distance and the liberal moment is to solve this by bringing the law closer to people, making it more friendly and, as we shall see in chapter 5, 'scientizing' it.   This nearness however does not change the fundamental control that society and its law exercise.   In the preceding sections we have shown how this control appears both in 'high bourgeois legality' and in the new liberalized version.   In this section we want to deal with practical examples of what the 'new dimension' of law means.

We start with the attempts to make law tribunals more 'informal' and 'relaxed';   a system where tribunal chairmen do not bother over-much about strict rules of evidence and procedure, where lawyers are discouraged from appearing and where the dictate of formal legal rationality is forced to give way to a kind of 'kadi' justice. The idea running through this new provision is that justice should somehow be 'socialized';   that the law should actively be doing things for people.

Unfortunately, those who would come bearing gifts often succeed only in dominating by kindness.   Law may appear in a new guise, but it is still law.   Thus the tribunal, for all its claims about 'full participation', still presents intact the old model of law-givers on the one hand, and law-takers on the other.   The chairman may, indeed, be a genial fellow;   there may well be flowers in the room, carpets on the floor, comfortable chairs and all the other paraphernalia which taken together enables us to declare that the bourgeois is at home.   But it is his home;   you are invited there and must behave on his terms.   Nor should 'kadi' justice be mistaken - as it sometimes is - for a 'popular' justice.   Indeed, the sharp individualizing of decision-making which is implied by the former means that even the circumscribed safeguards of the traditional adversary system are lacking, i.e. a system of what Selznick (1965) has called 'institutionalised criticism', and the formal rules surrounding it that help limit the arbitrariness of magistrates and judges.

What tribunals have done is to bring in the law-advocate in significant numbers.   These, however, are less likely to be the 'friend' of the claimant applicant than a social worker or some other professional figure.   Social workers, in particular, find the advocate's role a congenial one.   For them the attractiveness of the role can be reduced to the following terms.   It seems to offer the prospect of more effective, or a more 'rounded' social work practice.   Again, tribunal representation satisfied the social worker's search for fresh 'territory' (expansion of influence and areas for professional practice).

The debate about the efficacy of social workers as lay-advocates is basically an argument by liberal reformers about how best to 'bring law to the people'.   As such, the potential of social workers as advocates is usually contrasted favourably with the shortcomings of an unreformed legal profession.   This juxtaposition would seem to raise important political questions. First, do we want a reformed legal profession? That is, one willing and able to spread into the areas patrolled by social workers. Second, what actually happens when social workers take on the mantle of the advocate? One answer to this query is provided in Rose's (1973) research into different styles of representation before social security tribunals.

In this tribunal the appellant tended to be aided either by a Child Poverty Action Group (CPAG) representative, or, when Claimants' Union (CU) members, by a fellow claimant. Rose observed that the different representatives had markedly different styles of approaching the tribunal. These variations were described by Rose in this way (1973, p.411):

Where the middle class advocate may cite research evidence, the levels of unemployment or the range of local rents, the CU member will talk from direct experience about the length of the dole queue and the impossibility of finding alternative accommodation. The predominantly middle class character of the tribunals means that they can relate more easily to the middle class language with its impersonal courtesy of the CPAG advocates than to what is seen as the demanding hectoring style of the unions....

There is a tendency for a form of middle class co-option to emerge, whereby the educated and the expert enter into a compassionate complicity, where the chairman and the well-briefed middle class representative retreat into an expert's world leaving the appellant no longer an actor in his own destiny but merely the object of the case at issue....

Not only do the unions have a continuous relationship with particular tribunals through appearing frequently before them, they also have a continuous relationship between represented and representative, roles may be reversed and both are equal members of the same organisation. Representing at an appeal is not a service carried out by an expert advocate but is part of an ongoing membership activity of CU members helping and defending one another. Thus although in actuality it happens that some CU members are better than others at representing at appeals, and among members there is sometimes a feeling that they would rather be represented by one of the 'experts', there is at the same time an attempt to minimise this growth of alternative experts and to subordinate it to a practice of equality between members. Not only because of class differences between the advocate and the appellant, often skilfully exacerbated by chairmen, the advocate is essentially an alternative expert. The potential appellant applying to CPAG cannot demand representation as a right regardless of the nature of his appeal, as the CU member can and does. For the CU the appellant is a person who would take an active part within the union in the planning, organising and conduct of his appeal. Deciding the conduct of an appeal is seen as a practical experience within a philosophy of self activity. (31)

This is in sharp contrast to the style of representation adopted by the CPAG worker; no matter how well-intentioned they might be - in practice the social distance between the middle-class advocate and the claimant appellant tends to mean that in order to gain

the tribunal's sympathy for the appellant, and share the
advocate's compassion, the exposure of distress is employed and
the claimant is discussed as if he or she were not in the room.
Claimants, in the mobilising of compassion are thus confirmed
as objects and do not become subjects in their own right (Rose,
1973, p.412).
It is this form that the 'new dimension' of law wants to bring in.
What we see then, is the equating of the 'new' lawyer with that of
social worker.   The law then is to become a form of social work
practice.   But this social work version of the law is taken from
official versions of what social work is.   There is no regard paid
to the significant ideological disputes among social workers as to
what their profession does.   Social work becomes the new panacea
for law.   There is informality and there is compassion, but the
defendant still comes through this objectified and dehumanized.

This liberalizing largely takes place in tribunals;   judges and
the official law courts are still by and large resistant and
conservative.   That they are not all so can be seen in the writings
of Scarman and in the practice of Donaldson, who was President of
the now defunct NIRC.   He understood well that to bring the court
to the people was not to lose the control that it had - on the
contrary.   Indeed the court worked hard at being informal and its
efforts did not go unappreciated by the newspapers of the time.
One report ran as follows ('Observer', 12 May 1974):

Considering that the Industrial Relations Court was the storm
centre of the week's great industrial crunch, its committee-like
atmosphere came as something of a let-down when we went to watch
its death-throes.   Tucked unceremoniously into the Royal Exchange
Insurance building at 5 Chancery Lane, it has none of the
hallowed pomp of the Law courts or the sternness of the Old
Bailey.   Court 1, where Sir John Donaldson sits, is a windowless,
conference-style room with white neon lights, black plastic
chairs and grey-suited men.   No wigs or gowns, no royal-coats-
of-arms, it's rather like a smoothly run board of directors
talking things over with its chairman, who in this case is the
informal, calm, bland Sir John, a lean 54 year-old with a week-
end sailor's tan.   It went down very well when he made a little
joke about doing his arithmetic on pension rights - the QCs
almost laughed.   The informality is deliberate.   When the
court was set up two years ago, only women ushers were brought
over from the High Court up the road - presumably to add a soft
motherly touch to the brutal contours of industrial law.   Great
favourites are Betty and Joan, two sisters from Hackney (one of
them, surprisingly, a grandmother), both extremely pretty and
carefully made up.   They cosset the court, looking not unlike
the best type of tea-room waitress, in their black pinafore
dresses and gowns, displaying a touch of lacy white shirt.
It is in this way that control remains with the law and lawyers and,
ultimately, with capitalist society.   The law, though seeming to
give away everything, does not let anything of value go.   People
are shown that there is nothing that they can do to organize their
lives in freedom and that the law must do it for them.   They are
to give up their humanity to the law.   We close this section with
three examples of how this happens.

In a television programme on legal aid one image stood out.
The aim of the programme was to establish legal advice centres as
a progressive new force in socio-legal welfare.   By way of contrast
it showed a system of charity at work.   In one scene a city-dressed
lawyer talked in an impeccable accent to an old man.   He told him
to leave the papers and forms concerning his problem with him and on
his return they would be prepared, ready for signature.   What is
the ideological meaning of this scene?   First, there is a picture
of an old man who is seen as alone, poor and friendless.   The only
thing that he has which he can call his own is his problem.   The
lawyer takes away the last thing that the old man has which enables
him to think that people still react in some way to him, his
problem.   In taking it away, the lawyer takes away the last of the
man's battered humanity.   The meaning is plain - he is being
confirmed as a failure.   The only thing that he can do is sign his
name.   The image that we portrayed was not simply a product of
'the bad old ways' to be changed by the new breed of lawyers and
the legal advice centres.   The essence of that situation is all
too often repeated there, only the accents and the clothes have
changed.   People are still being dehumanized, although more 'nicely'.
Their problems are being removed.   Their experience of how things
are solved is being negated.   They are told that the only way of
solving their problems is to leave them to the expert;   to the
lawyers, to the planners, to the doctors, to the social workers.(32)
They are the ones who know, they are on your side, they will solve
your problems.   Law establishes professionalized ways of solving
social problems.   It uses as its model, 'the expert', and as its
yardstick, 'efficiency'.   In chapter 3 we present detailed empirical
evidence for this claim, we confine ourselves here to its ideological
message.
     The key words are 'reasonable' and 'rational'.   One argument that
some lawyers have developed to defend tort law against its total
abolition and replacement by insurance schemes is the notion of
'tort law as ombudsman'.   Thus, by using the law of torts people
can exert power over situations like the nuisance of an oil refinery
and the lorries that drive to it, day and night, where insurance can
give no help.   They can exert power by 'rational means' instead of
'just throwing rocks'.   The message of this argument is to defuse
the situation and take the forum of argument away from the location
of the incident.   Give it to the lawyers who will talk about it in
a language that few understand.   In the meantime nothing happens.
A year goes by and still nothing happens except that the people who
live in the neighbourhood become increasingly distraught, they are
unable to live in peace because of the nuisance.   The social
services try to defuse the situation.   People are calmed.   Nothing
happens.   In this situation is it not more 'rational' to throw
rocks at the lorries and the refineries?   We think that the answer
is obvious and that it is a tribute to the power of law that more
people do not see it. (33)
     The final example of taking over people's lives and struggles
can be seen in the Industrial Relations Act 1971.   Five shop
stewards were gaoled for contempt of the NIRC which forbade them to
picket (34) because they were acting against union policy.   They

were finally released, for the court held that they had acted as
agents of the union.   Therefore, it was the union that should be
proceeded against and not its servants.   The ideological message
is that the struggle was to be transferred from the grass roots to
the central bureaucratic machine.   It was not to be the dockers'
struggle, but the struggle of the Transport and General Workers'
Union.   This was part of the ideological significance of the
Industrial Relations Act.   The Act recognized the fact that unions
were losing power to the grass roots and tried to remedy that
situation by strengthening the union structure.   The aim was to
clamp down upon unofficial union activity.   It gave incentive to
the unions to reassert control over their own members, for
'responsible and fair' activity was not frowned upon and one of the
ways of being 'responsible and fair' was to have the activity
controlled by the union.   'Irresponsible' unofficial activity was
excluded because that results in workers searching for their own
power.   The struggle must not appear to take place between the
worker and his employer but between the employer and the trade
union machine.   These are the political consequences of seeking
the law in a form which confirms this sort of organization of
society.   Law is the celebration of the professional mode: the
institution of the society 'fit for experts to live in', a society
where people are dehumanized by being denied the capacity to
determine, self-consciously, their own lives.

'LAW HAS GONE AWAY'

We have so far argued that law can only be understood in terms of
the material base of society and that its ideological function
(apart from its overt repressive one) is to legitimate authority
and so deny the propertyless class their power.   They are symbolically emasculated by the insistence that there is nothing that
they can do directly to better their lot, and by the insistence,
in the liberal mode, that the neutral means of law should be
employed to achieve this.   This liberal moment makes them more
powerless because increasingly they have to rely on the 'experts'
of capitalist society to solve their problems.   These problems
are - as we shall see in later chapters - in a large measure manufactured by that society itself.
    Briefly, our point is that the law will not change capitalist
society because it is absurd to suggest, as such an approach does,
that you can somehow make capitalism illegal or immoral.   Capitalism is neither of these things;   it is a way of organizing the
productive base of a society and for a society to be radically
different then that base must be changed.   The problem is two-fold.
First, it is to show what the society is really like.   This means
an analysis of that society without regard to moral outrage.   It
means, if the law is to be the focus of attention, looking at those
aspects of law that are important to the capitalist mode of
production and not those that are on its productive margins;   for
those obscure the reality of the society in trying to deny what it
really is.   By this we do not mean exposing the exploiters; naming
the names and generally showing the unacceptable face of capitalism,

we mean showing the hard facts of everyday productive life under
capitalism. (35) To do otherwise would be to fall into the trap
of moral outrage and to succumb to the desire to show that it is
really unfair; thereby accepting the bourgeois fact-value gap.
That is, to describe a system is not to give reasons for any action
that is to be taken with regard to it (Wood, 1971, pp.281-2):

> There is nothing problematic about saying that disguised exploit-
> ation, unnecessary servitude, economic instability, and declining
> productivity are features of a productive system which constitute
> good reasons for changing it.... no one has ever denied that
> capitalism, understood as Marx's theory understands it, is a
> system of unnecessary servitude, replete with irrationalities
> and ripe for destruction. Still less has anyone defended
> capitalism by claiming that a system of this sort might after
> all be good or desirable, and it is doubtful that any moral
> philosophy which could support such a claim would deserve a
> serious consideration.

This means that radicals who are law teachers would actually have
to work at subjects that they tend to disdain because they are 'for
the rich'. Capitalism is what is being studied and their laws,
the ones that protect them, should be scrutinized; not just the ones
whose purpose is to neutralize proletarian power.

The second prong to the problem is to show the people that they
have the power. Our model has so far shown that this is what all
law in capitalist society denies. Thus to use law in this society
can only exacerbate the feelings of powerlessness. The problem is
not how to use law protectively but how to build up proletarian
power so that the society can be reorganized into one that is truly
free. What is important is the taking over of houses that are
unoccupied and not the taking out of injunctions; the taking over
of factories and entire industries and not the implementation of
further nationalization and participation measures; the taking
over of the entire society and not making illegal the 'unacceptable
face of capitalism'. In this way the law becomes irrelevant to
the building of a free society. We will show in chapter 5 how, in
situations where people are forced to use the law because their
survival depends upon it, legal modes of control can be by-passed
by treating the situation not as a stage where legal victories are
won, but where political lessons could be taught the world.

We close this chapter with a word about 'socialist legal institutions'. It will have become clear that to talk of them within the
content of a capitalist society is a misconstruction for no matter
how 'nice' the law is, it will still reflect the controls of a
capitalist society. This sort of society throws up a lot of law
for it has to maintain the property rights of those who control,
while at the same time having to neutralize the power of the
proletariat. 'Socialist legal institutions' can only be seen in
a society where these sorts of problems are not thrown up. For
the whole point of such a society is to eliminate such problems by
socializing production. In this way law and the state begin to
wither away. Society is organized upon the basis that power comes
from below rather than from the top. (36)

These sorts of organizations have been thrown up by working
class struggle in the past. In Russia in 1905 and 1917, in Germany,

Italy and Hungary after the First World War, workers' councils
were formed more or less in direct opposition to the bourgeois
state.   These councils were the main deliberative bodies, to which
all in the factory or group belonged.   Delegates to central or co-
ordinating committees were never full-time and were instantly
recovable.   In that way the emergence of full-time leaders is
impossible.   It is these organizations that are the models for mass
democracy and the way in which the working class can communize the
relations of production.   In this sort of a society law will
genuinely wither away.   But capitalist law assumes that the State
is permanent; that there always has to be some central body in
society necessary for leadership and organization.   Thus today the
self-activity of the working class is channelled into more and more
bureaucracies and legal modes of participation.   To achieve a
libertarian revolution people must learn to organize their own
liberation.   We do not claim that what we advocate can be achieved
easily.   Undoubtedly it will be hard and in striving for it we
tread the knife edge between freedom and barbarism but the struggle
is worth while.   It is better to try, and fail, than to do nothing
even where the very freedom of the organization makes it more
susceptible to defeat.

This then brings us to the 'problem' of 'law' as a form of
administration in a complex but free society.   As we have claimed,
many of the present functions of law will disappear.   The policing,
and many of the complex regulations for maintaining a highly fragile
social system will go, to be replaced by the system of councils that
we have mentioned.   But problems will still remain; for, though
law will wither away, there will still be the difficulty of running
a free but relatively complex society.   The argument is well put
by Wolff (1970).   He argues that the sort of vision that has been
put forward here is a variation on the theme of mass democracy.
This argument, he goes on to claim, falls foul of the fetishism
of majority rule.   Council democracy, unless there is unanimity,
still assumes that in the case of disagreement one side will win
against the other.   Thus in this society, Wolff argues, law will
be the expression of community power over a member of the community.
What is wrong with his argument is that it is not seen within the
context of a socialized means of production.   Obviously there will
be difference of opinion, but that need not make the law oppressive.
Law will be the product of socialized decision-making and control,
and man as socialized being will be free, even though he disagrees
with individual decisions.   The Wolffian argument implies the same
sort of private realm that capitalist society lays down; disagreement will be important in the way that individual agreement and
individual action are important within a capitalist society.   The
point is that within capitalist society the only public life that
you can have is a private one.   In a society where man lives as
a socialized being the meaning of private will be different and
these manifestations of his individual importance will not be the
blockages to living communally that they are now.   Man in a different world will be a different man. (37)

It is in this way that we can also look at Mills's problem;
how are we to act so as not to infringe another's occupations?   In
a society where men will pursue different activities, a society of

'socialist diversity', (38) 'legality' will in some sense reappear because it will help to ease the problems of clashing diversities. But within the context of a socialized means of production, these problems, unlike Mills's, will not have individualism built into the statement of the problem and therefore cannot figure in the solution.

The aim of socialist society is to make men's relationships with each other, and with the world, obvious and not obfuscated by various ideologies.   This is done by constructing a society where the individual is not king and where socialized man reigns.   Only then, as Marx said, will human history truly begin.

Chapter 2

LEGAL PROBLEMS AND SOCIAL PROBLEMS

INTRODUCTION

The aim of this chapter is to establish how certain situations
come to be defined as either 'legal problems' or 'social problems'.
Our enquiry is into different aspects of those phenomena designated
as problems, and the differences of approach between lawyers and
social scientists in considering such 'problems'. Law students
assume, or are educated, that legal solutions are normally the
only worthwhile solutions to problems. We challenge this approach
ab initio.

   This chapter also serves as an early introduction to some of
the issues which inform the design of the remaining chapters in the
book. These issues include the character of 'legal knowledge',
the education and socialization of law students and lawyers; the
power of the legal profession vis-à-vis both the public and other
professions; and the general domination of law in our society. We
open this chapter with an account of how 'legal problems' and the
'need for law' are commonly defined, explained and presented in
basic textbooks of law.

SCHLOCK TALK: THE LEGAL PROBLEM AND THE LAW TEXTBOOK

The term 'schlock' (1) has been coined to describe the way in which
the authors of texts on social problems and 'deviance', frequently
resort to broad and bland generalizations to avoid concrete study
of the uses of power in the creation and labelling of 'deviance'.
In this section we look at some of the features of commonly used
textbooks of law which help define the contents of such books as
'schlock' law. We begin with a brief study of a professional
ideology as it is exhibited in a set of law textbooks. The texts
are not randomly selected; instead, they represent those most
commonly offered as a first course to university and polytechnic
law students. (2) They are textbooks which help define, for the
noviciate, the character of law in general and of the English legal
system in particular. In other words, we seek to show how a number
of key textbooks of law set about conceptualizing the nature of the
'legal problem'.

First, we borrow a question from C. Wright Mills. (3)   To what
type of society are these texts oriented and how do they present
and explain the development and contemporary form of law in England?
Most of the texts open with an historical review of the English legal
system and stress the essential continuity of English law.   This
is explained by emphasizing the 'processional' and 'organic'
character of English society.   The texts draw upon a range of anthro-
pomorphic imagery, where the 'state', or 'society' or the 'country'
are awarded needs and dispositions which personalize them and render
them manageable for textbook purposes.   Moreover, the evolution
of English law is seen not merely as a fit subject for study, but
as a proper object for celebration and admiration:

> It is a constant source of wonder to foreigners that our law is
> built up to so great an extent on assumption: that in the most
> fundamental matters...there are so few direct commands and
> prohibitions.... In all branches, the assumptions on which our
> law is built are so many and so vital that it is tempting to
> regard them all as spontaneous outcrops of the national genius.

Nor should 'our law' be construed in any other way (Kiralfy, 1954,
p.3):

> Experience of revolutionary changes in other countries...suggests
> that our traditional methods of reasoning and our tried
> procedures will prove the best, even in such decidedly altered
> conditions.

But if 'the law' did not evolve entirely spontaneously how did it
attain its present form?   In the majority of these texts, the
'administrative reforms' of the nineteenth century are seen as the
crucial turning point.   'Crucial', that is, in so far as a legal
system that had previously been stricken by poor organization and
incompetent stewardship, was put firmly back on the rails.   According
to one account (James, 1972, p.39):

> The nineteenth century was an age of turmoil and reform.   The
> reform movement was largely due to the exertions of one man,
> Jeremy Bentham who, throughout his long life, set himself the
> task of publicly criticising legal institutions and of writing
> books suggesting the means for their reforms.

There was 'cause for concern' and only 'sweeping legislation could
clear the dead wood'.   The 'nineteenth century saw a change of
attitude'.

The vehicle for reform was the Royal Commission and the Victorian
period saw the 'rationalization' and 'cleaning up' of the legal
system (G. Wilson, 1973, pp.10-12).   'Rationalization' for what,
however, is never made entirely clear.   While 'concern' about the
legal system is acknowledged, the discussion of law reform is seldom,
if ever, linked to questions of antagonistic interests, social
conflicts or group struggles.   Instead, law is presented as capable
of reproducing itself in the style of an hermaphrodite.   Where
'outside influences' are conceded, they are usually acknowledged
in the form of a variant of the 'Great Man Theory of History'
thesis.   'Class' and capitalism receive no mention and for good
reason.   Since law textbooks encourage the idea that 'the law'
is somehow above 'politics' or separate from it, then it is not
surprising that they turn away from the study of how different
conflicts of interests have impinged upon and shaped the law.   The

student of law learns to accept the 'system' as inherently self-directing, the whole project being grounded in the alleged 'neutrality' of law, where politics is seen as something 'out there'.   What is given instead is a partial (in the sense of being both incomplete and partisan) constitutional history, situated in a context of incrementalism, gradualism and accumulating decency. History, in so far as it is systematically analysed, is read in the light of subsequent preoccupations, and not as in fact it occurred. We are left, through these texts, with what E.P. Thompson (1968, p.12) has called 'the "Pilgrim's Progress" orthodoxy', where history is ransacked for early exemplars of the present state of things. In Thompson's words (1968, p.13) 'Only the successful (in the sense of those whose aspirations anticipated subsequent evolution) are remembered.   The blind alleys, the lost causes, and the losers themselves are forgotten'.   The sternest invective of these text-book authors is reserved for the pre-nineteenth century English legal system.   Up to that juncture it is possible to find aspects of the law being categorized as 'oppressive'.   Williams (1973, p.208), for example, writes: 'The lawyer must feel a sense of shame about the part played by the legal mechanism in repressing the poor in the eighteenth and nineteenth centuries'.   Thereafter - beyond the 'great age of the Royal Commission' - criticisms of the legal system are articulated in more muted terms.   The language of the textbooks, for this period, is replete with notions of 'problems', 'inconsistencies' and 'inadequacies'.   It would seem, if we take our cue from these authors, that law is about domination only when we have a distant memory of it.   From this perspective the 'modern' legal system, while still seen as beset by certain 'shortcomings' is nevertheless taken to be in reasonably good health, in contrast with that system which preceded it.   In this way, the authors draw their reified histories of the English legal system to a close.

A more recent text (Scarman, 1974) has the dubious distinction of repeating all of the old errors in trying to identify cause and effect in changes in English law (p.34):

> A short reference to two of the somersaults of English law can
> illustrate the superb flexibility of its muscles.   It conserved
> and regulated the feudal system for centuries: but when the
> divine right of kings, feudal tenure and the burden of feudal
> services were laid to rest finally in the seventeenth century,
> the law adjusted itself without any sign of stress to the
> principles of the freedom of man - limited only by the need to
> preserve society itself - a philosophy of which Locke was the
> finest English exponent.   When freedom was found to leave the
> problems of the weak and the socially exploited unsolved, the
> law changed direction under the guidance of Jeremy Bentham and
> John Stuart Mill.

Sentiments such as these are part of the staple fodder of the English legal system textbook.   By this light law is seen as healthily parasitic on 'society'.   It also touches upon what Midgeley (1975) has called the 'profound influence of Bentham theory' of legislative developments in the nineteenth century. (4) But what Scarman does not do, and in this respect he marches behind the same banner as these authors we have so far considered, is to

make intelligible the 'why' and 'how' of legal and social change.
As Griffith has put it (1975, p.38):

> Reform of the law was not achieved by double-jointed judges
> but by politicians, philanthropists, some industrialists and
> many tough-minded members of the artisan and working classes.
> The reforms had nothing to do with the common law and everything
> to do with political protests, governments and Parliament.
> Indeed, the main contribution of the common lawyers was to make
> decisions in the courts which restricted the reforms to as small
> an area as possible.

Let us turn again to the idea of the 'rationalization' of law,
and to the question - 'rationalization' for what purpose?   The
'administrative reforms' of the nineteenth century, and hence the
reclassification of legal problems, are depicted either as the
fruits of a polymathic talent such as that of Bentham, the outcome
of the agitation of other 'critics' or, as the expression of some
'general concern'.   Such ways of seeing divorces law from the
influence of political action and imputes to it a pristine and
olympian quality.   This becomes clearer if the textbook exegesis
is compared with Weber's (1965) explanation for the 'rationalization'
of law.   For Weber rational structures of law (and administration)
are derived from the demands of 'the peculiar modern Western form
of capitalism' (1965, p.24).   According to Weber (1965, p.25):

> Modern rational capitalism has need, not only of the technical
> means of production, but of a calculable legal system and of
> administration in terms of formal rules.   Without it adventurous
> and speculative trading capitalism and all sorts of politically
> determined capitalisms are possible, but no rational enterprise
> under individual initiative, with fixed capital and certainty of
> calculations.   Such a legal system and such administration have
> been available for economic activity in a comparative state of
> legal and formalistic perfection only in the Occident.

Here, then, lies the principal force for the 'rationalization' of
the legal system, but it is one which finds no echo in the law
textbook. (5)   In contrast for G. Wilson (1973, p.17) the modern
English legal system has arrived 'trailing clouds of history behind
it', but the content of that history is seldom spelt out.   Instead,
processes of change are reified;   it is 'the law' which changes
because, and for, reasons of 'administrative convenience'.   Thus
when James (1972, p.20) refers to 'the struggle of the law to keep
pace with change' the tendency to reify and mystify the sources of
English law is increased.   We are told that 'the law' and 'change'
are sometimes at odds with each other but no attempt is made to
examine the status of either notion.

Going beyond 'history' to the present, it is common to find in
the texts the classification of English law into its different
categories and some discussion of 'prospects for further reform'.
References to those social formations, or what Wright Mills called
'the larger stratifications and structured wholes' which determine
and reflect the content and form this law, are sparse.   When
totalities are considered it is usually in terms of such concepts
as 'society' the 'social order' or 'the country'.   For example,
Hood Phillips (1970) refers to 'a changing society'.   Kiralfy
(1954, p.5) talks of the 'heightened tempo of modern life' as a

source of stress and change for law; Jackson dwells upon 'the
complex pattern of our way of handling national affairs' while
G. Wilson (1973, p.1) employs the notion of the 'modern industrial-
ised country', with its 'complex legal system'. G. Wilson (1973,
p.5) insists that the English legal system be looked at as a 'whole',
although we are warned that it is a structure which is 'fragmented,
complex, changing, detailed and factual'. Consequently, we may
only reasonably hope, according to Wilson, to perhaps 'catch a
glimpse' of this chimeral organism. This approach comes close to
what C. Wright Mills (1963) called the 'safe, colourless, "multiple-
factor" view of causation' (p.536). In Mills's terms, 'A formal
emphasis upon "the whole" plus lack of total structural consideration...does not make it easy to reform the status quo' (p.537).
What this means, if we adapt Mills's point as a critique of certain
English legal system texts, is that the vague 'organic' orientation
of writers like Wilson will never help to explain why the English
legal system has taken the shape it has.

To return to an earlier theme, the basis of these 'changes', the
character of our 'modern life', the sort of 'industrialized country'
we live in, are issues left untouched. Consequently, the
'stability', 'order' and 'solidarity' that are thought to be derived
from 'the society' are ignored. There is more than an echo of the
idea of natural law relationships. These relationships were
considered necessary in the sense that stability and order among
the living could not exist without them. Individuals, according
to this view, could choose to live 'unnaturally', but this choice
would be disastrous to them because unnatural relationships would
eventually disintegrate into disorder and chaos. The 'secular-
ization' of natural law occurs in textbooks when it is suggested
social life without 'our law' would be unthinkable and degenerate.
The textbook author takes the omnipotence of law for granted. Nor
should this be otherwise given that the lawyer is seen, above all
else, as a pragmatic fellow. Thus (Kiralfy, 1954, p.2):

The great majority of people in every community spend their
lives without passing through the doors of law courts, just
as many healthy people never require the services of a doctor.
For the professional lawyer, as distinct from the social
scientist, however, this is really irrelevant. He is called
upon to conduct litigation, to draft legal documents or give
legal advice, in cases where disputes are possible or have
already arisen.

This is an argument for the dominance of the 'professional-as-
technician' role. He is the man who is reluctant to ask questions;
partly because his education has not equipped him to be able to
think of any, and partly because this exclusive definition of his
work role subordinate all other concerns to the pursuit of 'doing
law'. This puts us in mind of Chomsky's (1969) description of the
'new mandarins' in the USA; that is, those professional (mainly
university academics) who helped mastermind the war in South East
Asia. Chomsky was concerned about professionals whose 'professionalism' reduced the status of every political issue to a
'technical problem' or 'administrative exercise'. Such a cast of
mind reflected, said Chomsky (1969, p.24):

a highly restrictive, almost universally shared ideology and
the inherent dynamics of professionalisation.... The professional...tends to define his problems on the basis of the
technique that he has mastered, and has a natural desire to
apply his skills.

The comparison is not a fanciful one. The same division of the
world into 'problems' (relevant, interesting) on the one hand, and
'wider issues' (irrelevant, speculative) on the other, typifies
the occupational style of both Chomsky's mandarins and the professional lawyer. Both are self-styled 'trouble-shooters', even
though the canvasses on which they work may be different.

Some might argue that the law textbook reflects no 'highly
restrictive ideology' and indeed does record the totality of
disagreements and disputes within the contemporary English legal
profession. Certainly English legal system textbooks register
contrary opinions about law and the varying degrees of satisfaction.
Some typical illustrative comments are:

The modernisation of the machinery of justice will be a very
slow process unless the legal profession can cease to be backward
looking and fit itself for the conditions of a changing society
(Jackson, 1967, p.468).

In recent decades...the heightened tempo of modern life has
caused the slow pragmatic development (of English law) to prove
inadequate by itself (Kiralfy, 1954, p.5).

Cross and Hand (1971, p.429) refer to the problem, for the lawyer,
of how best to 'bring law to the people', and Zander (1973)
documents some of the shortcomings and failures of current attempts
to achieve a 'justice for all'.

But these are the murmurings of men who are deeply in love with
the law. This is the reason why the rage is directed against what
is perceived to be the incompetence, the selfishness, the narrow-
mindedness of certain lawyers, and against the 'inadequacy' of some
areas of law. But the claim of the need for law goes unquestioned,
as does the particular style of its control and administration. It
is part of their taken-for-granted world - a world that Auden (1966)
portrayed

Law is as I've told you before,
Law is as you know I suppose,
Law is but let me explain it once more,
Law is the Law.

Consequently, the only legitimate aim can, and must, be to make
that law better. As a result, those who would impair its
efficiency or injure its purpose, should be turned upon. In
other words, the actual parameters of the debate about the efficacy
of law are, in the final analysis, narrowly drawn. We can
illustrate this point in another way. Several years ago 'The Times',
in an editorial, was fierce in its criticism of the San Francisco
police for their violent treatment of demonstrators on a university
campus. Different points were made in the denunciation, the
violence was 'unnecessary'; it harmed the 'image' of the police;
the law was brought into 'disrepute'. Throughout the comment the
power of the police went unchallenged, the rights of the demonstrators went unrecorded and the political context of the event remained
unexplained. Having taken for granted the idea that such people

(demonstrators) should be 'dealt with', the remaining matter for
discussion is the most 'humane' way of 'dealing' with them.   So
it is with the critics of the English legal system we have mentioned.
As Rock (1974) has put it, our formulation of ideas about what
passes as 'central problems', depends on what we take for granted
regarding the rest of the world.

In law textbooks (as in any other), the 'facts' selected for
treatment are not 'random'.   According to Mills (1963, p.530):

> One way to grasp the perspective within which they do this is
> to analyse the scope and character of their problems.   What are
> the selecting and organising principles to be extracted from
> the range and content of these texts?   What types of fact come
> within their field of attention?

The direction of the law textbook is towards particular 'practical
problems', to the problems of 'everyday life'.   The emphasis
throughout is on practicality, on not being 'theoretical' or
'speculative';   law is a hard-nosed business and must be seen as
such.   For this reason the English legal system textbook is, in
equal measure, a book of instruction and of justification.   Thus
the legal system is explained not only as working in a particular
way but also that it is good that it operates in such a fashion.
The texts we have been referring to are bereft of serious historical
scholarship and of any discussion of social science.   True, the
latter is not entirely ignored, but is generally considered useful
in so far as its findings and concepts may be used to improve the
lawyer's handling of legal problems - in short, to make law
stronger.   For this reason the favourite social science handmaiden
of the law textbook is criminology, whose use to lawyers is seen
as offering techniques for both the exploitation and pacification
of criminals. (6)   By exploitation we refer to the criminal-as-
commodity for the lawyer, where a knowledge of criminology can
further professional self-interest.   By pacification (or control)
we refer to the threat of criminal to the lawyer-as-citizen, and
criminology's contribution to the regulation of 'outsiders'.

Occasionally it is recognized that the law may fall down on the
job of resolving legal problems (James, 1972, p.19):

> During the present century it has come to be realised that more
> direction is required in the matter of law reform than the
> traditional agencies of change and supply.   Special committees
> therefore came into being.... Even these have, however, not been
> successful in giving full impetus to the desire for reform.

We are back to 'schlock' talk again;   'it has come to be realised';
'Special committees therefore came into being';   'the desire for
reform'.   Why 'the law' is judged to be inadequate, who decides
what criteria should govern reform, who gains from any new arrangement, are questions never raised.

THE LEGAL PROBLEM AS PROBLEMATIC

In these texts there is little or no discussion of what is meant
by a 'legal problem'.   The status of such 'problems' are presented
as non-problematic.   It is assumed that everyone knows what such

problems are and that explication of them is unnecessary.   This
view rests upon two assumptions; that a 'problem' is either a
legal problem or it is not and that clear lines of demarcation
exist between different kinds of problems.   Second, that once a
problem is defined as legal, then only a lawyer (the agent who does
the defining in the first place) can sensibly be expected to take
care of it. (7)
    This mode of thinking merits careful examination.   We begin by
taking up points made by Lewis in an essay critical of orthodox
thinking on the nature of the 'legal problem'.   Lewis argues
forcefully (Morris et al., 1973, p.75):

> to say that someone has a legal problem is not a description of
> a state of fact; it is to suggest that he should take a certain
> course of action, or that his situation could best be dealt with
> by taking such a course of action.   Whether this is so or not
> will often be debatable, and it may be that the appropriate
> course of action will be such that we should prefer to speak of
> the person as having a political problem.

It would be wrong to infer from this that people either have 'legal'
or 'political' problems.   Clearly those who show a preference for
classifying issues as 'legal' rather than 'political' problems are
displaying their own kind of political commitment.   In other words,
what a person defines as 'political' or as 'non-political' is,
itself, a political act.   This is implied elsewhere in Lewis's
essay (1973, p.79):

> when someone says that a person has a legal problem or says that
> a particular problem under discussion is a legal one...the
> typical suggestion is that action should be taken before some
> court or similar institution or that the services of a lawyer
> should be employed.   Very broadly, the point I should like to
> make...is that if certain problems are spoken of as legal ones,
> and official support is given to legal methods of solving them,
> that is to take a particular attitude to problems of that kind,
> problems which may be capable of solution in some other way, and
> which may be seen by those most closely concerned as best solved
> in that other way.

This interpretation is possible if we recognize that law, by its
very existence, implies that situations are problematic.   In this
sense, law can be seen as a 'contrivance' and, as a result, legal
problems as problematic,. as socially constructed - the outcome of
what Rock called 'constant, complicated exchanges' between law
officers, other law enforcement agencies and lay opinion and
power. (8)   This point will be illustrated later in this and
succeeding chapters, but for the moment we seek further clarifi-
cation of the idea of the problematic character of legal issues.
We do this by looking at the notion of the legal problem in the
context of taking law to the poor and the 'socially disadvantaged'.
    The debate has centred upon the extent of legal problems among
the poor and has been enmeshed with the concept of 'need'.
Lawyers speak with increasing certainty about the extent of 'unmet
legal needs' and the best way of serving them.   But as Morris has
rightly put it (Morris et al., 1973, pp.50-2):

> 'Need' is socially defined.   It is important to stress that
> legal need cannot be viewed in any absolute sense, nor can it be

isolated from a more general idea of social need.   In discussing these issues there would seem to be an analogy with the wider field of social services and in particular with the implications of the Seebohm Report, where one of the major drawbacks of the report lies in the failure adequately to define 'social need'...the Seebohm Committee failed to ask how it is that people come to have social needs, they simply said we should find better ways of meeting them.   In practical terms, they redefined 'social need' in terms of an alternative administrative structure, without any clear criteria being established as to how need should be measured or detected, other than in terms of definitions used by existing services.   Such new administrative forms may in effect increase the strength of bureaucratic structures to the detriment of the individual who has 'needs' which, for the most part, are not of his making.

This seems exactly parallel with the present situation in relation to legal services: the definition of unmet need currently being used is that of the lawyer - legal problems are those problems for which there is at present a legal solution, and by a relatively simple head-counting operation which determines how many people have such problems yet do not consult a lawyer, and which discovers to what socio-economic class they belong, it is argued that one can assess, at least in a crude form, the extent and type of unmet need for legal services.

However, Morris goes on to point out that (1973, p.53):

Once one accepts the view that legal and social need are over-lapping categories, and that they are relative and not absolute concepts, then the issue has to be seen as coming within a political context - we are dealing with questions of values not with scientific objectivity.   The 'political' aspect is also reinforced if one considers that the legal profession itself occupies a unique political and social position in the community. Furthermore, it controls access to the formal processes of adjudication and, because of the interaction between the judicial, the legislative and administrative processes, it virtually (though indirectly) controls access to all the formal decision-making and rule-making processes in legislative and administrative bodies as well.

What Morris is, in part, talking about here, is the power of the legal profession to define events as 'legal problems', and the interest it has in doing so. (9)   This view, with which we concur, would seem to be at odds with textbook orthodoxy which suggests that lawyers are the last people to push people into litigation. Hence (Kiralfy, 1954, p.280):

It has always been regarded as being in the public interest that persons should settle their private differences without recourse to legislation.... Now that a high proportion of civil litigation is conducted under 'Legal Aid' the public has direct financial interest in the saving of expense.

At best, this is an disingenuous account of the interplay between public and professional interest.   It ignores, for example, the way in which the 'public interest' is often at odds with the profession's (financial) interest.   In this way the interests of

the latter produces pressure for the creation of legal problems.
This becomes clearer if the discussion of what is, or is not, a
'legal problem' is put in the context of the market situation and
economic terms of work among lawyers.   But because law textbooks
do not follow this line of enquiry, the idea that problems can be
'manufactured' is never seriously entertained.   Our interpretation
will be unacceptable to many lawyers, but the spread of legal aid
which Zander mentions (1973), now means that lawyers - more
precisely, that growing number who depend upon legal aid work for
a large part of their livelihood - have a direct financial interest
in increasing public expenditure.   In chapter 3 we show the
different ways in which this happens, when 'legal aid' becomes, in
effect, a generous subsidy for the legal profession.   In this way
the private practitioner is supported increasingly out of public
funds.
     The power of the legal profession to define events, as described
by Morris, should not be taken only as an expression of material
interests, for it is also linked closely to a concern with the
protection and ownership of legal knowledge.   The interest in the
defence of intellectual property has the consequence of perpetuating
the lawyer's domination of his client-public.   It is a relationship of a Prospero to a Caliban;   the clue to the former's manipulation of the latter is to be found in the mastery of a certain kind
of knowledge about the world, and the particular language which is
a vehicle for it.   If Caliban now rebels, breaking free from
Prospero's language, then Prospero's professed values can be self-
destructive.   To seize his knowledge is to seize the world.   The
rendering of a professional service (in our case, the lawyer-client
'service' relationship depends on maintaining the incompetence
of the 'other' - the client.   It is difficult to see how this can
be otherwise.   The knowledgeable client is a threat to the
professional, for the basis of the latter's expertise (special
knowledge) has been undermined as the mysteries are dissolved
through greater popular participation.   While we are still in the
world of law, the control if it is no longer a professional
prerogative, as the client-Caliban asserts himself.
     We present a simple illustration of our point about the problem-
atic status of the legal problem, by looking at the management of
drug-use and the ways in which the definitions of the act have
oscillated from seeing it as 'illegal/criminal' on the one hand,
to behaviour that is viewed as 'sick/illness' on the other.   There
is tension between two 'treatment' models;   one that defines the
drug-taker as largely a legal problem, the other which persists in
seeing him as a clinical case.   In concrete terms we can demon-
strate shifts in the debate by examining the career of drug
legislation in the USA.
     Drug legislation in the USA - the process by which a social
phenomenon comes to be defined as a legal problem - reflects the
dominance of particular social interests in legislative action.
In this context 'social interests' are seen to include Becker's
notion of the 'moral entrepreneur' (and the 'moral crusade'), as
well as an agglomeration of other pressure groups.   Becker (1963)
in his account of the passage of the Marihuana Tax Act, 1937, in
the USA, distinguished between two related phenomena;   rule creators

and rule enforcers. (10)   The 'prototype' of the rule creator,
he who Becker called the 'moral crusader' - the person(s) who
initiate the action, though others may draw up the actual rules.
According to Becker, the moral crusader is typically a person
drawn from the upper levels of the social structure and whose
superior social status helps legitimize (i.e. make respectable)
his agitation.   Examples drawn from English culture of this social
type would include Lord Shaftesbury, Lady Astor and, more recently,
Lord Longford.   These 'crusaders' will often draw in, as
supporters, others with motives very different from those of the
crusader. (11)   For Becker, the successful lobby for stronger
drugs laws meant a victory for the moral crusader.   But another
interpretation has been offered where, in contrast to Becker's
view of the 1937 Act as the outcome of a 'moral enterprise' the
impetus for legislation was seen to come from the law enforcement
agency involved.   In other words, rule enforcers also became law
creators, the significance of their activity being the manufacture
of a vast new 'legal problem'.

This view has been put forward by Dickson (1968).   The starting
point for his thesis was the setting up of the US Bureau of
Narcotics in 1930.   Like all public bureaucracies in the USA at
that time the Bureau had to convince the 'public' and Congress
that it was both serving an essential function and that it was
uniquely qualified to do so.   Since its inception the Bureau has
always tried to widen its legislative mandate by generating a
public outcry against narcotics and narcotics users.   The success
of the strategy depended on getting the use of narcotics defined
as a 'legal' rather than (as hitherto) largely as a 'medical'
problem.   Consequently, any redefinition that took place would
mean that the Bureau had managed to create a large 'criminal class'
for itself.   It also meant that the basis had been laid for
endless talk and dramatization about the 'growing problem' of
drugs.   Put another way, according to Dickson, the struggle over
the 1937 Act was, in large measure, an expression of bureaucratic
impulses geared to ensuring the survival of the Narcotics Bureau
itself.

The Bureau, like the typical moral crusader, achieved its
success partly through a careful orchestration of 'public opinion'
and a claim to represent both the 'national interest' and to be
able to divine threats to that interest.   In this setting, the
structure of 'the legal problem' follows the contours of power and
social influence.   This point is well made if we take a further
example, this time from the regulation of drinking.   In a study
of the American Temperance Movement, Gusfield noted that (1967,
pp.84-5):

> For most of the nineteenth century, the chronic alcoholic as
> well as the less compulsive drinker was viewed as a sinner.
> It was not until after Repeal (1933) that chronic alcoholism
> became defined as illness in the United States.   Earlier
> actions taken towards promotion of the welfare of drinkers and
> alcoholics through Temperance measures rested on the moral
> supremacy of abstinence and the demand for repentance.   The
> user of alcohol could be an object of sympathy, but his social
> salvation depended on a willingness to embrace the norm of his

exhorters.   The designation of alcoholism as sickness has a
different bearing on the question of normative superiority.
It renders the behaviour of the deviant indifferent to the status
of norms enforcing abstinence.... This realisation appears to
have made supporters of Temperance and Prohibition hostile to
efforts to redefine the deviant character of alcoholism.... The
soundness of these fears is shown by what did happen to the
Temperance movement with the rise of the view that alcoholism
is illness.   It led to new agencies concerned with drinking
problems.... Problems of drinking were removed from the church
and placed in the hands of the universities and the medical
clinics.   The tendency to handle drinkers through protective
and welfare agencies rather than through police or clergy has
become more frequent.

The different designations of drinking (as 'immoral', literally
'intemperate', 'sinful', 'sick', or as 'illness') has different
implications for those designated and those doing the designating.
(12)   When the values of certain groups or interests are threatened
this will often be the spur to having those values restated in legal
terms. (13)   In the circumstances we have been describing (that
of 'crimes without victims') the legal norm, as Gusfield points out,
is not the enunciator of a consensus within the community: 'On the
contrary, it is when consensus is at least attainable that the
pressure to establish legal norms appears to be greatest' (p.87).
We referred earlier to the way in which 'public opinion' or the
idea of the 'national interest' is frequently invoked by moral
crusaders in their campaigns for changes in the law.   We explore
this process in more detail, this time taking a recent 'crusade'
in Britain as our illustration.

In 1945, on learning the news of Labour's election victory, a
woman diner at the Savoy Hotel, London, is said to have exclaimed
'But they've elected a Labour government - and the country will
never stand for that.'   Her confusion of thought is paralleled in
Becker's moral entrepreneurs and echoed by all pressure groups who
seek to alter the law in the name of 'public opinion'.   Their
actions devolve upon persuading the public - as they have persuaded
themselves - that their lobby for legislative change is not theirs
at all, but ours;   that their activity is nothing more than a
reflection of the 'general concern'.

A recent instance of this phenomenon is provided by the attempts
by Lord Longford (1972) and his supporters to force a change in the
British obscenity laws, the object of the campaign being to secure
a law that would regulate more closely the activities of 'pornog-
raphers'.   One of the first tactics was to 'collect a large and
powerful committee', (14) which, under Longford's chairmanship,
would investigate 'the mounting (sic) public concern about the
great expansion of pornographic or near pornographic material' (p.11)
and who would, in turn, establish 'what means of tackling the
problem of Pornography would command general support' (p.12).

The committee's report began by '(recalling) the growing public
anxiety in 1970' (p.11) over the spread of pornography.   The
turning point in the 'age-long argument about pornography' was
seen, by Longford, to be the staging ('with impunity') of 'Oh!
Calcutta!' in London in the summer of 1971.   Longford commented
(p.17):

> Somewhere about that time large numbers of those hitherto
> unconcerned...began to share the anxieties expressed for many
> years by other citizens.   All sorts of people began to say
> for the first time 'things have gone too far'.

Who constituted this polyglot multitude who symbolized the growth
of 'public concern'?   Longford offered some examples (p.21):

> Bishop Trevor Huddleston, arriving back after eight years in
> Africa, gave voice to the kind of concern that many people had
> already been feeling.   'I love England', he wrote, 'but the
> moment I came back I felt that things had gone desperately
> wrong.   I think the country is very sick indeed.'   A married
> couple in their twenties, Peter and Janet Hill, were horrified
> on their return after four years in India at the changes they
> saw towards materialism and away from Christian morality.   They
> took up the challenge, and were largely responsible for the
> initiation of the Nationwide Festival of Light that was to be
> launched in 1971.

Others were also named.   Meetings were held and demands spelt out.
With this in mind what does the 'Longford campaign' teach us about
the formulation of 'legal problems'?   In the first place,
differences in the ability to make laws and apply them to other
people are essentially power differentials (e.g. Longford's 'large
and powerful committee').   Next, these processes suggest the
arbitrariness of norms and laws.   This is not to say that they are
all necessarily 'wrong' or 'bad', or indeed that any are necessarily
in that category.   What it does mean is that many laws are not
passed - and legal problems thereby created - and enforced because
they proscribe behaviour which threatens society with some
'objective' harm or damage.   They are passed and enforced, instead,
often because the action in question upsets and angers powerful
social interests. (15)

THE 'LEGAL' AND THE 'SOCIAL': THE DEFINITION OF 'PROBLEMS'

So far we have tried, in contradistinction to the method of law
textbooks, to show the problematic character of 'the legal problem'.
We have also said something about the role of moral crusaders and
of various bureaucratic agencies in the creation of law and legal
problems.   We have yet to comment on the role of the judiciary in
law creation.   English judges, traditionally, have been reluctant
to admit to such legal proclivities.   This has been justified by
one of them - Lord Radcliffe - in this way (1960, pp.38-9):

> However various the sources of our accepted law, no part of it
> has ever made itself.   At the centre there has always been the
> judge.   That is the necessity of the thing, since he alone is
> always at the seat of justice.   He had to ascertain, interpret,
> and here admit and there reject the rules of custom.   He has
> had to interpret and apply, sometimes to enlarge upon, sometimes
> to confine, enacted laws.... We know all this, it is commonplace
> among lawyers.   It recognises, of course, the judge's law-making
> capacity, a capacity which only judges themselves, and that for
> excellent reasons, are likely to dispute.   It is to me a matter
> of surprise that so much pen and ink has been employed by

commentators in demonstrating this fairly obvious conclusion.
If judges prefer to adopt the formula - for that is what it is -
that they merely declare the law and do not make it, they do no
more than show themselves wise men in practice.   Their analysis
may be weak, but their perception of the nature of the law is
sound.   Men's respect for it will be the greater, the more
imperceptible its development.
The basis of this reasoning is expediency.   Acknowledged policy
choices would, in Radcliffe's view, undermine the respect for and
legitimacy of the judiciary.   Such a cast of mind promotes, in
effect, an overt conspiracy against the public.   According to
Palley (1972, p.67): 'Apparently judges think law enjoys esteem
through ignorance of the methods of its creation.   Such an attitude
exhibits contempt for the democratic process.'
     In the remainder of this chapter we examine some of the findings
of modern 'deviancy theorists'.   We draw upon the work of these
researchers for their explanation of the genesis of social - including legal - problems.   Their research tradition is one which has
emphasized the problematical character of 'problems'.   In the
words of one of its principal exponents (Cohen, 1973b, p.12):
     The older tradition (in the study of crime, deviance and social
     problems) was canonical in the sense that it saw the concepts
     it worked with as authoritative, standard, accepted, given and
     unquestionable.   The new tradition is sceptical in the sense
     that when it sees terms like 'deviant' it asks 'deviant to whom?'
     or 'deviant from what?';   when told that something is a social
     problem, it asks 'problematic to whom?';   when certain conditions
     of behaviour are described as dysfunctional, embarrassing,
     threatening or dangerous, is asks 'says who?' and 'why?'.   In
     other words, these concepts and descriptions are not assumed to
     have a taken-for-granted status.
If we compare the approach advocated by Cohen, with that adopted
by Kiralfy (1954) the different modes of thinking about the sources
and nature of 'social problems' are brought into focus.   According
to Kiralfy (1954, p.1):
     There are many matters of morality, decency and good manners on
     which some generally accepted standard exists but which are not
     fit matters for legal compulsion.   On the other hand, there are
     many matters where there is no obvious moral preference one way
     or the other, as in the case of the 'rule of the road'.
This is a testimony to the taken-for-granted status of everyday
life which is symptomatic of the law textbook.   It contrasts
sharply with the perspective that Cohen and others have brought to
bear (Cohen, 1973b, p.13):
     the student of deviance must question and not take for granted
     the labelling by society of certain powerful groups in society
     of certain behaviour as deviant or problematic.   The trans-
     actionalists' importance has been not simply to restate the
     sociological truism that the judgement of deviance is ultimately
     one that is relative to a particular group, but in trying to
     spell out the implication of this for research and theory.   They
     have suggested that, in addition to the stock set of behavioural
     questions which the public asks about deviance and which the
     researcher obligingly tries to answer (why did they do it?   What

sort of people are they? How do we stop them doing it again?)
there are at least three definitional questions: why does a
particular rule, the infraction of which constitutes deviance,
exist at all?   What are the processes and procedures involved
in identifying someone as a deviant and applying the rule to
him? What are the effects and consequences of this application
for society and the individual?

The law textbook typically leaves students on or about the low
water mark left by Kiralfy. Invocations about 'morality, decency
and good manners', or references to the 'rule of the road' or to
traditional beliefs, tell us little about the kind of moral
calculus that underpins the selection and management of social
problems. Thus what is picked out as a social problem and how
and why it comes to be picked out is all but ignored. Law textbooks show a liking, instead, for the idea that 'problems' are
lodged in some kind of objective social structure. From this
perspective, social problems are attributed to 'structural strains',
the 'breakdown of social norms', a 'clash of social values' or,
more popularly, to 'a decline in standards'. Such a view generates
a strong moral impulse for 'dealing' with problems. This, in turn,
rests upon a combination of strong purpose and limited vision which
puts us in mind of the following anecdote on the forming and
solution of one social problem of its day (Blythe, 1964, p.49):

   Homosexuality was something scarcely comprehensible and never
   mentioned before 1914. 'I thought that men like that shot
   themselves', said George V with astonishment when he was told
   that someone he knew quite well was homosexual.

THE CHANGING CHARACTER OF LEGAL AND SOCIAL PROBLEMS

Gusfield (1967) closes his paper on the legal regulation of
drinking with some general remarks on changes that have occurred
in the classification of social behaviour. He talked of how
certain previously unacceptable - in the sense of being both legally
and morally proscribed - attitudes and behaviour have become 're-
designated' as acceptable (though he does not, or cannot, explain
why this happens, or why such behaviour came to be condemned in the
first place). Our aim in this final section is to describe a
different sort of re-definition of 'problems' that is taking place.
One where the labels are not shifted by 'society', but by those
who bore the label acting for themselves.

   We have chosen to concentrate on the classification of a specific
kind of phenomenon, namely the overwhelming definition of most
forms of crime as social (legal) rather than as political problems.
This tendency persists even though it means ignoring the fact that
the decision to treat crime as a social problem is, itself, a
political decision; in other words, what we define as political
is, itself, a political act.

   Against this background some authors have recently gone so far
as arguing that the distinction between crime and 'political
marginality' is now becoming obsolete. For example, Horowitz and
Leibowitz (1968) - using ghettoes in the USA as a backdrop - have
suggested that behaviour in the past conceived of as criminal (the

legal problem) is now assuming clear ideological contours. Thus
it becomes possible to begin to talk in terms of the politicization
of groups like drug-takers and homosexuals. The claim of these
groups to the label of 'political' is derived from their attempts
to resist stigmatization or manipulation in the name of theory -
which may be seen as a self-conscious move to change the social
(including, of course, the legal) order. On the other side,
political marginals such as the Yippies, Weathermen and Black
Panthers have sought to create new styles of political activity
based on strategies traditionally considered criminal. In other
words, the distinction between the 'criminal' and the 'political'
begins to dissolve through the activities of such groups.

The different ways of defining a problem (in this case, the
reversible imagery of the 'criminal' and the 'political') creates
problems in fixing the appropriate label. As Cohen (1973a) pointed
out, there is much confusion about the line beyond which 'stealing'
becomes 'sabotage', or 'hooliganism' becomes 'rioting'. At what
point, to consider another example from Cohen, do 'reckless maniacs'
become 'freedom fighters'?

It would be wrong to dismiss our examples as merely portraying
or hinting at the exotic and esoteric. It is not difficult to draw
major examples from the mainstream of our own society, to underline
the thesis. Consider, for a moment, the laws on picketing and
conspiracy and the manner in which these are made to impinge upon
the activities of trade unionists. The extensive miners' picket
during their strike in 1971 provoked little in the way of legal
action. This was partly explained away at the time with references
to ambiguous laws (which was, and is, true) which it would have been
difficult, or indeed, even unjust, to apply. But is is difficult
not to draw the conclusion that a reluctance to administer the law
stemmed more from the political fear of organized labour and the
consequences of labelling a form of trade union agitation as a
legal issue, than from any concern about problems of 'interpretation'
on a particular legal statute. In other words, the collective and
strategic strength of the miners was sufficient to resist any
pressure to have their action defined as unlawful (i.e. the pre-
empting of the creation of another 'legal problem'). While their
picketing was often condemned (as 'intimidation', 'unlawful', etc.),
it brought forth no legal action, no charges of conspiracy.

This outcome can be compared with the result of the picketing,
by building workers, of selected building sites in North Wales in
1973. There, the labels were reversed; charges arising from the
act of picketing were laid and successful prosecutions made. Why
did this occur? It is hard to escape the conclusion that the
classification of the actions of several building workers as a
'legal issue' ('a matter for the courts'), when the miners received
no such censure, was a reflection of the differences in power between
the two groups of workers. Thus at no stage in their struggle could
the building workers match the solidarity of the miners (because of
differences in the conditions and organization of work). These
events because they effectively illustrate how legal problems are
socially constructed.

The law textbook teaches that to break the law is to offend a
central societal value. We are taught that it is an offence against
the 'democratic way of life'.   But the sanctification of law and
'society' asks no questions about what kind of political activity
is 'guaranteed' by the law.   Where political activity is exclusively
defined the range of legitimate legal problems deriving from it will
be narrowly circumvented.   The 'legal problem' reflects an imperial
code;   it allows of contrary opinions of itself only within itself -
that is, within the context of the law.   Those who insist on
constructing reality in this way deny the validity of other ways
of looking at the world.   Though they recite the litany of the
problem-solver ('helping', 'adjudicating', 'justice') it is little
more than self-idolatry.   For them there is only one true problem
and it must be the task of the lawyer as shepherd to show the way.

Chapter 3

UP AGAINST THE LAW

INTRODUCTION*

The aim of this chapter is to look at the tensions in the liberal
ideas of 'bringing law and lawyers to the people' and the reaction
to this in the way people fight the encroachment of law and lawyers
by evolving new styles of representation, by civil disobedience, and
by treating the trial as political. We have chosen to examine the
notion of 'bringing law to the people' through the study of an
important recent innovation in legal servicing; (1) the duty
solicitor scheme and the neighbourhood law centre. Our analysis
is directed toward these phenomena for the following reasons. First,
we have undertaken a substantive piece of research into a particular
duty solicitor scheme. Next, the two innovations, taken together,
seem likely to be a crucial part of any future attempt to set-up a
'national grid' of legal services aimed at, what we chose earlier
to call, bringing law and lawyers to the people. (2) Finally,
between them they raise many of the issues we consider in the course
of this book; the debate on the necessity of law, the nature of the
hegemony of law, the dominant concerns of the legal profession and
emerging relationships between law and the state in this country.

BRINGING LAW AND LAWYERS TO THE PEOPLE I

We open this section by referring to our work on duty solicitor
schemes, and we use our research as a vehicle for discussing the
relationship between law, lawyers and society at four distinct
levels of analysis. We begin, as our research began, with an
account of how a local law society sought to improve the spread of

* Although much of the research for this chapter was carried out in
  Cardiff (there can be no secret about this) we must, in fairness
  to all Cardiff solicitors who might otherwise have considered themselves defamed, make it clear that criticism of particular firms
  whose location in Cardiff might otherwise have been assumed is not
  intended and this chapter should be treated as applicable, as a
  generalization, to similar cities throughout England and Wales.

its legal services by setting up an agency whose avowed public aim
was to help the unrepresented defendant in the city's magistrates'
courts.

Next, the development of the agency is examined in relation to
both power struggles inside this local law society and to the form
and content of deviance in the legal system.   On this latter point,
our analysis will explore the notion of the lawyer as 'hustler', the
devices that lawyers use to obtain and keep clients, and aspects of
the relationship between lawyers and the police with regard to the
distribution of legal business.

Third, we move on to consider some facets of the relationship
between the law and the state.   We argue that the present and
growing effort to 'bring law and lawyers to the people' may be
viewed as the vanguard of what will almost certainly be increasing
state mediation in the affairs of the legal profession.   Mediation
arises, according to Johnson (1973, p.77):

> When the state attempts to remove from the producer or the
> consumer the authority to determine the content and subjects of
> practice.

The final section comprises a critical examination of the notion of
'bringing law and lawyers to the people'.   In recent years we have
witnessed the emergence of law centres, legal advice clinics, duty
solicitor schemes and the like.   We seek, in a tentative way, to
isolate the assumptions and ideology under-pinning this 'movement'.
Further, we have also tried to indicate how the present concerns
and sentiments of 'liberal' (especially academic) lawyers - expressed
through this idea of 'law-giving' - has the effect of actually
increasing and compounding the domination of the law over the lives
of the people they set out to 'help'.

(i)   An innovation in legal services: social service and private
      gain

When an altruistic glint gets into the bourgeois eye, then you
      can be sure that someone is about to get it. (E.P. Thompson)
In March 1973 we began a study of the duty solicitor scheme in a
large provincial city. (3)   The scheme was sponsored by the local
law society and presented to the public as an attempt to aid those
defendants who would otherwise go into court - especially a magistrates' court - without legal representation.   Solicitors who join
the scheme are asked to put their names on a duty-rota;   each duty
solicitor is on call for 24 hours and the service runs throughout
the week.   Currently, at least twenty-three such schemes are running
in England and Wales and there is a widespread belief among lawyers
that the national Law Society (4) will shortly recommend that a
nationwide network of duty solicitor schemes be established.

In our own area - as in others - the setting up of the scheme was
justified by officers of the local law society in terms of improving
the profession's service to the public.   There was much talk at the
time, as there still is, of a need to secure a more equitable and
efficient distribution of legal services.   A concern was declared on
behalf of those clients in magistrates' courts who were unaware of
their legal rights and their right to legal aid in criminal cases.

Here it was thought that the duty solicitor had a part to play; according to the local law society the new scheme offered the promise of a unique system of legal counselling. The scheme was (and is) widely publicized as a social service, staffed by solicitors who were interested in nothing more than the ethic of public service and the personal satisfaction accruing from a good job well done. (5)

We argue that the most powerful covert reason why this scheme was established and continues to draw strong support from most local solicitors was not a concern about 'social service' but the outcome of an on-going struggle for power inside the local law society. Moreover, there are good reasons for suspecting that similar struggles - which have at their core the competition for clients and hence the economic terms of work - are being enacted else-where.

Before taking up these issues, we examine the idea of 'social service' in this context, in rather more detail. Our enquiry was not about listing 'good intentions', but of actual behaviour at work. It was clear from our interviews that some solicitors did articulate what might be termed genuinely altruistic sentiments. Members of this group were willing to sit in court all day when it was their turn on the rota, dispense advice and look for no payment of any kind. In these cases however, although no-one was holding out his hand for money, alternative pay-offs were sought and expected.

For most solicitors of this kind, participation in the scheme was seen in terms of 'putting something back into the community'. As one of them explained it:

'Quite frankly we don't make a bad living out of this business. Let's make no bones about that. For this reason I support the scheme; it should be a duty - a way of putting something back into the community. After all, we're only asked to appear once every month for a few hours.'

Such philanthropic impulses can only be fully appreciated if some-thing is known about the general economic terms of work that solicitors enjoy.   Solicitors work in a highly favourable market situation, at least until recently. Viewed from this perspective, the community is asked to pay a heavy price for the operation of a duty solicitor scheme; namely the preservation of the right of solicitors to work without interference and with high profit at their usual line of business.

The ethic of 'social service' was stretched to cover other contingencies. The setting up of the scheme was seen as a way of improving the public face of the local legal profession. According to one solicitor:

'The scheme ought to be publicized more. We generally get a picture of the money-grabbing solicitor which is not really true you know. At least, it doesn't apply to me.'

Again:

'The scheme might do solicitors generally a bit of good, since we don't get a particularly good press at the moment. The general public seem to think we do nothing but skin them.'

Or as another solicitor put it:

'The scheme is very good for the image of the profession, especially nowadays when we're not really all that good towards

the public. I mean we're not really a happy profession as such
in the public's eye. We don't have an excellent reputation as
a profession; our public relations aren't too hot. The scheme
should help quite a bit here - you know, by showing the public
that we're willing to give up a bit of our time to help them.'
A final point about the idea of 'social service'. There was an
interest in 'helping' but some solicitors in this group made it clear
that not everyone deserved their help. They operated, like so many
other counsellors of personal welfare, with certain well defined
stereotypes of 'deserving cases'. These were the contrite, the
humble, the grateful; specially favoured here were shoplifters,
first-time offenders, particularly women - with honourable mentions
being given to 'little old ladies', 'nice young ladies who really
shouldn't have been in the court at all' and the 'confused'. In
these instances the solicitors clearly felt that a worthwhile job
was being done. Other kinds of defendants, however, could expect
a less welcoming and comfortable passage. As one solicitor put it:
'you get a lot of people in the courts who just won't be helped
by the duty solicitor. Not that I feel much like helping them
anyway. I'm thinking of what we call 'drop-outs'; 'hopeless
cases'. Quite frankly they don't really deserve a scheme of
this kind.'
Such strong condemnation of those regarded as 'undeserving' was
taken up and endorsed by other solicitors that we talked to:
'Occasionally a person will turn down the offer of the duty
solicitor's services. He's the kind of person who would probably
reject the offer of any kind of solicitor. He's probably a
lunatic, or wants to act for himself, or doesn't trust you -
since a cells officer has introduced you to him he thinks you
may be some kind of detective in disguise. These would have to
be mentally deficient sorts of people.'
'So many defendants are, well, just stupid. They never seem to
remember what they've done, or to understand what's happening to
them when they come into court. You lose patience with some of
them sometimes.'
This refusal to consider seriously the motives of those defendants
who 'wouldn't be helped' or who failed to show due deference and
respect for professional authority achieved its fullest expression
in attitudes toward the recidivist. Faced with the habitual and
apparently 'uncaring' offender, the cry of bewilderment: 'the
criminal heart is very fickle' quickly turns to righteous indignation
and even rage:
'The criminal mind is always on the defensive. The criminal
whines; he's never satisfied.... After a while the hardened
criminal bores you to tears. He just can't get out of his dirty
habits. How much sympathy can you have for a man who keeps on
robbing or committing sexual offences?'
We return to this problem later. For the moment we suggest that
this insistence on the 'fickleness' and 'stupidity-dullness' of
many clients has certain implications which professionals seldom
pause to think out.
As Friedson has put it (1972, p.377):
This very real problem is, however, characteristically evaluated
only from the professional point of view which stresses the

ignorance and irrationality of laymen without concern for their
counterpart in the ignorance and irrationality of professionals.
In none of the instances we have cited can the interest in providing
a 'social service' be linked directly to concerns about personal
advancement. This group of solicitors define their primary aim as
one of wanting to 'help' and, within the limits mentioned earlier
and in their own terms, they did help and do help. But the matter
cannot be allowed to rest here. A price is exacted for the provision
of this 'service'. In the first place, and as suggested earlier, it
is a form of displacement activity that has the effect of drawing
attention away from the highly profitable relationships which
characterize most routine legal work. Again, although solicitors
speak of a 'service', it is a service given entirely on their terms.
The concept of 'public interest' is still one defined by lawyers
and by no-one else. Under these conditions, the freedom of the
public is the freedom to be grateful.

Lawyers set about defining the 'public interest' - and then think
of the best way they can 'satisfy' it. In other words, the limits
of the so-called 'public interest' come to correspond mysteriously
with the ability of the profession to 'serve' this 'interest'. The
claim to 'know' the public interest is, of course, inseparable from
the legal profession's claim to a special knowledge and expertise.
It is an assertion of the claim that what is good for the profession
is certainly good enough for the rest of us. The limits of
professional autonomy have been well summarized by Friedson (1972,
p.367) when writing about the profession of medicine:

the profession, I believe, cannot be left wholly autonomous in
undertaking the task of setting up an organised form of practice
which contains a system of self-regulation adequate enough to
justify its claim. The technical expertise of the profession
of medicine does not include reliable expertise about social
organisation and its consequences. The profession's habits of
organisation seem to involve traditional usages modified by
practical experience and ideology. Lacking reliable expertise,
the profession lacks the resources to make its own decisions
intelligently and accurately. And, because the profession's own
self-interest is involved in the social as well as the economic
organisation of practice, there is the danger of bias in the
exercise of autonomy in organising practice, a danger of not
being able to recognise and honour the perspective of the layman,
whether client or general public.

A final comment on the notion of 'personal service': lawyers (like
doctors and many in the welfare professions) present themselves in
a rather disingenuous way. What we have in mind here is the way in
which these professionals talk readily enough about having 'influence'
and giving an 'important service' - but will rarely admit to having
power in the world. The point here is the way in which their choice
of rhetoric serves to mystify the idea of 'service' in that it
obfuscates the real nature of the relationship between them and
their clients, and between their profession and the public.

(ii) The profession in process

We turn to the relationship between the setting up of the duty
solicitor scheme and on-going power struggles inside the local law
society.   The scheme - like all others in this country - bears
largely upon the practice of criminal advocacy in magistrates'
courts.   In recent years this kind of advocacy has become increasingly profitable.   The reason for this is that more successful
applications for legal aid in criminal cases are being made now in
magistrates' courts.   As a result legal aid - especially since the
passing of the Legal Advice and Assistance Act of 1972 - has become
big business in England and Wales.   In 1970-1 the cost to the
exchequer of criminal aid was £8 million and the figure is thought
to have nearly doubled since then.

The questions now become - what groups inside the legal profession are benefiting most from these developments? and according
to what principles and under what procedures are the new monies
distributed?

(a) Deviance in the legal system: One recent attempt to
answer some of these questions was a study by Pauline Morris and
Michael Zander (1973) of the factors influencing the division of
legal aid in the fourteen Inner London magistrates' courts.   They
interviewed the clerks to the courts and a sample of local
solicitors.   The sample included those who spent considerable
time in criminal advocacy, those who did some but wanted to do
more, and those who did none but wanted to participate in this
legal work.   (The information that we give from these findings
applies only as at the date when the research was completed.)

All of the Inner London courts were found to have a 'working
list' of solicitors available to undertake criminal legal aid cases.
The lists were drawn up by the clerks to the courts but, according
to Morris and Zander, it was difficult to discover on what formal
basis the different lists were compiled.   There seemed to be a
heavy reliance on the discretionary power of individual clerks in
determining which names went on the list.   There appeared to be
only one court where this could automatically happen as a result of
a firm simply writing in and asking to be included.   This point is
important because a solicitor who is not able to get his name on
the list is severely disadvantaged when it comes to competing for
legal aid cases.

It became clear in the Morris and Zander study that little was
very clear.   The clerks were vague about the criteria they employed
when drawing up lists.   Solicitors complained that the criteria for
'acceptability' were unclear.   Many went on to point out that the
only challenge to the clerks' use of discretionary power lies in a
complaint to the Law Society, an action which several of them had
tried unsuccessfully, and others felt it would be a fruitless
exercise.

The first problem for many solicitors is getting their names on
the list and thereby putting themselves in a position of gaining
access to profitable legal aid work in criminal cases.   The second
problem took the following form: once a solicitor had his name on
the list, how could he be sure that defendants would be likely to

choose his name rather than the name of another solicitor? There
is, as Morris and Zander discovered, widespread suspicion among
solicitors that a small number of law firms were receiving a dis-
proportionately large share of criminal legal aid work.

The present system seemed, in Morris and Zander's words, to
'allow opportunities for improper conduct on the part of all those
concerned: court staff, police and prison officers, as well as
solicitors' (1973, p.2372). What was this 'improper conduct'?
What form did this deviance in the legal system take? Morris and
Zander were reluctant to push their interest too strongly. As they
put it: 'We chose not to ask direct questions on this issue since
we thought it would arouse both strongly negative reactions and
evasive answers' (1973, p.2372). As it happened, no prompting by
the researchers was necessary. Their respondents volunteered
information on how defendants are given the name of one firm of
solicitors to represent them rather than another. Morris and
Zander reported that 'no fewer than seven of the fourteen clerks
mentioned touting in the courts or prisons, and/or bribery, as
important sources of nominations.' They went on to write: 'one
chief clerk referred to the actual bribery of clerks in magistrates'
courts, and even, he claimed, in one court "up to a very high level".
Another clerk claimed that a firm of solicitors had been...repri-
manded for trying to make gifts of cigarettes to members of his
staff, and another chief clerk...said that bribery definitely
occurred between solicitors and court clerks' (1973, p.2372).

This issue was also taken up by the solicitors who were interviewed (via postal questionnaires) by Morris and Zander. Their
complaints were nearly all variations on one theme: that there was
no proper system of allocation and no known principle on the basis
of which cases were assigned. Some solicitors talked of 'favourit-
ism', while others suggested that the process of allocation was
tainted by corruption. In their words:

  'Some legal aid clerks at magistrates' courts are not supervised
  and, therefore, are able to allocate solicitors of their choosing.
  It's an open secret that inducements are offered to them.'
  'The field is rife with corruption. The decent experienced
  practitioners face unfair competition from the unscrupulous.'
  'Too many cases go to the same firm...the court staff recommend
  a name that is familiar. It's a vicious circle. If you go to
  court, you get more cases. If you do not, you get overlooked.
  Without proof one cannot allege bribery, although one is very
  suspicious that it goes on' (quoted in Morris and Zander, 1973,
  p.2372).

There are three main points that emerge from the Morris and Zander
study. The first is the cartel arrangements that determine the
distribution of criminal case work in the Inner London magistrates'
courts. The second is the elaborate 'sub-culture of deviance' that
underpins it and makes the operation of the monopoly successful.
It seems not to be a question of an individual solicitor 'doing a
deal' with a particular clerk or policeman, but of a small number
of law firms tying together policemen, prison officers and court
staff into a structure of what might be called 'professional
racketeering'. Third is the fact that while such practices have
been the subject of private talk among solicitors for years, today

there is a special interest in seeing the racket undermined.   The
reason for this is that legal aid is such big business that other
solicitors are anxious now to move in on it.

When the Morris and Zander findings were published they were
strongly attacked by the principal chief clerk to the Inner London
magistrates' courts, by the secretary of the Justices' Clerks'
Society and by the chairman of the Law Society's Committee on Legal
Aid in Criminal Cases.   On close examination the attacks were of
little substance: one writer simply asked for the names of
respondents and vaguely threatened police action;   another tried a
smear tactic, talking about 'interviews being carried out by lady
sociologists', while the third was upset more by the authorship of
Michael Zander than by anything else.

What was of interest, however, was the degree of support for the
finding among solicitors in local law societies in different parts
of the country.   The following extracts are taken from two letters
which were typical of the general support.   The first is from a
solicitor in Birmingham (like all the correspondence on this subject,
the letter is anonymous):

> the root cause of the legal aid accumulation into the hands of
> the few is really caused by touting.... Touting is big business,
> especially among ethnic...groups, as more than one solicitor will
> tell you.   The real villains of the piece are not magistrates'
> clerks, but police, prison warders and outside touting by
> solicitors' junior clerks.   These are villains of the piece - and
> talking about pieces, it always helps to cultivate the friendship
> of a member of the opposite sex who belongs to the ethnic group
> which you set out to represent.

The second letter, though on a more sober note, raised the issue
that was worrying most solicitors who are trying to obtain more
criminal work:

> The lengthy article published recently (3 October) concerning the
> situation as to allocation of criminal legal aid cases by
> magistrates' clerks reveals a situation which must come as no
> surprise to the many firms who are willing and able to undertake
> such work.   The situation out of London is no different from
> that as stated in the article.
>
> As a firm having four partners with two offices well able to
> cope with legal aid cases (all partners being experienced
> advocates) covering a very large catchment area in South East
> England, and indeed our practice extends into the areas covered
> by at least nine magistrates' courts, it appears that in some
> three years we have had only one or two cases sent to us by
> magistrates' clerks despite our application a few years ago to
> be placed on the various Court lists, and an indication of our
> willingness to accept legal aid cases, and indeed numerous
> appearances by all partners in non-legal aid matters in many of
> the courts in question.
>
> My partners and I wonder if the situation is the same all over
> the country - it certainly appears to be so - and indeed perhaps
> the situation is so serious as to warrant some sort of official
> investigation.
>
> Solicitor, Tonbridge.

But it is clear that no sort of 'official investigation' is likely
to be forthcoming. As we mentioned before, complaints have been
made but no action was taken. The art of concealment is a highly
developed one in prestigious occupations; finding 'proof' of
deviance of the kind we have described is difficult. Solicitors are
reluctant to make their criticisms public or even to take their
grievances to the national Law Society. There was, in other words,
no obvious way in which solicitors could resolve these conflicts
and restructure the economic terms of work.

There was no obvious way, that is, until recently, and at this
point the duty solicitor scheme reappears. The scheme has, from
the start, been seen by many solicitors as one way of legitimately
breaking the monopoly on criminal case work, and on legal aid in
criminal cases in particular, presently enjoyed by a small number
of law firms in different towns. In the city researched, criminal
advocacy is dominated by five law firms, known to other solicitors
as the 'Big 5' or, rather more evocatively, the 'Barons'. Until
the setting up of the duty solicitor scheme in 1972 the five firms
were thought, between them, to have a virtual monopoly of all
criminal work (including legal aid cases) in the city. Other
solicitors were aware of this and saw the scheme as a means of
forcing a re-allocation of such work.

This state of affairs tells us much about the segmental nature
of the English legal profession. (6) Its segmental character
depends not only upon the division of labour that exists inside all
professions (in the case of law this would include certain kinds of
work specialization such as probate, conveyancing, etc.), but also -
in the case of criminal advocacy - upon the maintenance of vested
interest and privileges by deviant means, within segments.

What then are these 'deviant means' and what processes are
involved? Organization and maintenance would seem to depend - at
least in our area - on three factors:
1   collusion between sections of the police and the 'Big 5'.
2   solicitors from the 'Big 5' acting directly as hustlers for
    clients.
3   solicitors' employees - articled clerks, managing clerks, and
    ex-policemen - hustling for clients, in the courts and elsewhere.
First, let us consider the existence of collusion between the 'Big 5'
and some sections of the local police force. The system of exchange
and obligation here is a complex one but there seemed general agreement that the 'understanding' was in part secured by the 'Big 5'
through the devices of gifts of drinks and cigarettes and party
invitations.

Local solicitors were clear about the kind of service that the
police concerned offered in these cases:
'One thing they have tried to do is sabotage the scheme. They
put difficulties in the way of the D.S. when he tries to reach
potential clients in the cells. There's a lot of obstruction
and unco-operative attitudes.'
'The police have never been co-operative with those solicitors
who don't do criminal work regularly. When they recommend
solicitors to clients they only give a list to clients that show
a marked preference for certain firms.'

'There has been a closed shop...there is a close liaison between
the police and a few solicitors in this city. You don't get very
far unless you've got the police on your side.'
'Why is it that 90% of defendants are represented by the "Barons"?
Many of them have never been in trouble before, some come from
outside the city so they don't have solicitors, but somehow they
get to the "Barons". The police play a major part in this. The
senior officers are very good people - I've rarely met a man above
Inspector level who was not a thoroughly nice man - but the
others are much less good. They're ill-paid and ill-treated, so
it's no wonder they try to make a bit on the side, is it?'
Seen from this perspective the police - and especially the lower
ranks who man the cells and carry out the first routine interrogation
of suspects - are powerful definers of reality. They have the power
to discipline solicitors (by denying them access to clients or
placing clients elsewhere), and an ability to determine the degree
of success or failure of this kind of innovation in legal servicing
by refusing to co-operate with solicitors other than those representing the 'Barons'.

We can give two further examples of police 'hegemony', both
relating to the distribution of clients to solicitors by policemen.
The first concerns the way in which some members of police are able
to provide clients for solicitors working for the 'Big 5' and in
return demand a particular kind of 'favour' from the lawyer involved.
It was explained to us that if such a police officer made an arrest
in the evening or early morning part of the day, a check would be
made if the person arrested had a solicitor he could turn to. If
the answer was 'no', then the officer concerned would contact a
solicitor from one of the 'Big 5', offering the accused as a client
or as a possible client. If the solicitor accepted the offer then
the stage was set for the 'pay-off'. In these cases what the
police sought were not material rewards but an 'understanding' from
the solicitor that he (the policeman) would be allowed what was
described to us as an 'easy route' whenever the case concerned
reached the magistrates' court. By an 'easy route' is meant a
courtroom encounter where the policeman is not too strictly cross-
examined by the solicitor for the defence. The 'understanding'
also includes an arrangement whereby the solicitor, happy to get a
new client, does not press to see his new client in overnight
police custody; nor is the solicitor 'expected' to draw the court's
attention to the fact that the accused, his client, was interrogated
and charged overnight without at any time being granted access to a
solicitor. The existence and organization of such exchanges and
tacit understandings implies a network of close and informal social
relations between some policemen and some solicitors. We explain
in chapter 4 other manifestations of such relations and the
mechanisms which sustain them and make them possible; for the
moment, however, we can note that this system of favours, together
with the moral calculus which is used to justify it, is arranged
primarily for the convenience of the police and lawyers - and not
the defendant.

Our second example refers to the 'discretionary' powers of cells'
officers in this context. It was explained to us on several

occasions, by solicitors, clerks to the court and ex-policemen, that
a principal factor in the successful maintenance of a monopoly of
criminal law work by the five big firms, was the mediating role of
the cells' officers.   Cells' officers were known to recommend
particular law firms to people in custody - 'advice' that was likely
to be followed, in particular, by those who either had never before
had a solicitor or had never before been in trouble, let alone in
custody: people, in other words, who are highly susceptible to
advice coming from apparently disinterested, yet seemingly knowledgeable, sources.

The apparent vulnerability of the scheme to police 'censorship'
is borne out in the two quotations which follow.   In both instances
the solicitors concerned are describing the effect of trying to
'graft on graft', that is, to superimpose a reform in legal servicing on a market situation where supply and demand are determined by
a pre-existing network of gifts, favours and obligations.   Thus:
'The duty solicitor scheme was partly a reaction, by those who
regularly did a little advocacy work, to the fact that the
monopoly of criminal work enjoyed by a few firms seemed to be
getting greater and greater.   I can well remember attending a
meeting with the Clerks to the Justices, the Stipendiary Magistrate and those local law society solicitors who were then
practising in the courts.   It was put to the Chief Clerk and the
Stipendiary that this channelling of work into a few sources was
to be deplored.   They both agreed it was deplorable, but said
they were powerless to stop it.   If anything, the way the work
was being channelled was the result of police activity they said,
and had nothing to do with them.'
'At the cell level there are a lot of complaints about certain
firms pinching from other firms.   It arises from the tendency of
the police to steer work to certain firms or to steer work away
from certain firms.   Selected firms have been favoured by police
in the past, which adversely affected the duty solicitor scheme
in its early days.'
In the event the 'deviant sub-culture' seems to have survived almost
intact despite all the strictures delivered against it.   The reasons
for this are simple enough.   Confrontation was avoided because the
scheme has created work for the previously 'disenfranchised'.
Everybody has grabbed a bit of the action, and for the moment, the
hubbub has subsided.   But, as we shall suggest below, the present
stability may not be long-lived.   However, we note that the often
bitter disputations about the terms of work are conducted exclusively with reference to the interest of the professionals themselves.
The client-defendant is nowhere to be seen;   like the child under
the firm stewardship of the Victorian pater-familias, he is out of
sight and sound.

The concept of the 'solicitor as hustler' can also be invoked in
this context. (7)   The Law Society's rules against 'touting' take
a stern moral stance but are, in practice, quite easily evaded.
Some examples will illustrate the point here.   'Touting' is
expressly forbidden.   In practice, however, solicitors (or their
surrogates) representing the 'Big 5' find it relatively easy to make
an approach to defendants in custody, while other solicitors are
effectively prevented by the police from directly approaching such

defendants. This exercise of police 'patronage' is well illustrated
in an account of it given by one solicitor we interviewed:
'The fact is that most of the Big 5 operate with former police
officers acting as clerks (i.e. as "support staff"). By reason
of the camaraderie they have with members of the police force
they are given perhaps preferential treatment when seeking access
to the cells than perhaps duty solicitors - or other solicitors -
are. One has only to consider the activities of X (one such
ex-policeman clerk). He goes straight into the duty officer's
room - which I'm not normally allowed to enter. I'm pushed
straight into the interview room. I consider the granting of
these preferences most improper. This is "tout work"; it's the
only way to describe it. And it's still going on.'
Not being able to compete directly because of this discrimination
was viewed by solicitors as a serious handicap in trying to build
up a criminal practice. As one of them pointed out:
'you can't break into criminal work by sitting in your office
all day waiting for people to come and find you. It just doesn't
work like that. You have to spread your name around, be seen
around the courts, make contacts. That's the only way to build
up your criminal work.'

(b) The multiplication of criminal legal work: The larger the
law firm the more sophisticated the organization of its hustling
(touting) can become. This is one of the reasons why, before the
arrival of the duty solicitor scheme, solicitors working solo or
perhaps with just one other partner found it very difficult to
break into the cartel. Thus law firms as large as the 'Big 5' are
able to deploy articled and managing clerks around the courts and
cells to pick up clients, and to employ ex-policemen to tout for
clients in pubs and clubs in the city.
Against this background the duty solicitor scheme was seen by
many solicitors as a way of re-allocating criminal work. A sample
of their opinions is emphatic on this point:
'There is a strong feeling against the five firms who do most
of the criminal work in the city. It's my view that the D.S.
scheme was set up by certain parties to break this monopoly.'
'Many solicitors in the city feel that there ought to be a
wider spread of solicitors undertaking legal aid work. I thought
that the scheme might help in this direction...and I don't care
who knows it frankly.'
'It's a very good scheme from the viewpoint of those solicitors
in the city who want to try and break into the monopoly of
criminal law.'
'One wants to break the power of the "Barons". The scheme offers
the opportunity of doing extra magistrates' courts work.... I
should like to say I joined the scheme out of humanitarian
concerns, but to be honest it was with a view to increasing
business.'
'I joined the scheme because I wanted to extend the criminal
scope of my practice and this was one way of doing it. It's a
good way of getting more contact with the courts and with
prospective clients.'
If this was a major advantage to be derived from enlisting there

were also four important subsidiary ones flowing from it. The first
was the increase in the amount of 'cost-chasing' undertaken by
solicitors in the scheme. Cost-chasing is an extremely profitable
legal ploy. It occurs when a solicitor insists on fighting every
case, entering a plea of 'not guilty' thereby bringing up the costs.
The increase in cost-chasing corresponds with the increasing
availability of legal aid in criminal cases in magistrates' courts.
The particular form of this phenomenon was outlined to us in this
way:

'My own view is that more often than not, with the greater
availability of legal aid, some firms tend to advise their
clients not only that they should plead "Not Guilty" when
perhaps they should plead "Guilty", but also that their best
course of action would be to proceed to trial by jury. This
"conveyor-belt" process which is being adopted by some of the
larger firms has the effect of course - whether intended or not -
of inflating costs.'

Second, the scheme allows, in practice, a system of 'licensed
touting' to come into being. This operates, first of all, by giving
the solicitor a base from which he can begin infiltrating into the
structure of informal social relations that characterize all magistrates' courts in process.   The importance of being in a position
where personal skills could be set to work was stressed by several
respondents. The scheme provided the forum where the aspiring
advocate could learn to market himself. In their words:

'The duty solicitor scheme gets our name known better; it is
valuable in that you get to know the clerks and some names on
the Bench. The scheme certainly helped me right at the beginning
when I was starting up as a criminal lawyer.'

'I would like to expand my criminal practice. The scheme helps
me to get my face known in court, and with the police. In the
long term it must surely generate more work for me in the
criminal courts.'

The duty solicitor is, at the same time, permitted to approach
clients in the area of the court, and defendants are also sent to
him by the clerks to the court. These concessions, more than anything else, have helped to undermine the mechanisms which supported
the old monopoly structure. Under the new arrangements everybody
becomes a 'hustler' as new referral systems are built up. As it
was explained to us:

'The duty solicitor scheme makes inroads into the old system of
recommendations. Under the old way, a man in custody would
probably be told by police that "X" or "Y" were good solicitors.
The man would never get the opportunity - especially if he came
from outside the city - to learn of other names. Now, of course,
he may be channelled away to a solicitor whose name might
normally not get mentioned at all.'

Third, the setting-up of the scheme has, as we hinted earlier,
helped create much more work for those specializing in criminal
advocacy in magistrates' courts. Quite simply, more lawyers means
the construction of even more 'legal problems'. Thus the growth of
'trouble' is inseparably linked with the expansion in the numbers
of solicitors doing criminal work. Professionals - lawyers or
anybody else - are, not surprisingly, reluctant to accept this

interpretation, yet the point has been tellingly made by Tony
Gibson, and it is instructive to consider his argument here.   It
will be an unfamiliar one to most professionals who define themselves as 'helpers':

> It is arguable for instance, that one of the roles of the police
> force is the generation of crime.   The police is a well-
> established body with its niche in society, just as are the army,
> church, stock exchange, judiciary, etc.   None of these bodies is
> going to operate towards its own dissolution: rather they will
> act to increase the range and power of their spheres of operation.
> It is in the interests of the police force, then, that the volume
> of crime should not decrease but rather increase.   This preserva-
> tion and generation of criminal activity is not, of course, a
> deliberate and cynical policy directed by police chiefs and
> corrupt officers, but the sum total of the operation of the
> police force.
>
>   The idea that the police actually increase rather than reduce
> the level of criminal activity may seem strange at first sight.
> The consideration of an analogous mechanism may help towards
> understanding just what is envisaged.   If I suggest that the role
> of the medical profession is to promote disease, such a conten-
> tion appears manifestly absurd, for we all know that doctors cure
> diseases and prevent their occurrence through measures of public
> health.   Yet the medical profession never works itself out of a
> job.   There are always just as many people suffering from diseases
> queueing up for treatment as there ever were, in spite of the vast
> advances in public health.   There are just as many people demand-
> ing treatment because, in a sense, the medical profession is
> always 'creating' new diseases.   New diseases are 'created' in
> several ways;   first, by improvements in diagnosis, so that some
> people who would previously have been regarded as not too un-
> healthy are now regarded as definitely sick and requiring treat-
> ment;   second, the general rising standards of public health make
> people less tolerant of ailments which would previously have been
> regarded as within the range of normality;   third, by prolonging
> the general expectation of life, the medical profession has
> created an enormous problem in terms of the multitude of degener-
> ative diseases of old age which hardly existed in former times.
> In a very real sense therefore, the medical profession does keep
> on increasing the bulk and variety of what are recognized as
> diseases in the community, and there is no prospect of disease
> being abolished, however efficient the public health services
> are (1970, p.57).

The creation and maintenance of legal problems by lawyers follows a
very similar pattern.   Though we cannot go into the matter here, the
interesting and significant thing about the production of legal
problems in the way described is that the process pushes us steadily
towards the litigious society.   Legal aid is an invention of those
who want to dispense 'proper' (i.e. legal) representation.   Whether
'proper' means 'better' we have no means of knowing, in empirical
terms, because no-one has yet come up with a measure of what is
'good' advocacy.   What is certain, however, is that when 'proper'
becomes synonymous with 'legal' and 'paid' then there is created
a pressure to abandon extra-legal means of dispute settlement in
favour of legal ones.

We suggested before that there exists no criterion of 'good' advocacy; but many of the solicitors we talked to had firm ideas of what constituted a 'good case' to handle. The good case was never simply the case that had held some special legal interest (unlike the medical profession, where the good case is almost always seen as the clinically interesting one), or even one that was financially profitable in its own terms. Instead the good case was the one that might conceivably lead on to a bonanza. An example illustrates the point. Several solicitors in our sample told us a story of a solicitor in the city who had so far made 'many thousands of pounds' by acting for different members of a single family, on both civil and criminal matters. We heard how the route to this veritable Aladdin's Cave of riches began when the solicitor concerned had represented one of the family on a small criminal charge. This provided the lawyer's entrée to other members of the family so setting him up as their legal broker. Whether this story was true or not is beside the point. The real point is that the solicitors who repeated the story both believed it to be true and wanted it to be true. The network of rumour and gossip among solicitors which sustained the tale (and which, incidentally, was attenuated by the closed, caste-like occupational order of the legal profession) also shaped opinion about the idea of the 'good case'. One result of making legal aid more available was to increase speculation on the chance of finding more 'good cases'. It was perhaps inevitable that the criteria of good/bad should evolve along these lines. Doing criminal advocacy work in a magistrates' court offers no great excitement to solicitors, particularly those who have been practising for a number of years. No great knowledge of law is required (see below) for this type of legal work; a form of work that demands little in the way of creativity and exceptional initiative. (8) Consequently, then, the only events of special moment are likely to centre upon rumours and speculation of client El Dorados.

Fourth, the arrival of the scheme, taken together with the relatively generous availability of legal aid in the city, has made it possible for new styles of legal work to evolve. More precisely, the scheme encourages the growth of entrepreneurial sentiments among young solicitors. It becomes easier for them to go 'solo', using the relaxation of the rules on touting to develop their own network of contacts and clients. Becoming an independent practitioner in the area of criminal advocacy in magistrates' courts is not regarded as difficult by solicitors. (9) As one of them put it:

'Criminal advocacy is not very taxing mentally...overall the standard of advocacy in magistrates' courts is quite appallingly bad, looking at it objectively. It's a matter of acclimatisation, not skill.'

According to another solicitor:

'I consider that compared with civil work as a class criminal work in magistrates' courts can be done almost with one's eyes closed. It doesn't compare as far as expertise is concerned. Anybody can tackle criminal advocacy; just learn the mumbo-jumbo, that's all.'

These observations have a double significance. The relative ease with which young solicitors can strike out by themselves will have the effect of altering the social structure and social character of

local law societies in this country in the long term. But more
important - for us at least - are the lessons that may be drawn
from these remarks by those who have thought of representing themselves in magistrates' courts.

The emphasis on the importance of techniques in advocacy (i.e.
the celebration of social skill rather than any insistence upon a
detailed factual knowledge) is suggested in the following comments
by solicitors:

'Criminal advocacy is like criminal behaviour - in the sense
that it is learnt.'

'I think that the duty solicitor is a useful training ground for
the young would-be advocate. Through it, they can learn how to
behave in court, because this is something that comes only by
experience. You get the whole thing into you almost by process
of osmosis. You pick up the finer points of technique and it's
this, rather than a detailed knowledge as such, that's really
important in advocacy.'

The difficulty of trying to establish any criteria for professional
competence in the area of advocacy is borne out by the debate over
the composition of the rota. So far, the criteria for membership
has gone through three phases: a 'free-for-all'; a restriction to
two solicitors per firm; and finally granting access to all those
who judge themselves to have 'substantial criminal court work
experience'.

It seems clear that these shifts of policy have come about
because of internal political reasons, and for these reasons almost
alone. In other words, the interest of the client and any concept
of professional excellence remained purely notional, coming a very
poor second to arguments about the economic terms of work. We
illustrate this by referring again to the three 'stages' mentioned
earlier. The first, the 'free-for-all', invoked the opposition of
the smaller and one-man firms who argued that the rota was being
'swamped' by representatives of the largest firms - including members
of those firms who did not currently or had never undertaken criminal
work. The formula of two solicitors per firm was objected to,
predictably, by the largest firms, who claimed 'under-representation'
on the rota. The present solution suggests something of an uneasy
truce, since the notion of 'substantial experience' follows the
contours of political expedience rather than standing for attested
and accredited expertise.

(iii) Legal services and the state

In this section we consider some aspects of the relationship between
the law and the state. Innovations in legal services, such as the
duty solicitor scheme, may be seen - as we suggested before - as
the vanguard of increasing state mediation in the affairs of the
legal profession in this country. Following Johnson (1973), the
main consequences for the legal profession would seem to be these:
  1 Since one of the consequences of state mediation is the creation
     of a guaranteed 'clientele', so we can expect to see the slow
     erosion of the traditional type of referral system that has
     operated inside the legal profession.

2 As Johnson pointed out, 'the effect of state intervention may be
   to support for a time at least, existing institutions of
   professionalism' (1973, p.77). Legal aid, in many instances,
   operates in just this way, by supporting under-employed
   practitioners who might otherwise be a source of dissension
   within the occupation.
3 It is possible to foresee the weakening of the notion of the
   'professional community' in law as new services and new styles
   of work increase specialization within the profession.
4 One of the major ideological orientations accompanying state
   mediation is a stress on social service. This forces practitioners to relate their policies to the social and political
   consequences of their actions. Consideration of social welfare,
   law reform, etc., will bring solicitors, especially, more
   explicitly into the political arena.
5 Finally, the role of the state as mediator may also lead to
   ethical questions being removed from the control of solicitors.
   In other words, decisions about how and where to practise may
   pass increasingly into the hands of different public governing
   bodies.

If we take these points in turn, we can consider their implications -
for the public as well as for the profession - in more detail. We
argue that mediation, seen as a form of 'intervention', has the
effect of still further increasing the power of lawyers and the
domination of law in society.

Turning first to 1, we find that new referral systems do evolve -
but the only result of this is to make it more difficult for people
to evade lawyers. More generally, the extension of the 'legal
franchise' inevitably forces the re-classification of political and
social issues as legal 'problems'. In other words, the possibilities for the collective resolution of issues (e.g. tenants'
associations, political groupings) are co-opted and redefined in a
'manageable' form. 'Manageable', that is, for lawyers; hence the
fragmentation of issues into units of case-work. The public and
the collective becomes transmogrified into the individual and the
private.

Regarding 2, it is clear that the duty solicitor scheme -
depending as it does upon the generous grant of legal aid cases -
has had precisely the effect that Johnson suggests. By creating
more work the scheme has acted very effectively as an agency for
heading off conflict and confrontation between factions inside the
local law society. But there is more to it than this. As we have
shown, the scheme was set up partly with a view to breaking the
monopoly on criminal legal work which included an attack upon the
devices which sustained the cartel - principally 'touting'. One
way of viewing 'touting' is to see it as a safeguard against the
inherent instability of a perfectly free client market. Admitting
more solicitors to the criminal work market will increase the
tendency towards instability - unless and only unless - legal aid
is made freely available. However, while more legal aid awards
will create stability in the short run (by providing the wherewithal
for the otherwise 'under-employed practitioner'), it may well create
more instability in the long run. This may happen if legal aid
attracts more solicitors than the market can bear. Should this come

to pass, then the only solution - if conflict within the profession
is to be contained - is to have legal aid awarded automatically to
every case appearing in magistrates' courts. In other words, the
pressure for more state mediation is likely to come from the
profession itself - since it will be very much in the profession's
interest to encourage this form of patronage. Thus the expansion
of legal services can be viewed as the outcome, primarily, of
intra-professional politics and professional self-interest.

Moving on to 3, it is perhaps difficult to see along what lines
any 'weakening' might occur. To a large extent, as in the duty
solicitor scheme, the service being offered is merely an extension
of an existing provision. Again, any erosion of the notion of
'professional community' would depend to a large extent on the
national and local law societies losing control over new innovations,
and there is little or no sign of a transference of powers.
However, if some control were conceded, it would devolve to the
state and not to the people. This would simply testify to yet
another form of 'corporatism', for it is difficult to envisage the
interests of the state on the one hand, and the legal profession
on the other, becoming incompatible.

Concerning 4, the stress on 'social service', as we showed
before, concedes nothing to non-professionals. The sacrament of
'service' in this context is simply a reaffirmation of the dominance
of a particular kind of professionalism. The ethic can be plainly
stated: 'The law helps those whom lawyers help.' There is no
better confirmation of the belief in excluding people from the
service process (other than as passive recipients), than the attitude of the Law Society towards self-representation and lay-advocates
before tribunals. They expressed it in this way:

> Upon what criteria would such representation be provided?...who
> would select and train those to undertake representation?....
> Though the idea of developing lay services might appear to have
> attractions, these fade upon an examination of the implications....
> With legal representation in the professional sense, the
> necessary organisation is already in existence.... The lawyer is
> trained to do (this work)...he is able to maintain the profes-
> sional detachment which enables him to present the case with a
> sense of duty to the client and also of his duty to the court or
> tribunal...(however).... The Council fully recognises the
> valuable help that has been given by laymen in tribunals to fill
> the gap in the availability of legal services. In some specific
> tribunals well-trained laymen have become specially experienced
> (1974, pp.399-400).

These phrases capture perfectly the Weltanschauung of the leadership of one half of the legal profession. Those lay advocates
judged to be good are those who aspire to be like lawyers. (10)
Indeed, for the Law Society, the only conceivable kind of lay-
advocate is one properly trained to the task; one who is sensitive
to the grand design of orderly service - a man who is not afraid
of his total incorporation in order. All that the Council - like
most lawyers - is able to grasp is the idea of some sort of
'circulation of elites'. If the circumstances are propitious ('to
fill the gap in the availability of legal services'), then the
client-defendant may be allowed to exchange masters. That he might

be permitted to speak directly for himself is, for the Council, not only going beyond the bounds of decency - but of common sense itself. Any suggestion that people may have no interest in 'a sense of duty to the court or tribunal', may see them as alien and not sacred places, is something regarded as both intolerable and, worse, unmanageable.   The debate on self-representation reveals the Law Society standing at a cross-road.   To move off in one direction (i.e. toward more and more self-representatio) would be to threaten their entire importance;   to follow an opposite path (i.e. toward the increasing confinement of self-representers) is to guarantee it. There is much more to be said on this matter, and we take up the theme again at the end of this chapter.

Johnson puts forward the notion that the stress on social service may well 'bring solicitors, especially, more explicitly into the political arena'.   We would argue that if it does, it will only be to bind law and state even more closely together.   The fact that the state looks increasingly benignly on the expansion and reform of legal services suggests that the state is not too fearful of the consequences of such reforms.   We have argued that these developments harmonize with the interests of the legal profession through the generation of work and influence which results.   More than this, these reforms also have the effect of strengthening the existing legal system and thereby compounding the domination of law.   Again the movement of lawyers into areas previously 'under-lawyered' could, as we have seen, exclude lay advocates.   In this respect, therefore, the growth of legal services, seen as a change-agent, has a dual nature.   Thus while it serves as a force for some change within the legal system, it is at the same time a force blocking the evolution of lay initiatives. (11)

Recently two self-styled 'radical' lawyers called for what they termed the 'nationalization' of the legal profession (Simons and Smith, 1972).   They put this idea forward as one certain way of 'bringing law and lawyers to the people'.   It was also, for them, a way of shaking the legal profession to its foundations. 'Nationalization' was invoked as a means of securing a 'better' profession and a 'fairer' distribution of legal services - a 'reform', from the top to be carried to those waiting below. Unfortunately, increasing state mediation, as the thin end of the wedge of 'nationalization' sends no such shock waves through law or the legal community, the reason being, as we have suggested, that state interests and legal interests converge.   Indeed, there is every reason to suspect that many 'non-radical' lawyers would be only too happy to accept the 'radical' mandate.   As one of our respondents put it to us:

'Even though I'm a Tory I'd have no objection to working for a nationalized industry.   It might be a bloody relief to have to stop worrying about where the next £1,000 is coming from, or the next £3,000 to carry the firm through the next month or so. So I wouldn't shout too loudly if we became nationalized.   Some would of course, but the noise would soon die down when people began to see some of the advantages.'

The notion of 'nationalization' used here would seem to closely correspond to what Johnson and others (12) have termed 'corporatism'. Corporatism is held to exist whenever any institution is character-

ized by two distinguishing and apparently contradicting features;
namely, private ownership but state control. For the legal profession this would mean retaining the idea of private practice - but
as a kind of ideological touchstone - rather than as a strictly
legal relationship. The obvious parallel here is with the economic
terms of work of the medical profession since the introduction of
the National Health Service in 1948. Indeed, the parallel can be
drawn out further, to cover the debate which took place among
doctors on the merits of 'socializing medicine' in this way. A
minority of medical opinion in the 1940s - the most influential and
also the most affluent, the consultants - denounced the 'state
control' of medicine. But at the same time, however, many other
doctors - less affluent and prestigious - saw the real economic
advantages that would accrue to them if the state exercised its
patronage. The advantages, that is, of a guaranteed clientele and
a high, stable and assured income - neither of which could be
counted upon in the period of private insurance schemes, 'charity
medicine', and a free and always potentially precarious market for
clients. Some lawyers - and we would argue that their numbers will
increase as the private practice market for law contracts - see the
advantages of corporatism, of 'socializing law', in similar terms.
True the state may insist on some minor concessions from the
profession (e.g. on the location of law offices, urging that more
'go out to the people', or that more law students should receive
instruction in 'poverty law' and the like), but since reform will
have its material reward, the changes required will be but tiny
crosses to bear. Some signs of the new corporatism can already be
seen; one example being the placing, by the government, of full
page advertisements in national newspapers explaining the new legal
aid schemes, and how to contact a solicitor, will do something to
generate a larger constituency for lawyers. The coming corporation,
then, is in no sense antagonistic to lawyers' interests; instead,
it will serve to further the course of law by other means. The law
and the state feed off each other. The consumer, finally, is
consumed.

(iv) Law-givers and law-takers: the rise of the neo-Narodniks (13)

In this final section we examine this notion of 'bringing law to the
people'. What does it mean? What ideologies underpin it? In the
last few years we have seen the emergence of community law centres,
duty solicitor schemes and the like. These developments are being
accompanied by changes in the education and training programmes
of many law students - where the current vogue is for 'clinical
legal education'. Indeed, so widespread is the enthusiasm for
innovations of this particular kind that we can talk in terms of
a minor social movement in some quarters of the legal profession,
designed to expand these new services even further, even faster.
For the supporters of these innovations the problem is the small
effect the law has on people's lives; the task is seen as one of
legitimating law and authority by making communication and access
to the law easier and by granting people a greater measure of

participation in the law making process. The question as to whether
people should have control is never asked because it is already
assumed that this can never be - there must always be law-givers on
the one hand, and law-takers on the other. The concept of 'choice'
presented by the powerful to the weak, of which the offer of
'involvement' in law is but one example, has been neatly characterized by Barber in this way:

> When we speak of expanding alternatives, the meaning of an
> alternative is not self-evident. Multiplying superficial options
> may actually obscure significant alternatives. The American
> consumers' freedom to choose between thirty-seven brands of
> deodorant may be repressive of true consciousness in that the
> choice between brands conceals the more significant choice of
> whether to mask natural odours or not; indeed, the overwhelming
> effect of the apparent choice is to make a real choice quite
> literally unthinkable. Similarly, the proliferation of candid-
> ates on an electoral ballot not only fails to guarantee signifi-
> cant options, but may prevent citizens from becoming aware of
> the possibility for systemic and programmatic changes of a kind
> not represented by the ideologically uniform state to which
> their duties have been confined (1972, p.75).

By this light, law is still seen as a benevolent institution to
which people might have greater or lesser access, but ultimately
no control. The indifference that people have to the law is interpreted as showing lack of publicity, the force of other social
norms, bad law, etc. - but it is never taken as an attack on
domination and as an attempt by people to run their own lives. It
is assumed that law dominates and, if it does, the problem is seen
as one of how to ameliorate the situation by providing greater
access and participation in order to make the domination 'fairer'.

The duty solicitor scheme is, we think, a good example of how
attempts to 'bring law and lawyers to the people' has the effect of
increasing the domination of law over people's lives. As we showed,
many local solicitors saw the scheme as a good way of 'helping'
people. Part of their concern was increasing people's knowledge of
available legal services. But this highly partial notion of
'sharing' is only aimed at securing a better distribution of
existing knowledge. No interest is shown, or credence given, to any
attempt people might make to construct different kinds of knowledge -
and through this, different ways of acting upon the world. (14)
The obsession is with 'spreading law around', pushing it into the
furthest corners of hearth and home. This taking of law to the
people is finally justified in terms of the importance of defining
and meeting 'needs'; 'needs', that is, that only the professional
can meet. In this way 'satisfying needs' becomes linked with an
extension and consolidation of professional control. Seen another
way, the end result of the ideology and practice of 'helping' is
merely to confirm again the supremacy and domination of law.

Quite apart from the interest of solicitors, the scheme was
unanimously welcomed by local magistrates and clerks to the courts.
For the latter especially, as the orchestrators of court business,
the scheme made for more 'efficient' justice - in their terms.
This becomes clear from the following comments:

> 'The scheme is certainly of considerable assistance to the courts,

who are less burdened by people acting without legal representation. They are probably the people who gain most.'
'It's in the interest of the clerks to see that people are
represented, as far as possible. Whether it's for this reason
or other reasons, their co-operation is very good.'
'The clerks like to use the duty solicitor. He helps speed
things up as far as they are concerned. They can almost use
him as a spare probation officer - you know, getting him to coax
along those defendants who haven't a clue what they're doing.'
'The scheme suits their (the clerks') book very well indeed.
Normally you get a lot of people who don't know whether to plead
"Guilty" or "Not Guilty". This wastes time, clogs up the list -
but if the duty solicitor is there the clerk can say: "Look -
whip this chap outside, see what he's on about, see if he's got
a defence. If he has we'll adjourn it straightaway." The court
is only too glad to get this type of case out of the way quickly
and easily.'

Some clerks also supported the scheme for a reason that had more to
do with intra-professional relations and the easing of tensions
between those who worked in the court, than it had with the furtherance of any clearly defined notion of defendants' interests.
Clerks to the courts are, to borrow a term from Tom Wolfe, the
'flak catchers' of the court organization; (15) that is, they are
often put in the front-line of criticisms about the allocation of
criminal legal aid work. While they are not necessarily to blame,
solicitors find them on occasions to be the easiest target for
complaints. As 'flak catchers' they sometimes take the brunt of
criticisms about legal aid work that perhaps should be directed
elsewhere (for example, the police; but although many solicitors
are, in their private moments, often dissatisfied with the part
some policemen play in allocation, they rarely make their criticisms
public for fear of police reprisals - the loss of possible future
work). Also, the management of the unrepresented defendant falls
to the clerks. The introduction of the duty solicitor scheme
removes the clerk from these 'sensitive' areas. In this way, the
scheme helps smooth intra-professional relations and seems to
provide for the better management of defendants. But here, again,
professional organizational imperatives are the primary considerations, not the best interests of the managed.

Clearly, cases could be dispensed with more quickly if defendants
could be persuaded to take the legal representation offered by the
duty solicitor. (16) Although at first glance this arrangement
seems to be classically Benthamite in its conception - with its
attempts to maximize the happiness of the greatest number possible
of those involved - in fact it bestows more advantages on solicitors
(more work, contacts and money) and court staff (a purer distil-
lation of some human mess) - than it does on defendants. Hence
we were told:

'I think it's of benefit to the courts as opposed to the public.
Having the duty solicitor on hand cuts out the time wasting.
The courts can get on with it.'

One likely result of these outcomes is to discourage still further
any attempts defendants (or some of them) might make to seek to
represent themselves, in magistrates' courts. Faced with a

formidable triple alliance comprising the celebration of organisational efficiency, a determined philanthropy and an elementary
acquisitiveness, the would-be self-representer is likely to retreat
or be smothered by good intentions. This is never a question of a
bloody and brutal repression but instead is born of the liberal
lawyers' belief that no reasonable and sensible person would ever
need to bother with such concerns when there is a lawyer on hand to
'help' him. 'Be sensible - be helped' is the rationalization
employed. It takes a strong-willed defendant to resist these
pressures and blandishments from kindly men. Some defendants, to
be sure, have tried from time to time to take a different stance.
On these occasions, the court is fair, but firm:

   'The occasion often arises when the court puts it to defendants
   whether they want the duty solicitor or not. Often they will
   refuse the first time, and a second time, but will often give
   way the third time.'

The idea of 'help' in the context is only help in choosing a lawyer.
As one solicitor observed:

   'The choice is effectively that of a solicitor who has represented
   you before, or the duty solicitor - the man in front of you.
   But you don't get any other alternatives.'

The concern of this lawyer was certainly in seeing the range of
choice widened but only in the sense of putting the names of even
more lawyers in front of the defendant. From such a list the
defendant would be 'invited' to select a name. A concept of 'choice'
such as this puts us irresistibly in mind again of the point we
drew earlier from Barber's work (1972, p.75).

   If we return to the notion of 'choice' in the context of legal
representation, it should be clear that one kind of choice is
altogether absent, and neither is it encouraged, namely, the freedom
of the defendant to represent himself, either alone, or with the
help of a friend.

   Put another way, the ethic of social service articulated by
liberal lawyers and their supporters among the court staff is
diametrically opposed to the interests of any one who may have
thought of self-representation in magistrates' courts. The essence
of the matter here has been well captured by Friedson in his
discussion of 'choice' and control in the context of doctor-patient
relations. Thus:

   it is my impression that clients are more often bullied than
   informed into consent, their resistance weakened in part by
   their desire for the general service if not the specific
   procedure, in part by the oppressive setting they find themselves
   in, and in part by the calculated intimidation, restriction of
   information, and covert threats of rejection by the professional
   staff itself. Such bullying, even if it does stem from a well-
   intentioned belief that the client's own good is at issue, must
   be replaced by greater attempt at instruction and persuasion
   and, if that should fail, by the humility of being willing to
   allow the client the greater value of the dignity of his own
   choice. I assert this to identify unequivocally my own moral
   posture in these recommendations; I do not believe that it is
   anyone's prerogative, profession or whatever, to impose his own
   notion of good on another; I believe that the greatest good is

each man's freedom to choose his own good even if in so doing
the result is one that others may regard as harmful to him;
and I believe that in imposing one's own notion of good on
others one always does the harm of reducing their humanity
(1972, pp.376-7).

One area where self-representation before the law is fairly highly
developed is in the area of tribunals. There are over 2,000
tribunals in this country, covering housing, social security,
national insurance, medicine and industry, and self-representers
have been active in most of these areas. The question though, must
be, for how long can they hope to survive? There is already
pressure from lawyers, and from certain pressure groups in the
welfare professions, to have the award of legal aid granted to
tribunal cases. When this 'struggle' has been won - as it surely
will be - it is not difficult to see self-representers in this
sector coming (like their counterparts in the courts) under increasing pressure from liberal lawyers who seek to help people in the
name of 'social justice'.   On a larger scale, the net result of
these attempts to 'bring law and lawyers to the people' will be to
force a redefinition of social and political issues as 'legal
problems'.

BRINGING LAW AND LAWYERS TO THE PEOPLE   II

So far we have isolated various images of law and tried to show how
their adoption accepts a view of the world as dominated by law, in
the context of an authoritarian society - even when the image is
one that seems to save people. We have also tried to argue how law-
centred the lawyer's world is and how he can only describe it and
history in terms of solutions to 'legal problems'. Finally, in the
preceding section we demonstrated the practical effects of these
sorts of views through a study of a duty solicitor scheme. Our aim
here, in closing our discussion on the 'bringing law and lawyers to
the people' theme, is to advance some more general remarks about the
implicit theories of man and the world carried in this particular
form of the practice of law. We illustrate some of our arguments
by referring to recent attempts in England and Wales and in America
to set up neighbourhood law schemes.
   The history of legal aid in England and Wales rests on the
premiss that only lawyers can operate the machinery of justice.
Such thinking is reflected in instruments like the 1949 Legal Aid
and Advice Act which regarded the problem of the inequality of
justice as simply a function of differential income and that the
situation could be effectively remedied by providing the services
of a lawyer (in private practice) at public expense to those
individuals who had a legal problem but insufficient means to
pursue it. As we pointed out earlier, the fact that legal aid is
more freely available now has smoothed the way for those lawyers
who wanted to help the poor. A large part of the new concern is
about satisfying 'unmet legal need' - a concern which, among other
things, has propelled neighbourhood law centres into existence.
The basic assumption underlying this notion of need is that a legal
problem can be defined in absolute terms; that is, a problem or

need for which there is a currently available legal solution.
However, we suggest that 'legal need' cannot be discussed without
reference to the distribution of power in society and to the class
structure; and that the emergence of phenomena such as law centres
pre-supposes that legal solutions to the problems of the poor are
the most suitable and satisfactory.

Westergaard (1972) has argued that the prevailing interpretations
of social structure hinged on two basic assumptions: (a) that the
substantive inequalities of earlier capitalism were both diminishing
and losing their former significance, and (b) that for these and
other reasons radical dissent is progressively weakened as new
patterns of living and aspiration cut across the older class-bound
horizons and loyalties. However, over recent years, this consensus
upon which the welfare state was imagined to rest has been systematically eroded. For example, Kincaid, in a study of social
security and taxation, has argued (1973, pp.10-11):

> My argument is, on the contrary, that the social security system
> as established by the Labour Government in the late 1940s was
> much less egalitarian in its effects than was widely supposed at
> the time, and more important, that over the past 20 years the
> modifications to the social security system which have been
> introduced by successive governments have on the whole made it
> less and less egalitarian in its consequences.

Moreover, Coates and Silburn (1970) claim that the fundamental
reason for the 'decline of the welfare state' is that welfare
policies must be located in the context of the market economy and,
therefore, we are obliged to evaluate the impact of social service
institutions upon the workings of the free market. They go on to
argue (1970, pp.185-6):

> In the case of Britain, welfare legislation has failed to
> humanise the economic and social system because it has been a
> policy of people who have avoided a confrontation with the forces
> of the free market on at least two crucial issues...the distrib-
> ution of income and the allocation of national resources.

Their argument continues that the limited effectiveness of welfare
services in reducing inequality in Britain is because these policies
do not so much modify the play of market forces but have themselves
been reshaped in the interests of the market. It is under these
circumstances that poverty has been 'rediscovered'. Therefore,
who are the poor and what is the nature of their needs which are
only recently being recognized? 'In the last analysis, to be poor
is to be placed in a particular relationship of inferiority to the
wider society' (Kincaid, 1973, p.171). A relative notion of poverty
in a society can only be estimated in terms of the degree of general
social inequality that exists. The more inequality there is between
standards of living and privilege at the top and bottom of society,
the larger the number of people it is reasonable to define as poor.
Therefore poverty and the broader pattern of social inequality are
inseparable:

> Our needs and enjoyments spring from society; we measure them,
> therefore, by society and not by the objects of their satis-
> faction. Because they are of a social nature, they are of a
> relative nature (Marx, 1946 edn, pp.268-9).

Legal problems of the poor arise from inequalities originating in the social and economic structure of society - poor housing, lack of worthwhile employment, poor educational facilities. The 'legally poor', therefore, cannot be discussed without reference to the factors that generate poverty itself, and to treat the problems of the poor in any other terms is to deny the more fundamental nature of their problems. In popular terms, if you wish seriously to discuss the condition of the poor, it is first necessary to ask questions about the privileges of the rich and powerful and how the came to possess them.

Those who seek to widen the dominion of law through, say, the setting-up of duty solicitor schemes and neighbourhood law centres derive much of their thinking about social action and legal reform from what has been called a 'pluralistic' political model of society. Pluralism, as Lemert (1970) pointed out, has as its objective only to modify sequences of overt action, through influencing decisions at points of power, rather than to attempt to change the values of those participating in the decisions. Put another way, a pluralistic model depicts a society in which widely varied groups compete with each other. In it, decision-making rests on give-and-take among the various groups; public officials and law makers respond to these various group pressures so that no one group will dominate.

With this in mind then, what are some of the policy implications of efforts to 'bring law to the people' and the efficacy of legal action as a strategy for social betterment? We follow these questions with reference to the emergence of neighbourhood law schemes.

The basic function of the law centre is to help the under-privileged to assert their rights by using the law to obtain redress and protection. In this view a lack of respect for law is derived from a lack of participation in the legal system. Here, it is possible to examine some of the contradictions of utilizing the legal process as a strategy for social change, by suggesting that first, efforts to bring law to the people which do not fundamentally question the legal system will be mostly organizational alterations which will not result in significant change; and second, in this context, the role of lawyer may have the effect of diverting or co-opting more effective forms of action.

These contradictions are illustrated by the experience of lawyers who were attempting to assert welfare rights of their clients in America. Edward Sparer, reviewing litigation to secure welfare rights, concludes (1971, p.79):

The welfare recipients' lawyer started his struggle in 1965 not merely a technician whose function was to assist the welfare system conform to what the elected representatives of the majority had decreed it should be. His mission was to utilise the legal process to help change the very nature of the welfare system.... And for a brief moment in the 1960s when it appeared that a majority were ready to accept some basic change, his mission appeared possible. In 1970, it does not. No more significant participant in grand change, he appears reduced to a technical aide who smooths the functioning of an inadequate system and thereby perpetuates it.

The strategy of legal intervention 'was vulnerable as soon as it

over-tried the limits of political tolerance' (Marris and Rein,
1972, p.360). If this was the conclusion drawn by some observers
from the American experience, there have also been signs that
English law centres run into similar problems whenever they have
tried to subordinate the practice of law case-work to attempts to
fight people's problems in other ways. Marris, for example,
illustrates this problem of control with respect to the work of
the first and best known of all the law centres in this country -
that at North Kensington, London, founded in 1971. Marris wished
to study the work of the centre carried out at community level
rather than at purely individual level - law reform test cases and
attempts to influence legislation or local government policy:

> I was told by one extremely influential member of the management
> committee (representing the Law Society) that it was not the
> policy of law centres to undertake work of this kind. Their job
> was to provide the services of a lawyer at an individual level
> in the same way that lawyer's services are currently available
> to paying clients (1973, p.8).

Turning again to the fortunes of law centres in America, several
points emerge from the failure of the American welfare rights
lawyer. First, as Marcuse (1969, p.71) remarked:

> there is no (enforceable) law other than that which serves the
> status quo, and those who refuse such service are 'eo ipso'
> outside the realm of law even before they come into actual
> conflict with the law.

Therefore, if the role of the lawyer is defined in these terms he
becomes severely restricted, if not irrelevant as an agent who can
transform the system. There is the inherent danger that the lawyer
for the poor may be increasing dependency on his services. There
are alternative possibilities to the increase of dependency; for
example, by creating institutions, forums, and ways for people to
air their grievances in which welfare officials can be held
accountable. In other words, to create the possibilities whereby
people can function without lawyers to create and to realize their
own potential.

> self-realisation...cannot conceivably be external, but only
> internal. This task cannot be done for man except by man
> himself (Meszaros, 1972, p.189).

Neighbourhood law centres in England and Wales have not emerged as
a result of any official policy. Nor can their emergence be
regarded as a result of pressure of public demand. Therefore the
lobby for law centres must be located within the legal profession
itself. What, then, have been the origins of the new concern?
In the first place there is the interest in helping and the belief
that the lawyer's services are not uniformly available to all
sections of society. Some of the arguments about the problems
generated by the ideology of 'helping' have already been mentioned.
But we can take consideration of it a stage further by enquiring
into the endemic character of poverty and the history of the
interest in 'poverty law' within the legal profession. There is
nothing new about poverty; the only disputes that it provokes
concern its extent and origins. Similarly, as Egerton (1945) has
shown in a meticulous historical study of legal aid in England and
Wales, there have always been a small caucus of lawyers interested

in 'law for the poor' and, in particular, in the part neighbourhood
law schemes could play in making the intolerable tolerable.
Remembering this, the question then becomes why is it only now that
a previously 'vanguard interest' has suddenly managed to attract a
more broadly based support from within the legal profession?

To begin with, helping people pays and it also serves to create
a whole new job-opportunity structure for lawyers, especially young
lawyers. Thus law centres, like duty solicitor schemes, give work
and profits to many more lawyers than those actually working on
these projects. It is now clear, despite some initial misgivings
among groups like the national Law Society and among sections of
the leadership of the British Legal Association, that these legal
innovations have had the result of generating more work for
lawyers. Indeed, their introduction in any particular area seems,
to borrow a concept used by economists in their theories of income
determination, to have something of a 'multiplier' effect on the
volume of legal business. Thus the greater the input of lawyers
and schemes for law reform, the greater becomes the number of legal
problems for lawyers to solve. To take the example of law centres
again, many of them may be seen to serve - though quite unintention-
ally - as 'touters' for the orthodox law firm. Located as they
usually are, in down-town or inner-city areas (since the concept
of 'legal need' is always held to be synonymous with the poor, an
anomaly we comment on below), law centres frequently find themselves
having to send a steady stream of clients up-town to the ordinary
law office. In this way the problems of the poor become the
vehicle for a larger and more affluent legal profession, even
though - and this is the important point - law centre workers
themselves may be unhappy about such an outcome.

This is one of the dilemmas for radical lawyers who work, or who
want to work, at bringing law to the people. Clearly such law work
is highly congenial for some of the younger lawyers and law
students. We have in mind here especially those recruits to law
who are 'atypical' in class terms - those with working class back-
grounds who perhaps feel they might not be well equipped, socially,
for a career in the more usual circles of private practice.

Another source of support for innovations of the law centre kind
came from those who were worried that any 'unevenness' in the
legal system (implied in the recognition of there being 'unmet
legal needs') could, in time, come to threaten its stability. For
example:

The absence of solicitors readily at hand leads people in these
districts to believe that the services of lawyers are not for
them - to the fear, often justified, that a solicitor will not
be interested in their case; and to the resigned conclusion
that the law cannot help them in their troubles. The traditional
distrust of lawyers is nourished...a very unhealthy situation
arises in which justice is felt to be unattainable, and respect
for the law declines accordingly (Council of the Law Society,
1969).

Earlier, we tried to show how the advent of duty solicitor schemes
has effectively resolved certain incipient conflict situations
among lawyers themselves. The argument we have just quoted from
adds a further dimension to the discussion, namely by recognizing

that any gesture towards helping the poor ends by helping law much
more, by increasing its domination-legitimacy, through making it -
law - 'accessible'. Any extension of the legal franchise, via the
device of the duty solicitor or the law centre, ultimately
strengthens the hand (and pocket) of lawyers. One of the obstacles
to the wider understanding of this relationship is the way in which
lawyers insist on a particular interpretation of their role and
social position. Hence lawyers, like most other professionals,
rarely talk of having power, owning up instead only to the ability
to 'influence'. Accordingly the work of lawyers becomes divorced
from any considerations of power, being described away instead as
an 'important service' of 'benefit to the community'.

Neighbourhood law centres, to turn to these again for a moment,
by definition require that we look closely at what is meant by the
concept of 'neighbourhood' and 'community' in these contexts. The
community law centre represents a specific manifestation of a more
generalized interest in the promotion of 'community action'
programmes by welfare workers, and social reformers; consequently
we can examine the two phenomena together. The community 'activist'
treads a well worn path which winds back to a base in certain
'vanguard theories' of social and political action. Under this
formula the activist serves as a self-styled catalyst for community
change. The areas chosen for propulsion into betterment are,
invariably, inner-city working class ones. Here the task is seen
as one of regenerating the spirit of 'community' in the areas that
have had better days. The key to arcadia is the community activist;
it is he who can revive dormant spirits and coax life back into the
corpse. It matters not whether he is invited by the 'community' to
play the part of activist, for he has come to help them. But why
is outside help necessary? And help for what?

For the activist the answers lie in the notions of 'community'
and 'organization'. 'Community' is held to be synonymous with
locality. The assumption of speaking of a localized aggregate of
people as a community, whether it has any shared values or not,
sometimes results in an attempt to make a community by pretending
that it is one. It is possible for the law centre to select issues
of 'community interest' and perhaps invoke a spirit of community.
But in realistic terms, the question is not whether the community
decides: it is a question of whether a community exists to decide.
In other words, the concept of 'community' is often used by
activists in a pronouncedly ideological way; they begin with a
romanticization of the idea of community implying some now lost
golden age when 'working class communites really were communities' -
going on from this to insist that the old ways can be resuscitated.
In so doing they strain after the image of a mythical communal past
and organize along authoritarian lines to achieve it. What this
impulse represents finally is not the 'community's needs' (however
these are to be measured), but the activist's demands. Organization
from outside is considered essential because people are deemed to
be incapable of helping themselves. From here it is but a small
step to conceiving of the catalyst function of the vanguard men.
'Help them to help themselves, lend them your brains.' Typically,
the activist plays down his indispensability. People are invited
to 'participate' in whatever scheme he sets under way; though if

they are invited to share what they share is his knowledge, his view
of the world. Finally, the community activist makes much of the
fact that the 'community' must never become dependent upon him; so
that when the community life has been restored, he should properly
become redundant.   The activist, according to this view, should
somehow 'auto-destruct'. Thus the man whose arrival on the scene
was a sign of the futility of waiting for people to organize themselves spontaneously, will himself spontaneously combust when the
moment is ripe, that is when the resurrection of community has come
about.   In practice, of course, such withdrawals rarely, if ever,
take place. This is not because the 'community' becomes dependent
upon its activist, but because he tends to become dependent upon
them. And the dependency of the activist derives from his
interest - money, a job - in maintaining himself as a perpetual
intervener. We do not offer this interpretation as a cynical view
of a particular market in ideas. Rather, we have tried to suggest
what happened when one man's (or community's) problem becomes
transmitted into another man's career structure.

It is our contention that many of the difficulties encountered
in 'doing' community action work, are reproduced in the setting-up
of the community law centre. In saying this we do not mean to
underrate these initiatives or to denigrate the motives of those
who work in law centres, but we do want to bring out some of the
underlying assumptions and some of the unintended consequences that
are reflected in attempts to extend legal services in this way.
First then, the law centres - where these are seen as part of a
more broadly based programme for community action - give rise to
similar problems concerning the concept of 'community' and the
precise role of the 'activist' (in this case the radical lawyer).
Next, the interest in 'community' is expressed in the most partial
way. Thus the quest for community is concentrated almost entirely
upon those areas where the poor are thought to live. These are
also the zones regarded as having the highest density of 'unmet
legal need'.   Entirely neglected in this approach - and we do not
make the point facetiously - are the 'unmet legal needs' of the
rich (or perhaps the non-poor), and the extent to which any sense
of community is absent from the more affluent areas of our cities.
Finally, some lawyers see the law centre movement as a forum where
the underprivileged can learn to assert their rights, and, in the
end, begin to function without lawyers. This thinking is close to
the community activist's ideas about 'auto-destruction'. As Wexler
has put it (1970, p.1055):

The hallmark of an effective poor people's practice is that a
lawyer does not do anything for his clients that they can do or
be taught to do for themselves.

While this falls short of the sort of self-abnegation advocated by
the community activist, it is doubtful that even this much will be
achieved. Our reasons for this judgment are two fold; first,
lawyers, in the long term, can have no material interest in
conceding very much to the poor. In other words, the more the
client knows, the less the lawyer is likely to be able to earn.
And second, a significant erosion of the monopoly of legal knowledge
is not in the lawyer's interest either, for if this base begins to
wither away then so does the claim of the lawyer to power and

privileges in society.   From this view it can be seen that the lawyer has need of the poor, but what we have yet to establish is whether the poor need lawyers.

Chapter 4

A POWER ELITE: THE LEGAL PROFESSION IN PROCESS

INTRODUCTION

Our aim in this section is to consider some of those factors which help to determine the ideology and behaviour of lawyers. These factors, which we examine under the rubric of 'professional social-ization', form the background of our analysis of the legal profession in action. We have, in studying the 'lawyering process', concen-trated upon the most publicly visible of all of the work situations of lawyers, namely client-defendant representation before courts and tribunals. We put forward four discrete perspectives on the behaviour of lawyers in such situations: (a) the courtroom-tribunal situation seen as a degradation ceremony, (b) the practice of law seen as a confidence game, (c) the 'dramaturgical' view of courtroom-tribunal settings, and (d) the practice of law seen as deviant behaviour. The chapter finishes with a consideration of the prospects for the radical legal professional, where we look at those - lawyers and teachers of law - who have sought to develop alternative ideologies and behaviours for the lawyer. We begin, however, with some brief remarks about the character of professions in general.

PROFESSIONS IN THE SOCIAL STRUCTURE

Historically, two contending paradigms have dominated the terms of the debate on the question, 'What functions do the professions play in contemporary society?' The first has broadly characterized the professions as organized conspiracies against the public. The second, in contrast, has looked to the professions as the locus not only of leadership, but also as the source of the moral reformation of capitalism itself.

Typical of those who have proselytized on behalf of the profes-sions is T.H. Marshall, who wrote, in the 1930s (1963, p.170):

it is their (i.e. the professions') business to study human needs and to construct a scale of human values...it rests with them, more than with anyone else, to find for the sick and suffering democracies a peaceful solution of their problems.

Similarly, Parsons (1939), also writing in the midst of the inter-war crisis of capitalism, argued that the very survival of the 'western democracies' depended upon the emergence of a 'new leadership element'. The role of guardian was to be assigned to the professions. Parsons, in company with others in this period, sought to resurrect the faith lost in the private entrepreneur, by suggesting a convergence between the values and practices of the world of 'business' on the one hand, and the sphere of the professions on the other. These projected new arrangements were meant to signal the end of the old 'rapacious capitalism'. Similar sentiments have been expressed in more recent texts, where the notion of 'moral reformation' has been given special emphasis (Halmos, 1970, pp.1-2):

> Science, technology, and economic growth have profoundly changed the division of labour in society and changes will continue along lines which are not altogether unpredictable. One line, the direction of which appears to be set for some time to come, points towards a continuing growth in the proportion of those of the total working population whose work is done in the personal service of health, welfare and education. The measure of this growth seems dramatic when we observe that those in the personal service professions make their mark on the sentiments and values of several of the leading elites as a whole, and thus exert an influence on society which is in excess even of their already large number.

The urge to 'reform', to 'save' society from itself ('from its own baser instincts') has carried its own idea of the 'good society'. The message is clear, though not always made explicit to outsiders, the public, that it is the duty of the professionals to make society unto their own image. That vision of the professions which, quite unselfconsciously allots to them a classically vanguard role in social change, comes close to confirming Friedson's view of the inherent pathology of professional power (1972, p.382):

> It is my own opinion that the profession's role in a free society should be limited to contributing the technical information men need to make their own decisions on the basis of their own values. When he pre-empts the authority to direct, even constrain men's decisions on the basis of his own values, the professional is no longer an expert but rather a member of a new privileged class disguised as expert.

Our analysis of the legal profession is located in neither of the two paradigms we have mentioned. (1) First, we are not sympathetic to that tradition which comes close to suggesting that not only are the professions organized conspiracies against the public, but that all professionals are aware of this and seek every opportunity to maximize the expropriation of those they 'pretend' to serve. Neither do we accept the ministrations of those like Marshall, which seem to lead only to the promise of a society fit for experts. Instead, we seek to trace the outcomes of the actions and ideologies of earnest and honourable men. The 'outcomes', that is, for those they try to serve. We suggest, in this chapter, that many of the consequences of good intentions (e.g. trying to offer a 'better service') have the effect not of widening the area of men's freedom but of compounding their domination. In other words, those who press forward claiming a solution to men's problems are, themselves, part of those problems.

PROFESSIONAL SOCIALIZATION

The occupational culture of law cannot be reduced to a matter of formal education and training because the lawyer never simply learns law through the mechanism of formal instruction.   The would-be lawyer is initiated into law; his definition of himself as a practitioner, his awareness of the formal and informal hierarchies within the profession, the reference groups he adopts and his sensitivity to the system of sponsorship and patronage within law, do not come to him from his textbooks, although some of the skills for survival may be picked up in articles or pupillage. (2)

Law textbooks do, however, as we saw in chapter 2, play an important part in the professional socialization of lawyers. Textbooks, as Kuhn points out, represent the emasculation of history (1962, pp.136-7):

textbooks have to be re-written in the aftermath of each scientific revolution, and, once re-written they inevitably disguise not only the role but the very existence of the revolutions that produced them...the depreciation of historical fact is deeply...ingrained in the ideology of the scientific profession.

Thus, instead of recording the contradictions, conflicts and paradoxes in the growth of knowledge, they offer instead only a simple cumulative knowledge.   As such they become, for the novitiate a crucial way of seeing.   The textbook functions as the depository of the profession's established truths, its articles of faith - all safely abstracted from the conflicts and contexts which helped shape them.   For the learner, a way of seeing becomes a way of not seeing. Law textbooks serve up a subject matter largely insulated from the social and political milieu which helped to define it. By reifying law in this way it becomes possible to rear the student on the myth of the 'objective' and 'olympian' character of law.   By 'dehumanizing' law these fictions are preserved.   The textbook, classically seen as an 'aid to understanding' functions instead to exclude the world.

Professional socialization provides the initiate with a knowledge (tacit or explicit) of the norms and values of the occupational community.   Socialization also serves as a source of formal and informal social control within the profession.   Clearly, the formal system of education and training for law provide the recruit with a certain definition of his professional role.   For this reason the legacy of, say, legal education - as theoretical, ahistorical, pedestrian and encouraging only a narrow cognitive sense of law - has to be treated as an integral part of the apparatus of professional socialization.   One consequence of such institutional instruction has been described by Mills in the following way (1963, p.535):

Present institutions train several types of persons - such as judges and social workers - to think in terms of 'situations'. Their activities and mental outlook are set within the existent norms of society; in their professional work they tend to have an occupationally trained incapacity to rise above series of 'cases'.   It is in part through such concepts as 'situation' and through such methods as 'the case approach' that social pathologists have been intellectually tied to social work with its occupational position and political limitations.   And, again, the similarity of origin and the probable lack of any continuous 'class experience' of the group of thinkers decrease their chances to see social structures rather than a scatter of situations.   The mediums of experience and orientation through which they respectively view society are too similar, too homogenous, to permit the clash of diverse angles which, through controversy, might lead to the construction of a whole.

Most professional associations strive for internal solidarity, an unambiguous and favourable public image, a clear definition of subject matter, and the establishment of universally accepted modes of practice.   The legal profession has achieved all of these things and more.   Law, for example, unlike other professions, has not undergone any 'crisis of identity' in recent years.   Those crises of varying proportions which have afflicted groups as disparate, for example, as teaching, medicine, science and social work have caused hardly a ripple inside the legal profession.   Such a crisis is usually provoked either by the reorganization of the profession (e.g. teaching and social work), or by changes in recruitment patterns (e.g. teaching, social work, science and medicine), or by a rapid growth in the size of the labour force (e.g. teaching, social work and science), or, finally by significant changes in its clientele (e.g. medicine).

The legal profession has been afflicted by none of these demons. Unlike nearly every other major profession, the law has preserved an institutional solidarity, a closed caste-like recruitment, a narrow range of professional services and a professional structure which has scarcely changed at all in the last half century.   These factors, which act to sustain the 'dynamic conservatism' of the government of the profession are reinforced by strict control of the legal hierarchy over the education and training of initiates.   In a situation of this kind, characterized by a high degree of social and cultural homogeneity at the point of entry to the profession, the initiate's subsequent path through the legal profession becomes a highly structured 'rite de passage'.   Against this background the imprint of professional socialization is likely to be particularly influential.   To turn to Mills again (1963, p.527):

With...a generally homogeneous group there tend to be fewer divergent points of view which would clash over the meaning of facts and thus give rise to interpretations on a more theoretical level.

The principal mechanisms of professional socialization in law include: the tightly controlled entry - and an important aspect of this process is the phenomena of 'self-selection' into the legal profession, given the barriers to entry into the profession, the motivations and anticipatory socialization of initiates is particularly well developed in law.   This social homogeneity and fixity of purpose eases considerably the problem of socialization.   This is in contrast to other professional and quasi-professional groups where the inculcation of occupational values has to contend with the (often) poor morale of entrants, law motivation and fragile commitment.

The social relations among lawyers and particularly the formation of informal groups among them are relevant to the work of law in at least two ways.   First, the pressure from the group for its members to conform to group norms is likely to influence client relationships and their behaviour as practising lawyers.   Second, research has shown that where there is a high degree of consensus among established occupational incumbents on appropriate professional behaviour there is strong pressure on initiates to conform.   This process is well documented, for example, in the teaching and social welfare 'professions'.   Consider, for a moment, the cause of young teachers;   many complete their training 'progressive' in their educational attitudes, but frequently change attitudes and behaviour after coming into contact with serving teachers, which usually means adopting more reactionary poses.   This pressure to change is known to be determined by a number of factors: among them, the sharing of work experiences, when the work is difficult and the initiate is deferential to the 'expertise' of existing practitioners, and when friendship of established practitioners is important for advancement within the profession.   Similar factors inside the legal profession, where their effectiveness is increased still further by the strong initial motivation and commitment among novices in law.   Established practitioners are of special significance as a source of the individual's norms and values.   Inside the insular occupational community of law they assume a heightened importance.   It is most usual, in socialization studies, to dwell upon the conforming or coercive aspects of colleagueship where these are seen to reinforce the 'mainstream' professional ethos.   This is a valid point and one which is easily applied to lawyers.   Thus, as a source of 'correct' professional attitudes established practitioners serve to support a behavioural and ideological conformism which ultimately is rooted in the marked social homogeneity of the legal profession.

If training provides many of the cues for initiates in law vis-à-vis the matter of 'correct' professional behaviour, a more important mechanism of social control within the profession is the system of patronage.   The problem of careers is central to any professional group.   The dependency of young recruits on a powerful sponsor, or upon the favourable recommendations of some influential patron, is a characteristic feature of all the senior professions and none more so than law.   The possibilities in these relations of acute dependency (in some cases, an almost perfectly asymmetrical relationship) for the strict control and socialization of initiates are, of course, immense.   Moreover, a system of this kind works with a special felicity in those professions which exert strict monopoly powers in the award of qualification and the placement of its graduates.   In this respect, the patronage system within the legal profession demands special attention.   The existing distribution of power within the profession would be seriously threatened only if there was a sharp change in the quantitative and qualitative (social class) aspects of recruitment to law on the one hand, and a broadening of the career structure in law on the other, (for example, by providing lawyers with the opportunity to study for practice in 'new' areas of law such as, say, consumer problems or welfare law).   At the moment however, the social organization of law directly influences its epistemology: in these circumstances professional socialization simply becomes a kind of dead hand which reinforces and endorses the structural rigidity of the legal profession.

The distinctive features of an insulated professional community like law include its system of language, its life-style and its mythologies.   Each of these critical ingredients plays a central part in professional socialization.   These items are legitimized in a number of ways.   Through an esoteric knowledge, protected by rigid institutionalization, and through the reification of legal roles.   The knowledge given to initiates is of two kinds: the textbook law, and a more subtle instruction in 'commonsense knowledge' concerning what is appropriate in style, content and purpose of the law.   This largely unconscious 'everyday' knowledge of legal practice is the pre-theoretical aspect of the preparation for law (i.e. 'what everyone knows is proper in law').   To this can be added the deliberate attempt to reify, to dehumanize, legal roles by denying that lawyers have any function other than strictly and impartially to administer existing law.   Such a denial of the policy making role of lawyers and the courts reinforces the myth of the 'objectivity' of law.   In this way, professional socializ-ation contributes to the fantasy that the lawyer propagates the work unaffected by the strivings of other men.

The mechanisms of professional socialization within law are further supported by two external agencies.   First, by the quality of the extra-occupational culture of lawyers, namely the social milieu of the conservative middle and upper middle classes, and by the intimate social contact with associates in other leading professions.   The precise significance of such inter-relationships has been explained by one lawyer, as follows (Plowden, in Zander, 1970, p.124):

There is also the more general point that the law must largely embody the values of the society in which it operates.   Some critics insist that if the law is to be regarded as a social service, especially by the less privileged sections of the community, it must be made to seem less forbidding, and less like an instrument of the ruling class.   There is something in this.   Michael Zander compares the reluctance of working class clients to seek the services of a lawyer with their ready acceptance of the doctor, who is no less middle class in back-ground.   This is used as an argument for recruiting lawyers from a wider social range.   But what distinguishes law from medicine is its necessary and intimate connection with social structures.   As long as British social structure is such that the traditional ruling class can still command some deference, the law, to be sure of respect, must partake of the style of that class.   Until the thought of a High Court Judge pronouncing a life sentence in a Birmingham accent no longer seems incongruous, High Court judges must speak with the tones of Oxbridge, and so must ambitious barristers, and so must solicitors who do not wish to be thought inferior to barristers.   This situation cannot be changed unilaterally by reforms in the legal profession, including changes in its members' education.

The second external agency is the needs and demands of the typical

regular clientele of lawyers.   This aspect of law has received
scant attention but there seems little doubt that clients can
serve to some extent to socialize those whose services they are
hiring.   Or at least, it is reasonable to suppose that lawyers -
and especially initiates - will learn those modes of behaviour
calculated to gain the confidence of the ordinary middle class
client.   In this way, the lawyer is partly defined by those he is
serving - an observation readily confirmed in other professions
(e.g. medicine and teaching).

Evidence that the status of the professional is partly determined
by the social status of those he formally serves is provided, among
lawyers, by the lower status of those solicitors who specialize in
doing criminal advocacy in magistrates' courts.   'Lower', that is,
in relation to other practitioners in the solicitors' half of the
legal profession.   The reason being the low social and economic
status of the great majority of defendants who appear in these
courts.

Although, in this limited sense, the poor client can make his
mark upon the lawyer, the social background of the lawyer makes it
difficult for the lawyer to understand the poor client.   As a
result, whatever explanations and accounts lawyers offer concerning
the situation and behaviour of such clients they frequently take
the form of crude stereotyping.   The detail of the stereotype, how
finely it is drawn, is an index of the social distance that
separates the definer and the defined.   We are put in mind, at this
point, of descriptions of attempts by members of the 'liberal'
professions (including law) in the nineteenth century to regulate
problems of the 'deserving' and 'undeserving' poor through the
formation of the Charity Organisation Society (COS).   According
to Stedman-Jones (1971, p.270):

> it was in the mid-nineteenth century that the 'liberal' profes-
> sions were first properly defined, and began to acquire the
> trappings of gentility: a process which Kitson Clarke has
> aptly described as the creation of a 'new gentry'.... as members
> of the liberal professions their new found prestige rested not
> upon wealth or birth, but upon education and the possession of
> appropriate professional credentials: even when they possessed
> independent means, they stressed primarily the value of a
> professional vocation.   This helps to explain the emphasis of
> the COS upon the indispensable value of expertise and its thesis
> that charity was a science with its own professional procedures
> which could not be safely practised except by those in posses-
> sion of the requisite skills.... But at the same time, this new
> urban gentry was perhaps least equipped by experience to compre-
> hend the behaviour of the poor...as a group who had attained
> positions of eminent respectability, not by accident of birth,
> but through the practice of austere virtues and long years of
> unrelenting hard work, they were prone to view the poor, not
> with the undemanding paternalism of the established rich, but
> with a hard-headed severity born of strong aversion to all those
> who stood condemned of fecklessness, indolence and lack of
> resilience.

In the next section of this chapter we look at some aspects of the
lawyering process in courtrooms.

THE COURTROOM-TRIBUNAL SITUATION AS A DEGRADATION CEREMONY

The concept of the 'degradation ceremony' has been developed in the
study of 'total institutions'. At the core of the 'ceremony' is
a precisely ordered exercise in role-stripping. By this we refer
to a systematic undermining of the self-identity of the individual
being 'degraded'. In Garfinkel's words (1955, p.420):

> a degradation ceremony (is) any communicative work between
> persons, whereby the public identity of an actor is transformed
> into something looked on as lower in the local scheme of social
> types....

The purpose of this planned subversion is to weaken the individual's
power to resist the demands of the organization or institution in
which he is placed. The more thorough-going the 'ceremony' the
more precarious the individual's individuality becomes. He appears
as a stranger to himself. He is stripped of his history and his
expectations. He is neglected, ignored and then abused without
warning. He learns to obey without hopes of reward. He becomes
an object to and for others; he is, in other words, reconstructed
by them as a non-person. Outside the total institution perhaps
the classic type of non-person in our society is the servant.
Mrs Trollope provides some examples (quoted in Goffman, 1971, p.151):

> I had, indeed frequent opportunities of observing this habitual
> indifference to the presence of their slaves. They talk of
> them, of their condition, of their faculties, of their conduct,
> exactly as if they were incapable of hearing. I once saw a
> young lady, who, when seated at table between a male and a
> female, was induced by her modesty to intrude on the chair of
> her female neighbour to avoid the indelicacy of touching the
> elbow of a man. I once saw this very young lady lacing her
> stays with the most perfect composure before a Negro footman.
> A Virginian gentleman told me that ever since he had married,
> he had been accustomed to have a Negro girl sleep in the same
> chamber with himself and his wife. I asked for what purpose
> this nocturnal attendance was necessary? 'Good Heaven!' was
> the reply, 'If I wanted a glass of water during the night, what
> would become of me?'

This is an extreme example but it is an attenuated form of a more
general phenomenon. (3)   According to one contemporary account
(Powell, 1973, p.142):

> I asked Mr. Kite what it was like working in those conditions,
> and he said 'Oh, they were real gentry.' 'In what way were
> they different from our employers here, then?' I asked. Mr.
> Kite said, 'Well, they were so far above the servants that they
> literally didn't see them. I remember one evening when I'd
> risen to be footman, I was waiting at the dinner table after
> the ladies had retired and the port was being circulated, and
> the gentlemen were talking about a very scandalous rumour that
> involved royalty, and they were all adding their quota to the
> rumour. One of the guests remarked, "We must be careful that
> nobody overhears us," to which the host replied, "How could
> they overhear us? We're alone here," and at that time there
> were three footmen in the room. But we must have been invisible.
> So that's how much above us they were; literally to them we
> weren't there.'

We leave our description of the degradation ceremony at this point
and ask what elements of the process we have outlined are reproduced
in the social setting of the courtroom and tribunal situation? What
we state below applies, in the main, to the social organization of
justice in magistrates' courts.

For many, the idea that a magistrates' court may, in some respects,
be viewed as the setting for degradation ceremonies, will be difficult
to grasp. For them the analogy will seem grotesque; it will be
hard to abandon the belief that the process of a court of law is
anything other than a festival of decency. Paradoxically, this view
will tend to be most strongly articulated by those who have never
been to a lawcourt. Those who depend upon certain media stereotypes
of the court in process will be steeped in the mythology of courtroom encounters: an arcadian sketch which draws together the imagery
of skilled and articulate advocates, of the protection of the meek
by the strong, of open and vigorous debate, of a contest of
principled and orderly minds - where the prize is the definition of
truth itself. A few years ago media portrayals of the police moved
from 'Dixon of Dock Green' to the filming of 'Z-Cars'. The shift
was symbolized by some 'de-idealization' of the police role. The
courtroom however, in television fiction, still remains at the
'Dixon' stage, represented by the highly conventional morality plays
of programmes such as 'Justice' and 'Crown Court' - where the media
assemble to praise law and lawyers and not to bury them. For all
who share these sentiments the notion of the courtroom encounter as
a degradation ceremony will appear as a bizarre intrusion into the
study of law. How is the analogy to be sustained?

In the first place, the defendant comes to the courts as a case,
a problem, not as an individual. Thereafter his identity is
publicly co-opted by those who seek either to defend or attack him.
Quite frequently details of his personal biography are discussed
openly in court - but without reference to him. He is of interest
only as a 'case'. The 'case', in turn, becomes the object of
negotiation among the leading players in the courtroom. The
defendant, although formally the focus of the bargaining is, in
practice, excluded from participating. He is 'represented' and
must wait patiently for the outcome of the deliberations of others.
He is a man taken out of his world and transposed to the world of
others. In that world he has no status (bar that of object), no
history and no understanding. His humanness is removed: he
becomes transmogrified into Goffman's 'non-person'. A crucial
agent in this de-personalization, in this subversion of personal
autonomy, is the chill hand of the language of the expert who
watches over him. Becker, in the following note, has caught well
the double tyranny of the strangeness of language and location for
those excluded from both (1972, p.102):

> We are uncomfortable in strange groups and subcultures largely
> because we cannot frame the appropriate verbal context for
> sustaining the action of the ceremonial. We do not hear cues
> familiar to us, nor can we easily give those that make for smooth
> transitions in conversation. The English invariably discomfort
> Americans because they seem to be saying just the right thing at
> the right time, and in the same language, but it is so unfamiliar:
> when they confidently terminate an interaction with a hearty
> 'Cheers', the American simply feels strange and uneasy. Some

subgroups have their own exotic jargon, and when we venture into one of them and hear words like 'Rorschach response' and 'tachistoscope' we feel quite like foreigners: left on our own goal line with no team members in sight and unable to sustain the game in which they are so warmly engaged.

The courtroom, too, has its exotic jargon. Its subject is the defendant, who cannot understand what it says of him. All too often the defendant is left to make of it what he can. No effort is made to bring him in, even on the court's terms. It is taken for granted that he cannot and moreover does not want to understand. He is universally seen as the recipient of whatever is judged to be appropriate for him. This arrangement puts us in mind of the circumstances of the condemned man in Kafka's penal settlement (1967, p.174):

> The explorer glanced at the man; he stood, as the officer pointed him out, with bent head, apparently listening with all his ears in an effort to catch what was being said. Yet the movement of his blubber lips, closely pressed together, showed clearly that he could not understand a word. Many questions were troubling the explorer, but at the sight of the condemned man he asked only: 'Does he know his sentence?' 'No,' said the officer, eager to go on with his exposition, but the explorer interrupted him: 'He doesn't know the sentence that has been passed on him?' 'No' - said the officer again, pausing a moment as if to let the explorer elaborate his question, and then said: 'There would be no point telling him. He'll learn it corporally on his person.'

Those who do not know the language of law are intimidated and mystified in turn by it. They are, in many instances, not separated by much from the condition that marks Kafka's victim. Moreover, any attempts to resist are discouraged by the court. The language and issues around which self-resurrection is built are likely to be declared as 'not relevant' by those who manage the courtroom. In other words, his history, his claim to authenticity, has to be reduced to their terms. The effect is to circumscribe further the individuality of the defendant by forcing him to merge himself into the amorphous mass of 'court cases'. The particular problems that defendants and their supporters (witnesses) have in getting attention on their own terms, was amply illustrated by some of the exchanges in the 'Oz' trial. The trial centred upon competing definitions of what constituted public morality. But the arguments of defendants and their expert witnesses are not easily deployed in the courtroom with its insistence upon an epi-grammatic and categorical style of discourse. As one observer of the trial put it (Dimbleby, 1971, p.145):

> Perhaps fundamental questions like: 'What is corruption? and depravity? and indecency? and how are people corrupted? and by what? are not susceptible to an easy 'yes, no or I don't know' formula, so favoured by the criminal law. As a result the witnesses were all but ignored.

The following exchange between the chief prosecutor and a leading expert witness for the defence (the social-psychologist, Dr Josephine Klein) in the 'Oz' trial underscores the point well (Palmer, 1971, pp.138-9):

> Leary stumbled on to an exchange that was, on reflection a key to

the whole trial. 'The girl on the right' he said 'has got her
right hand down on the pubic regions, hasn't she?'
'Maybe she has just got her fingers over the pubic triangle,'
suggested Dr Klein. 'What!' shouted Leary, even more astonished:
'In a Victorian attitude of modesty! Is that what you think?
Actually there's something else in that region, is there not?'
he added, mysteriously. 'And it is not her hand.'

Klein: Yes
Leary: Did you notice that before?
Klein: I had it pointed out to me.
Leary: Were you puzzled about it?
Klein: Yes
Leary: Worked out what it is?
Klein: I think there was a newspaper report which said it
            is a rat's tail.
Leary: Yes; you've read that report?
Klein: Yes
Leary: And having read the report, does it seem to you that
            it could very well be a rat's tail?
Klein: (laughing): It would have to be a very large vagina.
            You know, this really is a bit silly, this is what
            I meant about sick minds; this isn't a proper
            discussion?
Leary: Well, what is it? I'm simply asking you what it is.
            If it be not a rat's tail.
Klein: To me, it's just a pretty cover. There's no need
            to put it through the mangle 50 times.
Leary: Have you any experience with pornography?
Klein: Would you like to give some examples...?
Leary: I'm asking you; have you any experience of porn-
            ography?
Klein: Would you like to give some examples...?
Leary: I'm asking you a simple question, Doctor.
Klein: I do really need a little bit of information as to
            what is meant in this Court by the word pornography.
            It's not a concept which I use in my daily life. I
            don't divide things up into 'this is pornography'
            and 'this is not pornography'. I think most people
            don't. I can see that it may be important in a
            Court of Law; in fact I can't think of anywhere else
            that it is important. So you must explain to me
            what you mean.
Leary: Would you try, please to answer my question...have you
            any experience of pornography?
Klein: I think I must ask you what the definition is in this
            Court of pornography. I think I'm entitled to ask
            that.
Leary: The answer to your question is either yes or no.
            Or, I don't know.
Klein: That is my answer.
Judge
Argyle: She doesn't know because she doesn't understand the
            question.

To degrade someone, is, in part, to destroy all capacity for
self-determination, all ability, in Bettelheim's (1970, p.122)
words, 'to predict the future and thus to prepare for it.' In
court the future, for the defendant, is determined by others. More
than this, the defendant is also denied large segments of his past,
in the sense that the court allows only a partial glimpse of what
the defendant is and how he has become what he is. Thus the
actions of defendants - the culmination of which are the 'cases'
the courts consider are clinically abstracted from those cultural
contexts which originally gave them meaning and significance. Not
surprisingly, therefore, in the court the displaced even appears as
trivial or, worse, as meaningless. We return again to the 'Oz'
trial for an example (Dimbleby, 1971, p.144):

> The prosecution is nothing if not thorough. Each witness is
> taken slowly through the magazine stopping at length to examine
> some dozen drawings and strip cartoons, a paragraph here and
> there, and the small ads. The cartoons vary. Some are crude,
> some silly, some funny; often sexually explicit, usually
> fantastic. The magazine has been compiled by around 20 teen-
> agers at the invitation of the three defendants. The prosecution
> allows no detail to escape. Where is that hand? At what? That
> cane - what is it doing? What does this word signify? That
> smile? That gesture? The witnesses pore hopelessly over the
> pages, desperately trying to recall their first-year undergraduate
> skills at textual analysis; the concentrated stares of the jury
> diffuse into blankness; a policeman resumes his reading of
> Reveille; an exasperated witness burst out: 'But to go through
> it inch by inch, line by line..is judging it at an absurd level.'

Or as another defendant put it (Palmer, 1971, p.138):

> 'I think that you have to be in a place like a Law Court to look
> at these things so microscopically,' added Dr. Klein. 'Most
> people buy the thing and just have a look at it. But you have
> to be either in a Law Court or sick in the head to go into it as
> deep as you are doing.'

Unfortunately, it is the defendant who tends to emerge with the
label 'sick in the head' attached to him, after being exposed to an
inquisition of this sort. When questioned in such a manner it is
difficult for the defendant to give an adequate account of himself.
Treated as a 'case' his acts come across as 'irrational' or 'absurd',
without significance, value or purpose. The confusion is total;
those whom he cannot understand cannot understand him.

There are other ways in which, in Garfinkel's terms, an actor
in a courtroom encounter can be 'transformed into something looked
on as lower in the local scheme of social types'. Consider, for
example, this fragment taken from the 'Oz' trial (Dimbleby, 1971,
p.144):

Mr. Leary:	Dr. Klein, we know you are a doctor, what we don't know is whether you're Miss or Mrs?
Dr. Klein:	Miss.
Mr. Leary:	So you have no children?
Dr. Klein:	No.
Mr. Leary:	(slowly) I see.

He rubs his hands, pauses and glances significantly at the jury
sitting opposite.

The attempt is to impugn the witness's social and moral standing.
To try and deny their humanness by suggesting they are not like us.
In Klein's case her degradation was her 'atypicality'; she was
presented, as so many defendants also are, as different, as strange.
As an intellectual, as a woman who was without both husband and
children (and hence 'unfulfilled') she was defined as an outsider.
As such, she was someone to be guarded against, ignored in other
words; the principal elements in the individual's self-identity
become viewed as a kind of stigma.

There are other circumstances and events too, which, taken
together, have the effect of repressing defendants. One phenomenon
is the 'tyranny of objects and space' in the courtroom encounter.
We illustrate this notion by referring to a physical structure
characteristic of many magistrates' courts. The acoustics are
poor, making it difficult for defendants to hear or be heard.
This is important at those moments when defendants try to intervene
in the proceedings. If the effort required to overcome the
inhibition about speaking is met with the demand 'Speak up, I cannot
hear you', or 'Please repeat what you have to say', then it becomes
demoralizing and humiliating for many defendants. It is taken as
a slight on their competence. Their response, often, is to retreat
into silence. The court is satisfied; another prejudice is
confirmed, i.e. 'There's no advantage in defendants speaking for
themselves. It only leads to confusion and time-wasting. Much
better to let a lawyer do it for them.' Such folk wisdom is well-
intentioned but it has the effect of transforming the defendant
into a child - perhaps the final degradation of status for the
autonomous adult. But the tyranny of space and objects reaches
further. The elevated position of the Bench is symbolic representation of relationships of super- and subordination in the magistrates' court. It stands for the ambition to create a hierarchical
and deferential courtroom 'society'. Again, the location of the
dock in such courts serves to emphasize the isolation of defendants.
He is the thing apart, standing there he, himself, becomes an
exhibit: the object of stricture, deliberation and the moral rule
of others.

Finally, the tendency to treat the defendant as 'object' in the
magistrates' court must be viewed as a product of certain organizational imperatives. Large numbers of people pass through such
courts; if the person can be reduced to a case, so much the better.
To encourage defendants to assert themselves is, by this measure,
undesirable. It might result in a loss of control, and this, in
turn, would be administratively messy. The 'degraded' man is one
without a history, voice, or individual identity. So it is with
the typical courtroom defendant. He leaves behind no testimony.
Lawyers presume to know him but he remains largely silent. The
defendant, in the inferior courts, is the invisible man 'John Doe',
of legal history. He appears to us as a record card or as a
statistical nodule. He is no more known to us - or to those who
purport to 'serve' him - than we are familiar with the condition of
the medieval villein or the Sumerian slave.

We finish this section, however, by returning to an earlier
point, namely, the formal structure of discourse in the courts and
the inability of many defendants' witnesses to accommodate to it -

a failure to master, in effect, a new language and etiquette. (4)
We close by trying to underscore the importance of the consequences
of these arrangements for both lawyers and defendants. For the
former, it provides the basis for social control in the adversary
system, for the latter it helps confirm them in their importance in
court.   The dialogue which follows is humorous, but the problem it
illustrates is a serious one in the context of the earlier discussion.   We let the dialogue speak for itself (Heller, 1964, pp.86-8):

The colonel sat down and settled back, calm and cagey suddenly,
and ingratiatingly polite.

'What did you mean,' he inquired slowly, 'when you said we
couldn't punish you?'

'When, sir?'

'I'm asking the questions. You're answering them.'

'Yes, sir. I - '

'Did you think we brought you here to ask questions and for me
to answer them?'

'No, sir. I - '

'What did we bring you here for?'

'To answer questions.'

'You're goddam right,' roared the colonel. 'Now suppose you
start answering some before I break your goddam head. Just
what the hell did you mean, you bastard, when you said we
couldn't punish you?'

'I don't think I ever made that statement, sir.'

'Will you speak up, please? I couldn't hear you.'

'Yes, sir. I said that I didn't say you couldn't punish me.'

'Just what the hell are you talking about?'

'I'm answering your question, sir.'

'What question?'

'Just what the hell did you mean, you bastard, when you said we
couldn't punish you?' said the corporal who could take shorthand,
reading from his steno pad.

'All right,' said the colonel. 'Just what the hell did you mean?'

'I didn't say you couldn't punish me, sir.'

'When?' asked the colonel.

'When what, sir?'

'Now you're asking me questions again.'

'I'm sorry, sir. I'm afraid I don't understand your questions.'

'When didn't you say we couldn't punish you? Don't you understand my question?'

'No, sir, I don't understand.'

'You've just told us that. Now suppose you answer my question.'

'But how can I answer it?'

'That's another question you're asking me.'

'I'm sorry, sir. But I don't know how to answer it. I never
said you couldn't punish me.'

'Now you're telling us when you did say it. I'm asking you to
tell us when you didn't say it.'

Clevinger took a deep breath. 'I always didn't say you couldn't
punish me, sir.'

'That's much better, Mr. Clevinger, even though it is a barefaced
lie.'

THE PRACTICE OF LAW AS A CONFIDENCE GAME

The adversary system is the institution devised by our legal
order for the proper reconciliation of public and private
interests in the crucial area of penal regulation.   As such,
it makes essential and invaluable contributions to the maintenance of the free society.   The essence of the adversary system
is challenge.   The survival of our system of criminal justice
and the value which it advances depends upon a constant,
searching and creative questioning of official decisions and
assertions of authority at all stages of the process.   The
proper performance of the defence function is thus as vital to
the health of the system as the performance of the prosecuting
and adjudicatory functions (Allen, 1963, pp.10-11).
The idea of the courtroom as a setting for the practice of confidence
games is the product of the close study of the adversary system at
work in the lower courts.   In other contexts, the imprimatur of the
genuine confidence game is the total bamboozlement of the victim;
in the argot of the gamemasters, the 'mark' never realizes that he
has been 'conned'.   Were he to have this knowledge, the game would
be invalidated by the mark demanding retribution.   But in law
courts, the character of the game is different in some essential
aspects.   There, the successful practice of the game does not imply
that lawyers are acting 'unethically'.   In order to draw an
inference of this kind it would be necessary to show that lawyers
and court officials consciously conspire against defendants,
deliberately setting them up for the 'sting'.   We do not hold to
such a view but we do believe that many of the unintended outcomes
of courtroom procedures and behaviour, give the legal process
something of the character of a 'confidence game'.   Here, the
victim is manufactured by the good intentions of others.   In a
court of law the success of the game depends not on the idea of
conspiracy, or upon the ignorance of defendants, but upon the
complete domination of defendants.
Lawyers, perhaps, will not be willing to see their relationships
with clients, in the lower courts especially, as ones of domination.
For them, the routines and arrangements which we describe below,
will seem the only 'sensible' way to organize a court of law.   It
is to such ideas about the inherent naturalness of the lawyers' way
of doing things that we turn.
The notion of the practice of law as a confidence game has
developed largely out of the study of the 'plea-bargaining' system,
which is so highly developed in American courts.   In the USA 90 per
cent of all convictions in criminal cases involve some element of
plea-bargaining.   The basic idea is simple; the 'bargain' sought
by the defendant is a lighter sentence if he agrees to plead guilty.
Plea-bargaining, in the USA at least, is usually thought to rest on
the following factors.   First, certain bureaucratic imperatives
centring upon the pressure to 'clear-up' cases as quickly as
possible.   Thus, in the courts where there is either a huge back-
log of cases to be heard, or a heavy volume of daily business to
discharge (as in our magistrates' courts), the ingredients exist
for 'doing a deal', i.e. 'easing' the process of decision-making by
evading or modifying the adversary system.   'Modification' as we

shall see below, can take the form of pretending to work the
adversary procedures;   in other words, to substitute the idea of
the open contest (debate and challenge) for that of a charade of
conflict (the 'game').

Next, since the public prosecutor is paid to achieve convictions,
he will be ready to reduce a charge if the case is weak.   He is
ready to 'bargain' partly to secure even token triumphs in the
courtroom which presumably help make secure his reputation as a
'good' prosecutor (i.e. one who has a proven record of successful
prosecutions) and partly as his contribution to organizational
maintenance - 'making the system work'.   Finally, some classes of
defendants also have an interest in plea-bargaining.   For example,
the alternative to not bargaining may be a lengthy delay for the
case to be heard or case referrals leading to increased costs.
Again, by playing their part in the exchange, they hold out - and
are taught to hold out - some hope for leniency in sentencing.
Third, some defendants have a natural desire to avoid publicity in
certain cases, where the pressure to bargain is the exploitation of
sentiments of fear, shame or guilt.

There is of course, a price to be paid for exchanges of this
kind.   Decision-making in law becomes, in key respects, private
and extra-legal.   It is seldom clear, for example, on what basis
these negotiated settlements take place.   There is, however, more
than a suspicion that the terms of the 'bargain' are defined by
lawyers and not by the people they represent.   In other words, it
is the lawyer who declares what is 'reasonable', 'sensible' and
'realistic'.   And so it may be - for the lawyer.   As Blumberg
(1970) has pointed out, it is the lawyer who crystallized the
alternatives and who is, therefore, the critical element in the
defendant's decision to plead guilty.   In America, we have to
remember, it is only the final plea that is presented in public
after a series of negotiations in private between defence and
prosecution lawyers.   As Skolnick has put it (1966, p.13):

> The statistical pattern of guilty pleas and the reasons for
> this pattern are interesting themselves, but not so interesting
> as their implication that routine decision-making in the admin-
> istration of criminal justice is hidden from the public view.

In this country, plea-bargaining takes a different form, with a
more prominent part being played by the police - certainly in the
magistrates' courts which may, as we explain later, be seen in some
senses as 'police courts'.   Bargaining, under this regime, depends
for its success upon the ability of the police to dominate defendants.   As one group, commenting on police interrogation methods
has explained it (King, 1973, p.9):

> (these methods) depend to a large extent upon isolating the
> suspect, the idea being that once he feels that he is on his own,
> with no-one to come to his aid, he will succumb more readily to
> the various techniques that the police use to obtain confessions
> and information.

Against this background, the suggestion 'plead guilty - and we'll
put in a good word for you', sounds to the defendant less like a
bargain and more like a life-line.   In reality, it seems that he
has nothing to give in return, the police seem to be 'doing him a
favour'.   In these circumstances to plead guilty is part of no
bargain, it has become the common-sense action.

We suggested that the existence of plea-bargaining is linked with the notion of the practice of law as a confidence game. The argument goes as follows.   Social scientists, when trying to explain why certain groups of accused persons lose cases in the criminal courts, must often look at variables such as race, ethnicity or social class.   But they very rarely, as Blumberg points out, examine the variable of the court organization itself. (5)

If we view the court as a bureaucratic and administrative instrument, then the structural arrangements for the practice of the confidence game become more readily apparent.   Seen from this perspective, each court constructs its own 'Gosplan', its own commitment to maximizing production (in our magistrates' courts, this means developing strategies for 'clearing the lists', i.e. getting through the daily charge sheets as rapidly and 'efficiently' as possible).   Furthermore, work 'norms' and production quotas become inseparable from the career interests and career concerns of those who staff the apparatus.   It is these priorities (self-interest) that often predominate over the concern with the more abstract goal of the 'due process of law'.   In fact, organizational self-interest may frequently be inconsistent with any such commitment.

Put another way, 'the proper performance' of the adversary system is rarely given.   To do so would not only inconvenience the courtroom 'regulars', it would also, more importantly, bring the courts to a halt.   What this means is that the lower courts depend for their smooth functioning on extra-legal if not actually illegal arrangements.   Not that those who staff the courts see the choice in such stark terms.   For them the 'deal' (the 'bargain') and its concomitant, the 'game' are quite the most sensible thing to do. It is part of the taken-for-grantedness of the court milieu that the court system must step outside of the law if it is to be seen to do its business efficiently.   To keep strictly to the norms of legal rationality is of no interest here;   indeed, it is a dangerous practice.   Instead, let the lawyer and his support staff decide what's 'for the best', it would be presumptuous to intervene. If it has to be played as a 'game' then so be it.

We now turn to a closer inspection of the 'regulars' in the courtroom, those who develop their own routines and vested interests, singly or in co-operation with others.   By 'regulars' we refer, principally, to the following dramatis personae;   prosecuting solicitors, court clerks, police and those defence lawyers who specialize in criminal advocacy, and who consequently spend a great deal of time in and around magistrates' courts.

These groups are 'regulars' in the sense that while accused persons come and go they appear daily.   In this respect, the court becomes their court.   Regular attendance is the basis from which a complex of informal relations inside and outside the courtroom develop.   For example, defence lawyers become friendly with and dependent upon, court officials and the police.   Such friendships, and the often subtle debts, obligations and favours which hedge them about, serve to subvert effectively the adversary system in magistrates' courts.   A long familiarity with other 'regulars' makes it difficult - and rather embarrassing - for such defence lawyers to embark upon that 'constant searching, and creative

questioning of official decisions and assertions of authority at
all stages of the process', which is alleged to be the defining
characteristic of the adversary system.   Under these circumstances,
the regulars learn the value of discretion; they learn how to pull
their punches.   Thus (Skolnick, 1967, p.52):

> the public defender and the prosecutor are trying cases against
> each other every day.   They begin to look at their work like
> two wrestlers who wrestle with each other in a different city
> every night and in time get to be good friends.   The biggest
> concern of the wrestlers is to be sure they do not hurt each
> other too much.   They don't want to get hurt.   They just want
> to make a living.   Apply that to the public defender and
> prosecutor situation and it is not a good thing in a system of
> justice that is based upon the adversary system.

It is in this way that the defence lawyer learns the value of co-
operation, of being 'sensible'.   And the stronger these informal
social relationships, the greater the pressure to 'do a deal'
rather than be seen to 'cause trouble'.   Everyone, that is, except
the defendant who may need some persuading or reassuring on this
point.   The problem here, for lawyers, lies in convincing the
defendant that everything possible has been done for him, without
putting on a performance that will jeopardize those informal
relations mentioned above.   One device for easing this particular
dilemma is to reduce the adversary system to the dimensions of a
'game'.   A procedure where style and form triumph over content.
This is best illustrated if we again use an analogy drawn from the
world of wrestling (Barthes, 1973, p.22):

> It is easy therefore to understand why out of five wrestling-
> matches, only about one is fair.   One must realise, let it be
> repeated, that 'fairness' here is a role or a genre, as in the
> theatre: the rules do not all constitute a real constraint,
> they are the conventional appearance of fairness.   So that in
> actual fact a fair fight is nothing but an exaggeratedly polite
> one: the contestants confront each other with zeal, not rate;
> they can remain in control of their passions, they do not
> punish their beaten opponent relentlessly, they stop fighting
> as soon as they are ordered to do so, and congratulate each
> other at the end of a particularly arduous episode, during
> which, however, they have not ceased to be fair.   One must of
> course understand here that all these polite actions are brought
> to the notice of the public by the most conventional gesture of
> fairness: shaking hands, raising the arms, ostensibly avoiding
> a fruitless hold which would detract from the perfection of the
> contest.

The norm of existence for courtroom encounters carried out in this
spirit is one of co-operation and not conflict.   It is a demonstration of manners.   Thus the end of the game is invariably followed
by convivial chats and an exchange of pleasantries.   Under this
regime, the police, as witnesses, fare especially well, for the
dangers of pushing them too far (by dint of 'indiscreet questions',
or a tough cross-examination) are well recognized by defence
lawyers in magistrates' courts.   The police - as we showed in the
last chapter - have the power to punish lawyers.   If lawyers do not
'play the game', that is, treat policemen too roughly by the tacit

conventions of the courtroom regulars, they may find it more
difficult to get criminal work.

Bearing this in mind, we can now begin to see how magistrates'
courts might be defined as 'police courts'.   In the first place,
the police are courtroom regulars.   Second, their power to discipline
errant defence lawyers - mainly through controlling the supply of
criminal clients - underscores their influence and domination.
Finally the bench looks upon them benignly (King, 1973, p.16):

> Policemen do tend to be believed and defendants disbelieved on
> any points of conflict in the evidence.   There seems to be a
> general feeling among magistrates that to reject police evidence
> is to undermine the authority of the law.

The tendency towards collaboration between defence lawyers and
police in magistrates' courts was neatly illustrated in the course
of our research. (6)   Thus on more than one occasion we were
invited by leading criminal lawyers in the city for a drink in the
local police club.   This was regarded by them as a perfectly
natural thing to do - and indeed it was.   Since they spent so much
time in the company of policemen, it seemed only right to share
some leisure activities.   Though this is to assume, of course,
that 'work' and 'leisure' are distinct spheres in the context of
police-lawyer relations.   This we doubt;   thus buying policemen
drinks (and we never saw a policeman buy a lawyer a drink; and nor
did the police expect to have to pay) represents an extension and
elaboration of 'work' obligations by other means.

One of the potential problems of staging the 'game' is how to
cope with the new defence lawyer, particularly the younger men who
perhaps want to make their mark.   The police view on 'intruders'
is mixed;   on the one hand, a newcomer offers variety: fresh
performance to scrutinize and evaluate.   On the other hand, though
the new man might be entertaining he must also be taught not to
play it too seriously.   He must learn that it's only a game, and
that it is in nobody's interest (i.e. the regulars) to play the
part too enthusiastically.   As one senior policeman explained it
to us:

> We get the same old mitigation pleas time and time again.   It's
> all so repetitious and boring.   It's rather refreshing to see
> and hear somebody new in the court.   But they have to remember
> that it's all only really a game between solicitors and
> policemen.   I know they sometimes sound like enemies, but you
> don't want to take this too seriously.   They'll often go off
> for a chat or a pint afterwards.   They're not really bad friends
> at all.   After all, they're always both in court together.

The real imprint of the dominance of the magistrates' courts by
the regulars comes through clearly in the phrase: 'it's all so
boring and repetitious'.   The utter predictability of events is
the manifest sign of their control.   Indeed, so confident are they
in their control that plea-bargaining in such courts will occasionally take place in public.   That is, the huddle of regulars beneath
the bench;   that symphony of whispers and mutterings which marks
the exchange between lawyers, police and court clerks.   Not only
is the defendant excluded from these deliberations, lay magistrates
are also kept at arm's length.   They are not court regulars and

hence have no place in the network of informal social relations. Their function is to transmit the decisions of others; the impotence of the lay magistrate is eloquent testimony to the hegemony of the courtroom regulars.

The search of the regulars for a 'quiet life' is one of the factors which makes possible the practice of the confidence game. In Skolnick's (1966) terms, the organization of the game presupposes the guilt of the client, as a general matter, and the fact that pleas of guilty are so common tends to reinforce the presumption of guilt throughout the system.   It is a theory that stresses administrative regularity over challenge, and emphasizes decisions most likely to maximize gain and minimize loss in the negatively valued commodity of penal 'time'.

Playing the 'game' gives a mechanical character to advocacy. Those who observe it most often, the magistrates' court clerks, are well aware of the routinization of passion that occurs.   According to one clerk we spoke to:

> You see chaps (solicitors for the defence) in court every day with whom you are on christian name terms. You say to them after a case 'that was a good version of speech 33.' They get jaundiced themselves.   Luckily, the lay magistrates only sit a couple of times every few weeks, so they never really become aware that a set stock of speeches are being passed around.

If the game sometimes turns sour on those who play it ('becoming jaundiced'), the consequences for the defendant of this reliance on repetitive oratory may be an inefficiently conducted defence. Consider for example, the following two comments, taken from our own research file. The first comes from a magistrate's clerk, the second from a magistrate.

> 'How can they (the solicitors) stand up in court five days a week and keep presenting original defences for similar types of offences? No, defences have to be slotted into a category if the solicitor is to churn them out day after day.'

> 'The approach of the typical criminal advocate is to begin by suggesting possible defences to the client, rather than by examining what features of his client's case might lead to the presentation of an original defence.'

In other words, the mechanization of justice which is implied in these statements is a condition of the practice of the game.

We end this section by bringing in social class factors. Social class differences between, on the one hand, lawyers and court officials (excluding the police), and on the other, the typical defendant in magistrates' courts, underpins the degradation ceremony and the confidence game.   Its existence makes the passage and maintenance of both phenomena easier.   The factor of class and its attendant paraphernalia (dress, bearing, accent, speech) comprise an extra barrier for the defendant to negotiate and form the contour lines which help direct the social organization of justice in magistrates' courts.   Social class, in this country, is intimately linked with notions of deference and 'respect'. A lower class membership breeds its own fatalism; its own philosophy of the inevitability of oppression by 'them'.   'Them', in this case, are the lawmen and their functionaries.   The defendant who seeks to assert himself in a court of law has to cast off a double burden:

the dominance of the professional and the emasculating realities
of class.   Thus the defendant who would 'make himself' in the
courtroom will also have to set about re-making his entire social
world.

THE 'DRAMATURGICAL' PERSPECTIVE ON COURTROOM-TRIBUNAL SETTINGS

This view leads on from our discussion of the confidence game.
Part of the mythology of law is the notion of the courtroom 'drama'.
We shall argue that any 'drama' exists only in the sense of
'theatre', rather than as 'confrontation' or 'struggle'.   Our
earlier account of the confidence game suggests ways in which the
dramaturgical perspective applies to certain courtroom encounters.
The principles of 'dramaturgy' as a framework for social analysis
have been defined by Goffman as (1971, preface):
    the way in which the individual in ordinary work situations
    presents himself and his activity to others, the ways in which
    he guides and controls the impression they form of him and the
    kinds of things he may and may not do while sustaining his
    performance before them.
Clearly, central to this perspective is the idea of the 'performance'.   Performances can vary, but Goffman describes one kind of
behaviour which seems particularly apposite in the context of
lawyer-client relations.   Thus, Goffman introduces us to the
'cynical performer';   that is, one who is not 'taken in at all by
his own routine'.   Yet Goffman also suggests that such cynicism
is not simply rooted in indifference (1971, p.29):
    It is not assumed, of course, that all cynical performers are
    interested in deluding their audiences for purposes of what is
    called 'self-interest' or private gain.   A cynical individual
    may delude his audience for what he considers to be their own
    good, or for the good of the community etc.   For illustrations
    of this we need not appeal to sadly enlightened showmen such
    as Marcus Aurelius or Hsun Tzu.   We know that in service
    occupations practitioners who may otherwise be sincere are
    sometimes forced to delude their customers because their
    customers show such a heartfelt demand for it.   Doctors who are
    led into giving placebos, filling-station attendants who
    resignedly check and recheck tyre pressures for anxious women
    motorists, shoe clerks who sell a shoe that fits but tell the
    customer it is the size she wants to hear - these are cynical
    performers whose audiences will not allow them to be sincere.
These examples have some parallel in courtroom encounters.   As one
solicitor explained to us:
    'Provided the solicitor gives them (i.e. defendants) a run in
    the courts, they feel that everything has been done for them.
    After all, most defendants are guilty of offences.   They just
    form the centre of attraction for the day - when they become the
    "prisoner" or the "accused".   It is important to make them feel
    they've been looked after.   They expect a bit of a show to be
    put on, even when they know they're "done for", so to speak.'
The 'ceremony', the 'game', the 'performance' all depend for their
successful execution upon the ability of lawyers to dominate and

manipulate defendants.   Such control would be impossible to maintain if defendants were without fear and uncertainty.   The manoeuvres we have sketched symbolize the powerlessness of people in law forums.   Their alienation is partially expressed through their inability to act for themselves.   Seen from the dramaturgical perspective, the defendant is the 'audience'.   But he is the spectator and recipient in a theatre whose language he barely understands.   It is the theatre, moreover, of Artaud and the 'brutalists', where the end of the performance is signalled by the actors turning on the audience and chastising them.

Occasionally, however, the defendant experiences some feeling of the 'drama' in the sense in which we are using the word (Ifans, 1972, p.11):

> I felt I was taking part in a play and even expected to hear the applause of the audience, and to return with my fellow-players with the judge in the middle, to take the curtain call.

Here, the control over defendants has begun to dissolve.   In recognizing the 'play' aspect the defendant can also begin to put on a 'performance'.   Ordinary conventions and procedures are subverted as the defendant begins to rewrite and recast the script. But such departures are unusual.   Normally the defendant accepts what he is given, not necessarily because he can conceive of no alternative, or because he is unwilling to speak out but because of an appreciative sense of what will happen to him if he opts for the course of 'resistance'.   This point has been well made by Parker in describing the courtroom experiences of a group of working class youths in Liverpool.   The group - which Parker calls 'The Boys' - had a view of court proceedings which fitted in closely with a dramaturgical model of the court.   As Parker put it (1974, p.170-1):

> Sociologists have used a dramaturgical analysis of the Court with considerable effect.   The Boys themselves use several theatrical terms to describe the prosecution process.   To them the pomp and rigidity of nineteenth-century justice, still retained in today's Court, would be farcical were it not so powerful.   As we unravel their view of this crucial part of the prosecution process one thing should be made explicit.   The Court's kadi, the judge or the magistrate, is trying to assess the accused's moral character. Despite whatever else is meant to be happening the whole process is seen by The Boys as an attack or denunciation of the accused's character by the prosecutors, with the defence making a pitch in favour of his honesty, self-discipline, genuine remorse or what-ever particular personality trait could helpfully be emphasised at that moment.

> The Boys' part in the drama is usually a small one;   often it is a non-speaking part, seldom is it eloquent.   The more import-ant actors will often proceed without even looking to the dock or acknowledging the accused's presence.   The Boys thus continue to feel powerless and are even less willing to speak out than when arrested, believing that any attempt to do so will be taken by the bench as disrespect and aggression.   This may well be the case since the whole ethos of the Courtroom is aimed at intimid-ation, with the procedure quietly emphasising - you may not be guilty this time, but you're one of them, you look and speak like

one of them and you'd better respect this Court and take home
your experience as a warning.   This attitude beams out of Court
officials right down to the way the man on the door treats any
'public' who come to listen to the case and look like an ally
of 'one of them' in the dock.

Finally, we return again to the implications of the activities we
have sketched for the adversary system.   The system rests upon an
assumption of genuine conflict between the contending parties.   In
Skolnick's words (1967, p.52):

> The most striking example of an institution based upon conflict
> is the sporting event.   Not only are most sporting events zero-
> sum games in which one player must lose and the other win; even
> more fundamental is the condition that each player should try
> to win.... Otherwise, the (contest) is not considered genuine.
> Procedure is as important as outcome.

With the adversary system, however, the notion of the 'zero-sum
game' applies only to the fortunes of defendants.   Lawyers working
in the legal contexts we have described, seldom 'lose'.   The
primary concern cutting across all courtroom exchanges is that of
preserving intact informal social relations and obligations.   These
are more important to him than most clients, for they help determine
his economic terms of work.   Over and above this the lawyer will,
typically, have another primary referent in the legal system itself.
According to Hayden (1970, p.73):

> The law, like politics, is organized around a principle of
> 'representation' rather than direct participation by the people
> most affected.   The citizen is reduced to being a client.   He
> exercises choice only when he selects a lawyer.   The lawyer then
> takes over as the expert in how best to represent his client's
> interests.   The lawyer speaks for the client not in the partic-
> ular style of that individual but in a proper and formalized
> way.   Within this ritualized situation, the lawyer's highest
> obligation is not to the client but to the legal system itself.

It is from analyses like these that the first stirrings of interest
in self-representation before courts and tribunals took inspiration.
And any movement towards self-representation should largely be
viewed as a product of (reaction to) the practice of the 'ceremony',
the 'game' and the 'performance'.

THE PRACTICE OF LAW SEEN AS DEVIANT BEHAVIOUR

From one view, of course, the earlier accounts of the lawyer at
work may be defined as 'deviant' behaviour.   Lawyers, themselves,
would rarely be willing to concede the point but there are other
occasions when deviance takes a form that is impossible even for
lawyers to ignore.   Frequently, complaints about 'irregular' or
'improper' behaviour centre upon the organization of touting.   The
problem, for lawyers, is how to handle the issue without impugning
the honesty or integrity of all criminal lawyers.   In other words,
how might a potential scandal be redefined as merely a simple
mistake at work?   Friedson has suggested one strategy that
professionals find convenient to adopt at moments such as these
(1972, p.88):

Deficient behaviour on the part of a professional tends to be explained as the result of being a deficient kind of person, or at least having been inadequately or improperly 'socialised' or educated in professional school.   The most commonly suggested remedy for such behaviour is reformation of the professional curriculum rather than of the circumstances of professional work....

We are driven back here to the 'bad-apple-in-the-barrel' theory of deviant behaviour.   It is a sure way of minimizing and obscuring the significance of the act.   Thus instead of examining structural factors (such as work settings), the obstacle is negotiated by scapegoating particular errant individuals.

Among lawyers, a further device is also favoured: that of simply ignoring the existence of what Hughes calls the 'dirty work of the profession'.   In Hughes's words (1971, p.306):

A lawyer may be asked whether he and his client come into court with clean hands; when he answers 'yes' it may mean that someone else's hands are of necessity a bit grubby.   For not only are some quarrels more respectable, more clean, than others; but also some of the kinds of work involved in the whole system (gathering evidence, getting clients, bringing people to court, enforcing judgements, making the compromises that keep cases out of court) are more respected and more removed from temptation and suspicion than others.   In fact, the division of labour among lawyers is as much one of respectability (hence of self concept and role) as of specialised knowledge and skills.   One might even call it a moral division of labour, if one keeps in mind that the term means not simply that some lawyers, or people in the various branches of law work, are more moral than others; but that the very demand for highly scrupulous and respectable lawyers depends in various ways upon the availability of less scrupulous people to attend to the less respectable legal problems of even the best people.   I do not mean that the good lawyers all consciously delegate their dirty work to others (although many do).   It is rather a game of live and let live.

For the client-defendant the problem is one of what to do when he is the victim of deviant practices.   There is first - given the power differential in professional-client relations - a doubt if he will ever even know that he has been a victim.   And second, when his suspicions are aroused, there is the problem of penetrating the profession's conspiracy of silence.   This response is one common to all professions, as Goffman makes clear (1971, p.95):

In a recent study of the teaching profession, it was found that teachers felt that if they are to sustain an impression of professional competence and institutional authority, they must make sure that when angry parents come to the school with complaints, the principal will support the position of his staff, at least until the parents have left.   Similarly, teachers feel strongly that their fellow teachers ought not to disagree with or contradict them in front of students.   'Just let another teacher raise her eyebrow funny, just so they (the children) know, and they don't miss a thing, and their respect for you goes right away.'   Similarly, we learn that the medical profession has a strict code of etiquette whereby a consultant in the presence of

the patient and his doctor is careful never to say anything
which would embarrass the impression of competence that the
patient's doctor is attempting to maintain.   As Hughes suggests,
'The (professional) etiquette is a body of ritual which grows up
informally to preserve, before the clients, the common front of
the profession.   And of course, this kind of solidarity in the
presence of subordinates also occurs when performers are in the
presence of subordinates.   For example, in a recent study of
the police, we learn that a patrolling team of two policemen,
who witness each other's illegal and semi-illegal acts and who
are in an excellent position to discredit each other's show of
legality before the judge, possess heroic solidarity and will
stick by each other's story no matter what atrocity it covers
up or how little chance there is of anyone believing it.'
The ability to sustain these fronts is confirmation both of the
power of professions and the impotence of those they 'serve'.   In
the final chapter we examine other aspects of courtroom encounters
and of the trial: principally, the interest in some quarters in
using science to 'modernize' and 'humanize' the law;   the form of
the intersecting of law and science in the trial;   and the
construction of reality and the manufacture of knowledge in the
courtroom.

PROSPECTS FOR A RADICAL LEGAL PROFESSION

Having talked about the ways in which lawyers are socialized and
of some of the results of this conditioning, we finish this chapter
with some notes on the prospects for the radical lawyer.   In
recent years a new type of radical lawyer has emerged along with
the appearance of groups of 'radical professionals' in social work,
school-teaching, medicine, architecture, etc.   At the same time,
as we saw in chapter 1, a lobby exists among some teachers of law,
to 'radicalize' the law syllabus in the sense of aiming at what
they define as a more relevant and progressive course content.   We
wish to say a few words about both of these phenomena;   about, that
is, liberation and the lawyer and liberation and the law teacher.

(a)   Liberation and the lawyer

In chapter 5 we look at the distinction drawn by Hakman (1971),
Sternberg (1972) and others, between 'old' and 'new' kinds of
political trial activity.   Their descriptions and analysis are
largely worked out with reference to changes in litigation strategies
made by the defendants themselves.   But what interests us here,
however, is the way in which attempts, by defendants, to make the
trial political have been paralleled by the emergence of the 'new'
radical lawyer.   What, then, are the roots of this radicalization
and what are the prospects for the radical lawyer and for the
creation of a radical legal profession?   And more generally, what
are some of the problems, tensions and contradictions facing those
who wish to make their mark on the world as radical professionals?
   For us the search for 'causes' narrows down to four factors, none

of which can properly be considered in isolation from the others.
First, the radicalization of some lawyers cannot be viewed
separately from the changing character of radical politics in
general in this country.   This point is well made by Taylor,
Walton and Young (1975, pp.14-20) in describing the radicalization
of segments of what they term 'the non-commercial middle class'.
In other words, the construction of (or more accurately, attempts
to construct) a wider radical politics, which in part turned upon
a redefinition of the 'political' while turning away from established
major political groupings, provided some sort of supportive culture
for the development of a radical praxis within particular professions,
including law.   Second, since the radicalization of some defendants
(measured in terms of new courtroom tactics) preceded the radicalization of some lawyers, we have to consider the extent to which the
former determined the latter.   Taylor, Walton and Young talk of the
way in which ideological shifts among the non-commercial middle
class (by which they seem to mean those who man the welfare professions as administrators or face-workers) was 'paralleled by the
politicization of blacks..., prisoners and mental patients' (1975,
p.19).   For Taylor, Walton and Young then, it would seem that this
class and its clients-constituency all partake of the same radical
totality.   Thus the radicalization of the former is instantaneously
'paralleled' by the conversion of the latter.   Perhaps it really
was like this, although the authors themselves point to the prelim-
inary character of their enquiry into the non-commercial middle
class (p.59, note 6).   But we hold to the importance of seeing the
route to the radicalization of some lawyers as having its origins
in the politicization of their client-defendants.   In MacDonald's
(1971) words the defendants, in making the trial political (cf.
chapter 5) 'invited the (defence) lawyers to share their alienation'.
It has been a stark enough choice, but some lawyers have opted to
share and in this sense we can talk, to adapt a cosy piece of
rhetoric from the social case-worker, of 'client-centred radicalism',
and its imprint upon the professional.   It goes without saying too,
of course, that those lawyers who elect not to participate also
emerge with a political identity thrust upon them.
   Next, we suggest that the radicalization of some lawyers can in
part be traced back to the recent interest in 'liberalizing' law
which we outlined in chapter 1.   We do not mean to imply by this
that there exists some kind of natural progression from 'liberalism'
to 'radicalism' for those lawyers who begin by wanting a reformed or
more socially conscious legal profession.   In reality, those
lawyers caught up in the pressure to 'radicalize' have a number of
alternatives open to them.   They can either capitulate by running
away and leaving the profession; or they can retreat to the old
austere professionalism of the black letter lawyer, or they can
decide to keep to their liberalism.   But while the shift to
radicalism is only one of several electives open to the liberal
lawyer, nevertheless it is one partly rooted in this liberalism.
   Fourth and finally we introduce again a 'market-model' explanation of the radicalization of some lawyers.   We used a variant on
this model in chapter 1 to account for the spread of socio-legal
studies; and we employ it again in the next section of this chapter,
on liberation and the law teacher, when looking at the occupational

world of the radical teachers of law. (7)   The market-model can
be used to explain aspects of lawyer radicalization in terms of the
highly favourable market (i.e. work opportunities) that lawyers have
enjoyed in this country in recent years.   In chapter 3 we described
how some of these new opportunities have been created, through the
vehicle of state mediation-subsidization.   The amount of work
created by this intervention has helped bring about the 'liberal
hour' within the legal profession.   As we say in chapter 3 if
innovation pays, then most lawyers will tolerate legal reforms.
When everybody is doing well no-one minds very much if some lawyers
take up 'extreme' causes or make radical speeches.   Indeed, at
moments when the work to be done outstrips the number of lawyers
available to do it, then the radical lawyer can sometimes win a
kind of approval from the rest of the profession.   For he is a
tangible sign that the legal profession moves with the times.   In
these circumstances the radical lawyer is both tolerated and ignored;
tolerated, because his existence seems somehow 'good' for the
profession at large (by this light, making it representative of all
opinion) and ignored because what he does in the affluent liberal
hour threatens no-one.

   Taking this further, one result of state mediation (cf.chapter 3)
is to make the survival of the radical lawyer easier.   But if
mediation simplified matters financially, it complicates them
ideologically.   Thus mediation means, in effect, receiving a
mandate from the state to agitate;   the radical lawyer is granted a
licence to be a bolshevik in the legal world.   At the same time,
and this introduces another paradox, if the radicalism of the
radical lawyer is ever threatened or challenged he can protect
himself by invoking the canons of professionalism.   Hence in the
last resort the beleaguered radical professional can defend himself
by retiring behind the same institutional apparatus that his
radicalism would seek to subvert.   To put this another way the
radical lawyer (like any other radical professional) is entangled
in a situation where he is committed to undermining the very
structure that provides his own power base in the world.   We
discussed some of the dilemmas and contradictions implicit in
instances like these, at the end of chapter 3.   We have no easy
answer as to how they might be resolved except to repeat an earlier
point that might prove cautionary here;   that those who present
themselves as having the answers often turn out to be part of the
problem.

(b) Liberation and the law teacher

In the final section we look at the occupational world of the
radical teacher of law.   As we noted in the case of the lawyer,
liberalization - here in the shape of 'socio-legal' studies - has
an effect on this radicalization.   Again, we do not mean to argue
that there is some sort of natural progression from liberalization
to radicalism.   But the liberalizing movement is important for to
radicalize as law teachers necessitates the opportunity to see the
law outside of itself and at the same time be a lawyer.   Socio-

legal studies provide this opportunity, though, as we argue, these conditions are never met because of the structural pressures that force the whole movement to take a law centred view of things. Thus, those who begin to be radicalized through this route tend either to stay confirmed in their liberalism - the meaning of which we have already examined - or, if radicalized, either to bifurcate their lives, becoming political activists on the outside and austere professionals on the inside of the law school, or get out of law teaching altogether.   The option of radicalizing as law teacher tends to be the hardest to maintain.

We now discuss some of these structural pressures from the standpoint of the control and legitimation of certain subject areas within the academic legal fraternity.   What we have seen is how 'socio-legal' academics have had to define their own scholarship as centrally legal in order to legitimate their own activity and progress within the law schools.   In looking at it in this way we have not discussed an important dimension of control.   These academics do not have control over the legitimation process.   The control is vested in those who are at the top of the legal academic profession and it is they who enjoy control over the criteria and definition of legal scholarship.   An analogy from science will help explain this point.   Ravetz (1973) talks of the notion of quality control in science: the role of the journal and the referee in determining what is to be counted as scientific knowledge and hence a legitimate area for scientific study.   We can extend this model, analogously to law, by looking at the way in which criteria for legal scholarship are created.   Thus, by and large, the criteria are set by the established journals, the established law publishing firms and their associated readers.   These controllers have come up the old established way and in the old established traditions and it is their definitions that are powerful and prevailing.   Legal scholarship and knowledge, as scientific scholarship and knowledge, is not something 'out there', waiting to be found, gathered and weighed in, in the selling plate for promotion.   It is something that depends upon those who operate and control the system of quality control.   For the quality control system measures not only quality but also decides what is to count as something deserving of quality control.   It is the defining measure.

New directions and new advances have to be accommodated by the controllers.   This is done in two ways.   First, they ignored the phenomenon and refused to define it as legal.   As the tide of socio-legal studies becomes stronger, the more common response is to extend the hegemony of the old pattern of quality control.   Thus the phenomenon is to be defined as legal; as located within the law school;   as something that might have some connection with other disciplines but only in a service role.   Becoming legal means a reassertion of power by those who have control over the quality control mechanism.   The new subject and the new attitudes are defined as legal but only as being peripheral to the main trad- itional legal enterprise.   That is still the paradigm of the lawyers' activity;   the rest are luxuries that we can sometimes afford.

Those who started the liberalizing movement are caught, because, as we say, they have also tried to define their enterprise as centrally legal. In doing so they fall into the trap of social structure, for they allow what started off as their property to be taken away and powerful definitions of what is legal take over. They do not retaliate: they are also seduced and believe in the ideology of the powerful. They, after all, are law teachers teaching in law schools and their knowledge is to that extent controlled. They feel committed because they see themselves as in some ways committed to the law. The law teacher in this position is like a monk in a monastery who finds, to his horror, that he is ceasing to believe in God. He must either get out and start life anew - which after the personal investment that has gone into the religious life is not something that can be quickly or easily done - or he must find some way of working out his salvation within the monastery. The way to do this is to bury yourself in activity, in good works, anything that means that you do not have to think of the implications of your disbelief. And so you have the 'God is dead' school which is essentially concerned with making the world a 'nicer' place in which to live. Transfer this analogy to the law teacher and you have the same sort of thing. His crisis of disbelief is resolved by burying himself in activity, by making the law, in any way possible 'serve the people', by making law 'friendly' and 'nice'; anything to avoid thinking of the implica-tions of his crisis. This activity brings him centrally into the law again - he keeps the faith because he is forced to and because he wants to.

The radicalizing law teacher then, finds himself in a difficult position for he has to be inside and outside of the law at the same time. We finish the section by examining some of the ways that this might be achieved.

First we look at the creation of alternative structures. But in these alternative structures, because they are alternative structures, the debate about radicalization (if there is one) tends to be about whether to bring the structure back to law - in which case its autonomy is lost - or to drop out of law altogether. It does not really concentrate upon radicalizing as law teachers. (8)

The other way out is to use a structure that already is inside and outside of the law. Here we turn to the use of jurisprudence. Jurisprudence is a strange subject - in most law schools it is a mixture of the social sciences, the humanities, law, and almost anything that can be seen, on very loose criteria, as relevant. Traditionally it has been a compulsory subject in law schools but this status is coming increasingly under attack. One of the reasons adduced is that it is simply not legal, another employs the notion of the 'withering away' of jurisprudence. The idea is that jurisprudence need not be taught compulsorily because each particular legal subject can be taught, and indeed should be taught, with the theoretical insights of jurisprudence that are particular to it. Teaching in this way will do away with the need for compulsory jurisprudence. This locates any questioning purpose that jurisprudence might have firmly within the law. For juris-prudence is the subject which, because of its contacts with the outside, can show the law teachers other vistas and horizons. They can see a different world and then inform their students of it.

The aim of the argument that it is not legal is to exclude jurisprudence from 'legal' status altogether.   The aim of the 'withering
away' argument is to drag the stray sheep back into the fold; to
locate them firmly within the quality control system of law; to
enable them to teach students without asking important questions
about what law does but to accept law as an all-embracing, albeit
fickle, provider.   As the 'radicalized' law teacher seeks to
confront the myths of the law in his working life, he must simul-
taneously be inside and outside the law so that he can be legitimated as a lawyer - whilst denying the law.   Such a fence sitting
operation is difficult to sustain, for the pressures are always
there to make him fall off on one side or the other.   Jurisprudence
helps, for its status is vague and undefined in that it can be seen
as both legal and non-legal.   It is within this sort of structure
and protection that the radicalizing teacher of law can work.   It
is only in this uncertainty that he can work.

The need for jurisprudence teachers, however, is small, whereas
the need for 'law' teachers is greater and so the radicalizing law
teacher has to invest some of the traditional 'hard core' subjects
with its status.   To reclaim the area that, as we described in the
beginning of this book, has been deserted by the liberalizing
moment.   It is only in this way that this sort of 'radical
professional' can make sense of his world for it is only in this
way that his critical teaching will make sense to his students.

Having said all this two contradictions still remain for him.
Concentrating on his own activity can make him think that the most
important thing to be overcome is law and so paradoxically law
once again becomes the centre of things because it is the central
thing that must be overcome.   And so the concentration, by these
kinds of radical professionals, on making the content of the
subject radical - thus radical law and radical criminology. (9)
And finally concentration on teaching might make him forget that
professional socialization involved in becoming a lawyer outside
of the law school plays a far greater role than his teaching.   He
is more likely to produce radical teachers than radical lawyers.

EPISTEMOLOGY AND OPPRESSION

INTRODUCTION

So far we have looked at the way law prevents and defuses any sort of radical change. In so doing, we have concentrated on the ways that the law, in bringing its gifts, forces people to accept its own definitions of reality and so strengthen legal and thus capitalist society's definitions of control. We have also talked of the symbolic function that the law has in emasculating people and preventing them from taking any action at all. It is this abstract ideology of a bourgeois society that prevents any change. For what it does is to convince people that they have no power. It convinces them that the world cannot be changed; that things might become better but only with the help of autonomous agencies staffed by experts. As part of this general ideology of capitalist society, the law plays its part by channelling protest and guiding reform within its parameters. By mediating the relationship between people and their objectives, it prevents them from taking any form of direct action. Political action - as we see throughout the book - is transmuted into constitutional and legal change.

   The effect of these assumptions is to close the doors through which the oppressed must step if they are to transform our society into a free one. The doors that must be opened are those of an ideology and epistemology that tries to establish a consensus in society. That is, that everyone agrees to everything; that nothing changes but what is reasonable; where the aim is not to find the best society but to get one that all 'reasonable' men of 'good will' agree on. This takes place within the context of an epistemology that divorces man from the world. It claims that the world is a world of immutable, ahistorical, atemporal facts and is distinct from man's activities. Thus these facts are the guidelines towards any change in a society because they constrain all activity directed toward such change. This theory is implicit in the reactions against the advocates of a better society: 'things cannot be different, that's the way people are'; 'we have laws and leaders because of human nature and you cannot change that.' Such reaction reflects a view of the world that is static and stable,

where the only sort of change is exactly the sort in which the law
is already involved, i.e. piecemeal social engineering.   We can
make things better and, in some cases bigger, but we cannot radically
change them.   Thus the world is set out before us and man cannot
create and recreate it;   the only part he can play is to make it a
'nicer' place to live in. (1)
    The way this is to be done is to discover more 'facts' about the
world and here the epistemology that we have been describing ties in
with a more sociological theory about how, and by whom, the immutable
facts are to be found/constructed.   The historic mission of this
sort of positivism is to conflate rationality with scientific
rationality and to make knowledge dependent upon those trained in
science accepting it.   Knowledge then is only real knowledge if it
is endorsed by such mythical creatures as 'the international scientific community' or 'the community of scholars'.   Science then
legitimates society for it is the knowledge that will count towards
constructing a better society.   This celebrates a society where
there are experts who 'know best'.   It reflects the dichotomy of
capitalist society into the 'knowers' (the order givers) and the
'doers' (the order takers).   The world is saved by the scientist
and his surrogate in the guise of the 'reasonable - rational' man
heralding the 'end of ideology' where social change is left to
technology and the technocratic experts.   Social change then
becomes a weak-kneed utilitarian affair in that it takes on itself
the mantle of technical rationality.   Consensus about ends is
assumed - the way the world is settles that - and all that is
necessary is to find out how to achieve them. (2)   Lawyers themselves reflect this ideology as manipulators of a legal world that
only they understand.   This world is one that is only discoverable
by them and for everyone else remains arcane and inviolate.   Law
then regulates the kind of changes that are possible and denies
power to the 'consumers' by claiming that it, and the surrogate
scientists who service it, know best.
    Powerlessness then is shown in two ways: first, through the
claim that the world is constituted in a particular way and that
nothing radical can be done to change it.   Second, through the
insistence that what change can come about must come through a
certain class of people in society - the scientist or his surrogate.
In law this is transformed into the doctrine that the lawyer knows
best.   The problems that people have are only to be understood in
legal terms and so taken away from the 'consumer'.   People cannot
solve these problems directly because their fears and their worries
have first of all to be translated into the reasonable and rational
concepts of the law.   In so doing their worries, and their resolution become unintelligible and, somehow, unsatisfying.   Thus there
is politics, there is vested interest, there is polemic and partisan-
ship, there is irrationality and blindness - and there is the law,
which transcends it all, changing human activity into 'rational' and
'reasonable' activity.   Man then becomes a hollow creature who can
only act in the world through the institutions that scientific
rationality has set up. (3)
    It is from this sort of theory that men must be liberated because
it denies the possibility of any radical action in the world.   Thus,
self-representation often fails because the self-representors start
believing that law and human nature cannot change.   They leave it

to those who incontrovertibly know how; the lawyers.   If these
theories are accepted there is no way out of the trap.   There is
no escape because of the self-created image of the world.   If
freedom is an open door in a room, the only problem being that you
cannot see it, then that door does not exist.   It does not exist
because men will think it an illusion until they see that they can
create or construct that door.   In the kingdom of the blind, or
where people will not open their eyes, darkness is the only reality.
Light is the reality of those who can, or want to, see.

SEIZING THE LAW

In showing what is wrong with these particular theories we aim to
establish our view of man and the epistemological position that
sets it up.   Our aim is to argue for something that has been
implicit in the book so far: that man can create the world and
change it and that the possibilities of liberation lie in each
person's grasp.   That, potentially at least, man is a free and
creative being and, because of this, can break out of a society
which stultifies him.   As we have seen, the theory that we are
attacking denies this and makes man passive and malleable.   In so
doing, the theory reflects the social formations of a capitalist
society.   Our argument will take the form of showing that there
is a praxis which itself denies this prevailing ideology.   What it
needs is an epistemology to explain it; to show that this is
rational action in the world and not the activities of unscientific,
unreasonable men.
      We go back then, to the themes that we raised at the end of
chapter 1.   There we argued that change through law was a waste of
time and that the main way in which genuine political action was
expressed was through the building up of working class organization
and proletarian power.   It is through this that the bourgeois
ideology of powerlessness is denied. (4)   For, in this way, the
class can be seen as creating its power and making it felt.   But
this necessitates an epistemology which can explain this as the
self-conscious acting out of power.   For the sort of activity that
this involves - direct action, community politics and the like - is
too often defined as irrational, the activities of hooligans and
politically motivated subversives.   What is needed, it is claimed,
is modification of the law to enable the legal experts to solve
what real problems, if any, are manifested in this activity.   This
is particularly important when people are caught up in the coils
of the law, when they have to fight on the stage provided by it and
their liberty is being judged according to its norms.   Here the
law, in the way that we have described, works to emasculate self-
activity.
      What we have in mind here are trial and tribunal situations where
the arena is not of the players' own choosing.   These situations
multiply as manifestations of proletarian power increase.   For that
sort of politics inevitably brings those involved into direct
confrontation with the state and its apparatus.   These confront-
ations take many forms but the ones we will concentrate upon here

are trials.   For these, besides stopping and punishing those who
break the norms of the society, are also designed to force home,
symbolically, the message of a consensus society.   That nothing
can be radically changed; that everyone, except for a few 'crazies'
agree; that those who run the society know what is best for they
have the access to true 'scientific' knowledge.   Everything is as
well ordered as it can be and the law is well able to cope with any
necessary alterations.   It is here then, that the abstract ideology
of the law is set up for public gaze as something that denies man
the power to change the law himself.   Man's artifact takes on a
life of its own.   It slips away from man and his power to change
and becomes something that controls him.   Law becomes reified.
As Berger and Luckmann (1969, pp.106-8) say:

> Reification is the apprehension of human phenomena as if they
> were things, that is, in non-human or possibly supra-human terms.
> Another way of saying this is that reification is the apprehen-
> sion of the products of human activity as if they were something
> other than human products - such as facts of nature, results of
> cosmic laws, or manifestations of divine will.   Reification
> implies that man is capable of forgetting his own authorship of
> the human world, and, further, that the dialectic between man,
> the producer and his products is lost to consciousness.   The
> reified world is, by definition, a dehumanised world.   It is
> experienced by man as a strange facticity, an opus alienum over
> which he has no control rather than as the opus proprium of his
> own prductive activity.... The basic 'recipe' for the reification
> of institutions is to bestow on them an ontological status
> independent of human activity and signification.   Specific
> reifications are variations on this general theme.   Marriage, for
> instance, may be reified as an imitation of divine acts of
> creativity, as a universal mandate of natural laws, as the
> necessary consequence of biological or psychological forces, or,
> for that matter, as a functional imperative of the social system.
> What all these reifications have in common is their obfuscation
> of marriage as an ongoing human production.... Roles may be
> reified in the same manner as institutions.... The paradigmatic
> formula for this kind of reification is the statement 'I have no
> choice in the matter, I have to act this way because of my
> position'....

We do not want to argue that 'seizing the law' is a solution to the
problems of oppression in our society.   But for people who are
forced on to this battleground there are ways, by politicizing the
trial, by transcending the purely legal battle, of denying the
abstract ideology of the law and of putting forward a vision of a
new society.   Thus there are actions in the trial itself, which
can, given the right epistemology, be shown to be the self-conscious
political activity of men.   Making coherent a theory that shows
how man, in fighting back against the law, makes the trial political,
will explain how the abstract ideology of consensus society is
incorrect.   We look here at those defendants whose primary interest
was not in scoring legal points (even for the furtherance of radical
causes) but in seeking to expose the domination of law, and to de-
mystify law through the weapons of political speech, ridicule and
a contempt for courtroom convention.

We begin, thought, with a paradox.   In a sense all trials, all law in process, is 'political'.   Since courts are agencies of government and judges and magistrates part of the state apparatus, then all decision in law can be considered as political ones.   At the same time, there is a steadfast refusal by the state, in this country, to acknowledge the existence of political trials in the legal order.   The denial is, in part, a denial of the authenticity of those who seek to make the trial political (Levine, 1971, pp.127-8):

> Cross-examination of Miss Morse by Government Attorney Schulz.
> The Witness:... The Government of the United States has lost its credibility today; there is fighting in the United States today going on in cities in this country today.   People's Park in Berkeley, the policemen shot at us when people were unarmed, were fighting, if you wish, with rocks, the policemen used double-load buckshot and rifles, and pistols against unarmed demonstrators.   That is fighting, OK? There is fighting to regain their liberty, fighting to regain their freedom, fighting for a totally different society, people in the black community, people in the Puerto Rican community, people in the Mexican-American community and people in the white communities.   They are fighting by political means as well as defending themselves.
> Mr. Schulz: Your Honor, that is not an answer to my question..
> Mr. Kunstler: Your Honor, they are intensely political questions and she is trying to give a political answer to a political question.
> The Court: This is not a political case as far as I am concerned.
> Mr. Kunstler: Well, your Honor, as far as some of the rest of us are concerned, it is quite a political case.
> The Court: It is a criminal case.   There is an indictment here. I have the indictment right up here.   I can't go into politics here in this Court.
> Mr. Kunstler: Your Honor, Jesus was accused criminally, too, and we understand really that was not truly a criminal case in the sense that it is just an ordinary -
> The Court: I didn't live at that time.   I don't know.   Some people think I go back that far, but I really don't.
> Mr. Kunstler: Well, I was assuming your Honor had read of the incident.

The act of nullification depends on having 'political acts' against the law, redefined as 'criminal' ones.   To do this is to minimize the ideological basis of the behaviour of actors, and to sublimate the meaning of the act beneath the labels of conventional morality and wisdom.   For example, urban racial troubles in the USA were labelled 'riots', and their leaders seen not as politicians, but as 'hoodlums and gangsters'.   'Time Magazine', (5) commenting upon the troubles following the death of Martin Luther King, said: 'The majority of plunderers and burners in American cities last week were about as ideologically motivated as soldier ants.'   The persistent denial of the authentic nature of the act, in this context, is aptly illustrated by Taylor (1973, p.31):

> ... I... have in front of me a paper delivered at a recent conference which is entitled 'Flights to Fantasy among Skyjackers' The author attempts to demonstrate that the actions of sky-jackers are not political.   He describes their psychological

predisposition to such actions in the following way: 'At a
time of acute personal failure, their paranoid characterologic
system fails, they can no longer hide their feminine identifi-
cation. A sharp depression ensues during which they have
strong impulses toward murder - rape - suicide. These acts are
unacceptable to them. During subsequent depersonalisation with
psychotic disorganisation complex biologic, social and ethnical
symbols become fused into two impulses: to stand like a man and
to fly like a bird.

A refusal to accede to the concept of the political trial is, of
course, the obverse side of the argument that insists upon the
courts' freedom from political influence and patronage. From here
we get the claim that the law is 'essentially apolitical'; it is
made even on behalf of countries such as South Africa, where the
'independence' of the judiciary has excited must liberal approval
in this country. But if we examine outcomes, rather than ideologies,
we find a different picture. To continue with the example of South
Africa; on the one hand its courts are highly professional, decorous
and learned. Individual blacks might, indeed, win cases in court.
Yet these are pyrrhic victories; the law of apartheid still remains
and the courts who try to administer them 'fairly' merely help to
legitimize them. In this way 'apolitical' law functions as a
crucial agency in the domination of blacks. (6) But though this
is true and has been argued in greater detail in chapter 1, saying
that all trials are political does not get us very far. For we
have to distinguish between behaviour in a trial which does reflect
consensus reality and ways of acting which transcend that and make
taking part in the trial a political action in itself. The
distinction that we are seeking to draw is that of being tried for
a political act and making the trial political itself. Traditional
types of radical litigation tactics reflect the former well. Their
principal characteristics emerged in what Hakman (1971) has called
'The Classic Movement Case'. Such cases have a three-fold aim
for radical litigants - to discredit the 'Establishment', to
produce political sympathizers, and to change the law. But most
significant of all, from our viewpoint, was that the radical
defendants involved were usually prepared to give the preparation
and general conduct of the trial over to professional lawyers.
They were seldom reluctant to respect what Sternberg (1972) has
called 'conventional courtroom deportment'; that is, the acceptance
of the ground rules of the court room. In other words, the
militancy of such defendants always stopped short of the court room
itself. This point has been noted by one observer of the behaviour
of radical defendants in American judicial history (Macdonald, 1971,
pp.xviii-xix):

> In old style political trials, from the pre-revolutionary trial
> in which Peter Zenger was successfully defended against His
> Majesty's prosecutors on a charge of publishing seditious matter,
> to the recent trial of Dr. Spock, et al., in Boston, both sides,
> in dress and behaviour accepted the conventions of the ruling
> establishment.... The defence behaved as if they shared the
> values and life-style of the Court, even when they didn't, as
> in the big IWW trial of 1918 under the Espionage Act. There
> were over a hundred defendants, the entire leadership plus the

Wobblies.... But although the defendants were anarchists to a man...bold and ingenious in anti-establishment disruption outside the courtroom...they behaved themselves inside it.

Or as Spock himself commented (Sternberg, 1972, p.110):

We sat like good little boys called into the Principal's office. I'm afraid we didn't prove very much.

For political defendants to behave in this way means their tacit acceptance of the model of the traditional criminal trial. The model has been defined as comprising exclusively the following categories of active participants: the judge, and his auxiliary staff; the defendant(s); the public prosecutor(s); the defence lawyer(s); witnesses for the prosecution and defence; and the jury. And it also encompasses a further, passive, group, the spectators. By agreeing to accept the part already written for them in the 'drama', radical defendants, without a word being said, have submitted to the morality and procedures of the court. They take their place in a social world characterized by highly formal patterns of interaction between participants. There is a quiet celebration of style and manners. It is accepted that the judge 'guides' the trial; it becomes taken for granted that a defence lawyer speaks on behalf of his client, who should not speak out for himself; it is thought 'sensible' to ask only particular questions of witnesses - those put in a particular style and order. Witnesses, for their part, answer only those questions put to them by court officials and do not 'volunteer' information. This reflects an orderly consensual view of the world and shows the paradox in the traditional definition of the political trial; that of a prosecution launched with a political purpose. For then the political trial becomes totally apolitical in that it reflects the traditional trial and consensus society. Solzhenitsyn, when talking of Stalin's role in the Moscow trials in the 1930s puts this well (1974, p.374):

On the threshold of the classless society, we were at last capable of realizing the conflictless trial - a reflection of the absence of inner conflict in our social structure - in which not only the judge and the prosecutor but also the defence lawyers and the defendants themselves would strive consciously to achieve their common purpose.

Historically, the great majority of 'criminal trials of political radicals' involved labour and trade union struggles. But the emergence of new litigation strategies - making the trial political has different issues for confrontation, viz. race, sex, drugs, poverty and general problems of social change. At the heart of the new thinking is the attempt by radical defendants to wrest back control in the trial, to the extent of totally negating trial proceedings, if necessary. The operation of 'new model' trials is made possible by the refusal of radicals to accept traditional courtroom roles, rules and rituals. More than this, the audience, usually passive, is brought into the drama. The shift in tactics is summarized well in this comment on the Chicago conspiracy trial (Macdonald, 1971, p.xx):

In the new-style radical courtroom tactics, either the lawyers share the alienation and often the hair style of their clients,

or there are no lawyers.   Also, as in the Living Theatre and
other avant-garde dramatic presentations, the audience get
into the act; the spectators raise their voices, or, worse,
their laughter at crucial moments, despite all the beefy
marshals.   And the defendants, hitherto passive except when
they had their meagre moment on the witness stand - 'Please
answer the question yes or no' - feel free to make critical
comments on the drama when the spirit moves them.

The new tactics, though they offer the prospect of more vigorous
pursuit of specifically legal objectives, make the basis for the
transformation of courtroom proceedings into a form of 'political
theatre'.   The impetus for the 'new-model trial' would seem to
develop upon the following factors.   First, the left is radicalizing faster than lawyers (especially those in this country), and
confrontation is on issues with which even 'politically progressive'
lawyers have no empathy.   Second, the 'new-model' resolves the
problem of the personal predilections of lawyers.   Finally, and
crucially, the new tactics are a direct assault upon alienation and
serve as a vehicle for self-actualization in the courtroom.   Under
this regime the defendant is able to remain autonomous; the court
has to respond to him.   The resurrection of the defendant, under
rules of the defendant's devising, can only be prevented by actual
physical coercion.   And when this happens (as in the case of the
gagging of Bobby Seale in the Chicago conspiracy trial) action
serves effectively as testimony.   When the radical defendant's
primary interest is in political theatre (to return again to that
theme) in mockery and calculated subversion of sacred ways (rules
of evidence and procedure) and sacred places (the courtroom) the
results can be stupendous.

THE TRIAL AND SCIENTIFIC RATIONALITY

In this section we discuss how the English trial can be understood
as an arena wherein alternative versions of reality compete for
acceptance and how this enables us to understand, as self-conscious
political activity, the actions of those who attempt to make the
trial political.   The fact that the form of the trial can be seen
as a fight is neutralized by putting forward an epistemology that
makes it appear, in outcome at least, like the Moscow trials that
Solzhenitsyn (1974) describes.   Thus though there appears to be
a fight, what is portrayed is the state's version of reality, a
well ordered consensual world.   This portrayal takes two forms.
At the philosophical level it denies that it is by the dialectical
relationship of man to the world that truth and reality are created.
This it does by positing a timeless and immutable ring of facts
about the world.   At the practical level it uses that theory to
supply and endorse experts who are best suited to discovering these
facts.   And so the trial is scientized and professionalized so
that the state's version of reality wins, not by force, but by the
force of 'reason'.

We will first of all consider the epistemological problems by
looking at the attack on what might be termed 'the alternative
reality' theory of finding truth in the trial.   From this we will

develop the epistemological foundations of our own theory.   We
move on then to consider the writing of Frank (1950).   We use this
work because, in many ways, it has set the parameters of the debate
in talk of trials and juries.   In this work Frank develops the
scientistic attack upon the trial and jury system which, he claims,
has hampered progress.   He argues that the aim of the trial is to
seek truth and that the Anglo-American trial manifestly fails to do
this.   The essence of his approach is the distancing of the trial
from the notion of truth; truth is something that exists rather than
something that is created.   His argument takes the form of an
attack upon the accusatory method of trial procedure.   This is a
system which has its roots in the medieval trial by battle where
the contest was between the accuser and the defender, or their
respective champions.   The winner earned his right to establish
his version of what happened.   This is what Frank claims occurs
symbolically today.   The court, in the person of the judge, does
not play a major role in this process but instead is cast in the
role of the referee, making sure that the rules and some semblance
of fairness are observed.   There is no question of an impartial,
rational way of finding the truth.   Each side is literally
fighting using as many tricks as it can to establish its version of
reality.   Each side is in the nature of things partial and biased.
From this clash of opposites the truth will emerge.   But how, asks
Frank, can truth emerge when two sides are presenting essentially
one-sided versions, how can white emerge from two blacks.

He calls this theory the 'fight theory' and contrasts it with
the 'truth theory' which is in some ways equivalent to the
inquisitorial system. (7)   In this system it is the court which
is centrally involved in finding out what happens and it is the
court that impartially ascertains the facts.   What is portrayed
is a contrast between the ideologically motivated partisan who
interprets the 'facts' to support his position, and the impartial
scientist surrogate who, without any motivation but a keen love of
the truth, interprets the eternal and timeless 'facts' so that
what really happened is shown.   The implication is that the trial
of the future should be based on the scientific model;   the
reasonable man of ordinary reality is to be replaced by the rational
man of science.   Frank also directs this scientific attack towards
the jury system.   They are 'reasonable' but not 'rational' men.
Since they are not trained to sift the facts impartially they will
be the playthings of the trained eloquence of the prosecutor and
the defender.   Thus, we must pick experts and/or train judges to
be able to sift the facts impartially.   From here two major
strategies present themselves.   First, those who argue that the
trial as Frank describes it is dead and that we need to move to a
clear scientific way of finding the truth. (8)   Second, there are
those who claim that the present trial process can be made
scientifically rational by some tinkering with it. (9)   By and
large it is in this way that the neutralization of the trial as a
means of expressing alternative realities takes place.   Both of
these ways see rationality as defined in scientific terms and to
be the only true rationality left in the world.   Truth is seen as
being outside the actions of men;   as something that stands apart
and creates a timeless criterion.   Scientists are best fitted to

arrive at this truth because they are trained to view life objectively, to find the facts and come up with solutions that will not
be biased by a grand theory but are founded upon the things that
we really know.   Science has a legitimating function in our
society.   It is the sole criterion and justification of knowledge.
To be real knowledge, it must in some way be scientific knowledge.
Science has had this place for two reasons.   First, for the
practical reason that science has up to now at least delivered the
goods.   Second, there are the philosophic assumptions that
surrounded it and which comprised one of the reasons by which the
spectactular successes of science were explained.   Associated
very closely with the notion of science is the idea of objectivity.
The idea that science could be disengaged from the machinations of
ordinary men and that it was involved in finding out, disinterestedly, the 'true facts'.   These could be shown to be true irrespec-
tive of the ideological persuasion advanced.   Thus, science is
about facts: the hard, objective atemporal, ahistorical facts
that are the basic units of our knowledge.   Natural science, it is
claimed, is value free.   This means that science is supposed to
tell us how the world really is without fudging the picture with
the value presuppositions accorded to men.   Thus in our talk of
the world we mix up two kinds of statements; statements of fact
which are objective and can be proved and statements of value which
depend upon our feelings and passions.   It is the job of the
natural scientist to present us with the hard facts about the world -
the building blocks from which we can construct and develop our
knowledge.   The philosophy is one of reductionism for it reduces
what we say to statements that all men can logically accept.   These
statements are empirical in that they relate in some way to reality
independent of any theoretic construction.   It is these facts that
circumscribe what we say about the world for they are independent
of our volition.
    Science becomes the major discipline for it pursues these
objective facts by the only way that is available: by testing,
measuring, and observing.   This is the only way in which facts are
susceptible to proof: if they can be shown in some way to exist.
The social sciences are true and not soft sciences, totally over-
laid with value-preconceptions, in so far as they measure up to
the model of natural science.   It is in this way that the idea of
the 'international community of science' grew up: men of differing
ideological persuasions but all disinterestedly pursuing science.
(10)
    That this view is the philosophy of the status quo can easily
be seen for it stresses that the only true facts are those that in
principle are open to everyone. (11)   All can see that they are
true and these constitute the reality of the world.   Thus the
world is as in a particular society, it is, and it is from this
constraint that you have to work.   It is these facts that are
patently and incontrovertibly obvious.   We cannot have socialism
because 'men are greedy and that is a fact about human nature' as
shown by hard objective research.   What this view forgets is that
this is a fact about a particular society which is based upon
greed.   It is a fact about this world because the only way that

capitalist social formations can work is by greed.   We do not see beyond the society with a criterion that is based solely upon seeing what goes on in the society.

The theory rests upon the assumption that there are basic statements about the world which, independent of the observer, can be shown to be true.   We have chosen to concentrate upon this empiricist philosophy which is that everything ultimately stems from sense experience because we think that this philosophy is the philosophy of the bourgeois era.   It is this philosophy that has permeated the thinking of ordinary man and so it is here that we need to confront it. (12)

So far we have linked our exposition of the theory to our analysis of what law and lawyers do and shown how social engineering, the philosophy of piecemeal alterations to the status quo, becomes the order of the day.   We now intend to counter the arguments of Frank and his followers by showing that truth is not something that stands by itself but is the creation of man working on his environment.   This vindication of the 'alternative reality' thesis proves the accepted ontology wrong for it shows that men have the potentiality for freedom and that they can, at some stage at least, live in a free and creative way.   The form of the trial then shows man creating and recreating his world and not, totally, a prisoner of that world.

Let us look at examples illustrating that what seem to be 'hard facts' do not speak for themselves but instead depend upon the value positions of actors in the world.

Let us look at an example adapted from Cornish (1971).   He tells of a juror he interviewed who was judging a case where the facts were as follows (1971, p.174):

> A man was charged with receiving a coat knowing it to have been stolen.   His story was that he had innocently bought it from a stranger who knocked on his door and offered it at a cheap price.   The middle class members of the jury were inclined to believe the story, thinking him entitled to jump at a good bargain if he could.   But the working class jurors, some of whom lived on the same kind of housing estate as the accused, treated the tale with the utmost suspicion, having learned never to trust such a caller themselves.

What is important are the jurors' differing views of the world. The middle class juryman's inclination to acquit is not an example of class bias, 'lax' middle class morality, or stupidity but rather it portrays the way they have made the world for themselves and the way that it has been made for them.   In this example the accused claimed that someone had offered him a cheap bargain at his door. Does not this wonderfully reflect the suburban middle class view of life?   People are born with silver spoons in their mouths. Crime is not something that comes round to the door offering you cheap goods.   The shrewd and clever man is the one that can snap up bargains in the market place of life.   Thieves are recognized by their black and yellow horizontal striped burglar style sweaters, they do not wear sober suits and behave like 'respectable' businessmen.   Thus for them it is far easier to believe the story of the accused than for the working class juror.   His reality is very different.   In his world nothing comes easy, nothing comes cheap,

everything is a struggle.   Those who are in trouble with the law
are people who live next door.   They are part of everyday life,
not pale and shadowy figures.   When the accused excuses himself
by saying that he bought it cheaply he knows what that means.   He
knows that it 'fell from the back of a lorry' because in his world,
it does.   For the middle class juryman it is an incontrovertible
fact that men come and offer you bargains and for the working class
juryman it is an incontrovertible fact that men steal things.   They
are both right, for the worlds that are made for them are to an
extent at least, different.

Does this example show that we are wrong, that what is needed is
the unbiased scientist surrogate juror who can find out the real
facts?   What sort of picture would be drawn from the story that we
have given?   His attempts would be unsuccessful because he would be
unable to measure and test enough to obtain what he would consider
to be the real story.   His version would have to do with the
activities of men in his own world and away from the world in this
story.   He tries to look at something which he sees as objective
with the result that he sees his own distorted picture.   He is
rather like someone who says that the only way in which you can
explain man is by giving neuro-physiological and biochemical
descriptions of him.   This is seen as the only true description
because it is the only one you can prove.   But scientifically
that itself reflects value presuppositions - it reflects a view of
the world where people are considered and treated as automata.   The
value stance being the refusal to add more than machine status to
men.   This then becomes an 'objective' fact about the world and
society is organized in this image.   In this society men are
treated as, and so become, machines.   The image of man as machine
is an image that fits well within capitalist society.

Let us consider another example that will further clarify this
point.   In the Mangrove trial ('The Times', 16-17 December 1971)
nine blacks were charged with riotous assembly and affray and some
with assault and possession offensive weapons.   The incidents were
alleged to have occured outside the Mangrove, a 'black' cafe in
Notting Hill, an area notorious for its social tension.   In this
trial the defence asked for an all-black jury.   This request was
refused by the court with murmurings about the evils of juries
picked upon racially biased lines and the benefits of impartially
selected juries.   Why was the all-black jury requested?   It was
not due simply to the fear that the whites on the jury might be
racially prejudiced.   The application was made because few others
would understand and make sense of the world that would be portrayed
in the trial.   This was an environment where tensions between the
police and the local community were so high that there was always
the chance of an incident occurring such as the one that resulted
in the trial.   Those who did not experience this could not understand that particular reality. (13)   Take any example in the form
of a simple story that might happen in an area like Notting Hill.
A policeman comes along and sees some black youths.   He says:
'Hello, hello, hello, what's going on here?'   Then he is assaulted.
Those facts seem simple.   There has been an unprovoked assault.
It seems clear that the facts say what they say, but it is not as
obvious as that for those living in the area might not recognize a

friendly greeting but rather a calculated provocation. (14) People
not brought up in this type of area would be unable to understand it
as anything but a friendly greeting. Again, what we have are two
different worlds: the one where the police are friends and tell
you the way home; the other where the police are enemies and show
you the way to gaol. The first view would be that of a Hampstead
liberal and the second that of a Notting Hill black. Here are
situations when people cannot be neutral when they look at the
'facts' for the facts are reflected in their view of the world.
Thus it is not purely a question of conscious bias or prejudice but
rather a situation where even those who do not want to be biased
are forced to impose their view of the world - a quite, orderly
consensus view, upon a reality that is sometimes very different.

What would be the 'neutral' scientist's view of this? His
opinion would probably be that of the Hampstead liberals. If it
could be shown that he said the words 'hello, hello, hello', then
it is clear that it is an unprovoked attack for it is obvious to
everybody what these words mean. Now it could be claimed that
what is being done here is to establish the facts - what was said -
and then go on to make inferences from them.

Our argument has been that to say that is in itself a way of
looking at the world, that that view itself is not neutral. It
is like saying that the correct and true description of a chess
board is a block of sixty-four black and white wooden squares.
That may be the case if you are a specialist in wooden forms but
not if you play chess. It is a chess board and it is simply that,
we do not need to go further. You do not infer from sixty-four
black and white squares to a chess board. Value enters into
everything that we see - we do not observe through a vacuum but
rather through the categories that have been handed down to us.
The world that denies this is a world that claims that 'idiot' is
just a medical term; that it is purely descriptive and that it
has no other significance; that you can describe a man as a robot
without treating him as a robot. The decision is ultimately a
value decision not to see the facts as rich and complex, but as
stark and simple.

We have used the example of the trial as a microcosm of the
world - to show that what holds true there, holds true generally.
Thus the claims that we are making about the trial process are also
general epistemological claims and we use the examples to show how
people make sense together by acting on their environment and the
environment acting upon them. Thus truth comes from the
dialectic relationship of the subject and object, man and world.
Facts are not ahistorical and atemporal, but are constructed
through the actions of men and the world on each other. Reality is
constantly changing because we are constantly creating it. What
is also important is the way of seeing that world, For though it
can be full of stimuli to political change (a declining economy,
industrial disruption, etc.), yet an ideology that makes it seem
changeless and stable acts powerfully to prevent their influence.
Theory is not something that is harmless, it has a relationship to
society and acts to change or stabilize that society. We must
remember why systems of knowledge are constructed for it is the
reasons behind the knowledge that are important. They show us the
reality that is being constructed. (15)

MAKING THE TRIAL APOLITICAL

So far we have confronted Frank's argument about the trial, and by implication about the world, and argued for viewing the trial as an arena wherein opposing visions of reality clash. What the argument is pointing to is that the trial becomes political when the abstract ideology of the trial, as portraying an orderly consensus world, is shattered. But, as in men's political actions in the world, the prevailing theory fights back to neutralize and render impotent those political activities that attempt to shatter consensus.   And so, we move on to see how the state, ideologically and practically, defuses the embryonic attempts to make the trial political and establish another vision of reality. We turn, then, to the ways in which the 'natural reality' of the trial still appears to be that of a stable orderly world.

The thrust of liberal theory and research about the trial process is towards its scientification and objectification. Their reaction to the splintering of the consensus is to recreate it scientifically and rationally. The other form of reaction is to fix the fight so that the state's reality wins. It is in this light that we can view not only the Eleventh Report of the Crimimal Law Revision Committee (CLRC) (1972), but also the increased use of the crime of conspiracy and attacks on 'crooked' lawyers.

To illustrate these approaches let us look at reactions to the claims, made by Mark (1973) among others, that 'too many people who are obviously guilty are getting off'. Now in the context of our previous discussion they cannot be 'guilty' because the notion of guilty is a property of the legal meaning structure and it is the reality that wins that establishes legal knowledge and so guilt. So long as the trial works in that those who are 'obviously guilty' are incarcerated then everything is fine. When, marginally, this consensus about who are the guilty starts to break down, when the courts are attacked and the 'obviously guilty' start to win victories then the fight back occurs. Usually this takes the guise of a reactionary move to tighten up the machinery of the trial; to set the laws of evidence and rules relating to police behaviour in such a way that the state has greater chance of winning. The liberal reaction to such statements as those of Mark is more circumspect.   They are not so sure that the reality is really cracking and they aim dispassionately to find out if this is the case.   This involves the construction of a scientific justice which at the same time appears to humanize the law.   It is in this way that liberal and hardliner march hand in hand, their aim being to defuse and depoliticize the trial and the world, to make the world safe for a reality that they know exists.   Their aim is the establishment of consensus ideology and the methods are both harsh and 'human' and scientific.

Thus both tend towards the inquisitorial mode.   The liberal because the ideology of scientism points that way as the mode of finding real truth and the 'reactionary' because, though they attack the inquisitorial system as a way of giving the state too much power, they arrive at the same result in the end. (16)

We now examine, in more detail, some of these reactions. First, the CLRC (1972).   The concern here, is with the way the odds have changed in favour of the accused due to the way criminal trials are now being conducted.   This conduct is seen as the work of the 'professional' criminal and his 'shyster' lawyer. (17)   The activities of the majority whose conduct - in exhibiting the beginnings of an attempt to construct their own law simply by knowing about law - gives the committee so much concern, is thus defused.   King (1973, p.14) says:

On reading the CLRC Report it becomes increasingly apparent that what the committee meant by 'the growing sophistication of criminals' is often no more than the growth of knowledge amongst accused persons of their rights and privileges under the law. It is this, rather than a massive increase in 'professionalism', that the CLRC seem to be complaining about.   The police may well have found it an obstacle that accused persons are now less likely to make incriminating statements or to say anything in response to police interrogations.   Organisations such as Release and NCCL have been campaigning for many years now for people to be aware of their legal rights and to make use of them when the occasion arises.   Are the CLRC in effect saying not that the professionalism of criminals has reduced the efficiency of the police and the courts in trapping and convicting law breakers, but that the civil rights and privileges are to blame for this state of affairs, and, consequently, it is these rights and privileges which must be curtailed?

As the trial comes to be used more and more successfully then the rules have to be changed and procedures that shift the odds in favour of the state adopted.   The fight must be there but the result must be determined.   Throughout the report the emphasis is on reforming the rules of evidence, the criteria of knowledge in the legal meaning structure, in order that they might tell us what we already know.   And what we know is that too many of those who are obviously guilty are getting off.   Thus the recommendations tend towards an inquisitorial structure to let those who know get on with the job.   Again King (1973, p.28) says:

The abolition of the right to silence would produce a hybrid system of justice, a cross between the continental inquisitorial system and our own traditional adversary system.   However, the continental system provides adequate safeguards against abuse by the police and officials for, although the accused is obliged to answer questions, these questions are not put to him by a policeman behind a closed door of a police interrogation room, but by a judge in open court.   What the majority of the CLRC is suggesting is that we take away the citizen's only protection and at the same time put a powerful new weapon in the hands of the officials of the state.

King's book which is a useful analysis and attack of the report also shows signs of the liberal ideology that we have talked about.   In his discussion of the problem of police interrogation he presses for the idea of a quasi-examining magistrate;   one who will be neutral and impartial and get the 'facts' straight.

Second: the crime of conspiracy and how that helps to depoliticize and defuse the trial.   The offence requires agreement between two or more parties to effect some unlawful purpose.   But 'unlawful' here does not mean just a criminal offence.   Indeed the Law

Commission (1973) lists six other 'purposes' which, with varying degrees of certainty, can constitute a conspiracy.   They are (a) conspiracy to defraud, (b) conspiracy to defeat the course of justice, (c) conspiracies relating to public morals and decency, (d) conspiracy to do a civil wrong, (e) conspiracy to 'injure' and (f) conspiracies with a public element.   Even when the substantive act has been committed and is illegal there can still be a prosecution for conspiracy.   This helps the state in two ways.   First, because conspiracy is a common law offence not subject to statutory limitation as to penalties, it enables people to be punished by sentences ranging to life imprisonment for relatively minor offences or indeed behaviour that is not criminal at all.   Thus Peter Hain was found guilty of conspiracy to interfere with the lawful rights of persons to watch a Davis Cup match against South Africa.   The judge's instructions to the jury were that he was guilty if his methods were unlawful and 'of substantial public concern - something of importance to citizens who are interested in the maintenance of law and order.'   This though the actual methods running across the courts, using no force and disrupting play only for a short time while carrying civil legal liability, were not in themselves illegal (see Robertson, 1973).

Again one can be punished for offences for which there is no legal liability whatsoever but which are seen as, in some way, disturbing the good order of the state.   Among this category are conspiracies to corrupt public morals and outrage public decency, as in the 'International Times' case where the editors were convicted for publishing in 'International Times', advertisements soliciting homosexual acts (Knuller v. DPP, 1972, 2 AER 898). Again, those arrested for causing the explosion in Aldershot were charged with 'conspiring together with others unknown to effect a public mischief by means of possessing explosive substances for an unlawful purpose, i.e. by promoting by violence a political object, a United Ireland' (see Kay, 1973).   What this does is to transform political motives and realities into a legal and hence apolitical reality.   And so the state tries not those who want to transform the political reality, but those who are defined as breaking the law and nothing else.   Political acts are not specifically banned, they are hidden in the legal notions of 'public mischief', 'injury to the community', etc.

Second, conspiracy helps the state because its use enables the rules of evidence to be relaxed, to have matters of a political nature brought into the trial process in an apolitical way and so not inflame its orderly consensual nature.   Conspiracy is not merely a specifically made agreement.   It can also be 'a nod or a wink'.   In the case of the Shrewsbury pickets (18) this went further and guilt was inferred because they had been one of the many who were present at the sites in question.   In that case the judge said to the defence counsel: 'You know very well that it can be conspiracy when they never met or never knew each other' (Robertson, 1973, p.8).   What becomes clear from this is that the notion of guilt by association is creeping in.   For one of the ways, if actual serious agreement is not necessary, that it can be shown that people have come together as a purposive group, is to show that they have some form of logical similarity.   Conspiracies

have to be formed by the same sorts of people, and so if a group of
people are similar, in that they are all pickets, it becomes easier
to ascribe a conspiracy to them than to a group of ill assorted
people.   In these cases some similarity, apart from being co-
conspirators, is always to be shown for it makes the conspiracy
more plausible.   Thus evidence that they were all anarchists,
marxists, hippies or IRA sympathizers becomes not political
evidence but factual evidence to help prove a conspiracy. (19)
Presenting this sort of evidence is not seen as a way in which the
trial becomes political but legal devices to prove a legal charge
of conspiracy.   In the various trials of IRA bombers in England
copies of Guevara, Connolly, Mao and Carmichael were all produced
as evidence of conspiracy - the claim being that they must be
conspirators because they all had the same political beliefs.
Again in the 'Oz' and 'IT' trials evidence was adduced of the
defendants' 'hippy' life styles.   As Kaye (1973) puts it:

> In the Irish trials over the last few years, the prosecution
> has used material of a political nature - especially the posses-
> sion of marxist, communist and republican books, papers and
> membership cards - in order to prove motive.

Third: the role of the jury and jury research as a 'soft' establishment of the consensus.   Following our analysis so far, part
of the function of the jury is ideological.   Via the celebration
of the 'communion of peers' its aim is to legitimate the law and
legal institutions.   The jury appears not to be part of the
process that is the trial but as something that sits on the side-
lines, judging the 'facts' that come out of the trial.   It is
in this way that the 'scientific' researches of Cornish (1971),
Kalven and Zeisel (1966), McCabe and Purves (1972), see the jury -
as a device that is supposed to arrive at the truth.   The only
difference between them and Frank is that they are more convinced
than he was that it can actually arrive at the truth.   Thus the
thrust of their researches, through shadow juries and the like, is
to find out whether the jury can decide rationally.   The jury,
seen in this way, does not take part in the ideological message
and legitimating function of the court, but stands outside and says
what 'really' happened.   When Mark and others attack the jury for
legitimating a different reality from that of capitalist society,
this is seen as a scientistic attack on the jury and answered in
those terms.   If the reality cannot be sustained in the old and
traditional ways then science is the new way to do it.   As
Cornish (1971, p.278) puts it:

> It would certainly be foolish to dismiss too hastily the obvious
> fact that a great many people simply believe in the jury system.
> A measure of trust in the fairness of its criminal courts is
> something which it is difficult for any state to establish or
> to maintain.   The present public faith in the criminal courts
> has undoubtedly been encouraged by conscientious juries, and the
> system has the intrinsic advantage that in drawing upon a steady
> stream of ordinary citizens it is not only educating them in the
> work of the courts, but also, since they are generally satisfied
> with their own performance, sending them back to their ordinary
> lives with a sense of the fairness and propriety of the judicial
> process in this country.   However, it is an essential argument

of this book that the general public's faith in the jury system
should not be enough to ensure for it everlasting life.   The
fact that it has often been seen to function less happily than
it might is evidence enough that all is not well.   We have had
occasion to examine a number of recent instances in which the
jury has not functioned successfully and have adduced reasons
why another kind of tribunal might have done better.   The
extent of the breakdown now deserves proper investigation....
This quotation sums it up.   What we have here is the ideological
mystique of the communion of peers.   But the fact that the public
have faith is given only qualified approval.   For this might be
subverted when people use the trial for their own ends.   The right
result must also be achieved and the public's 'general sense of
fairness' must be directed towards the right reality, the 'reality'
of a capitalist society.

What is really important in jury research is the process of
learning to become a juror.   For it is this that enables the juror
to have a legal and so bourgeois view of the world. (20)   The
juror learns this in many ways.   He learns it in his normal life,
in the way that his everyday world is presented to him.   He learns
it in media representation of his role, from handbooks and advice
on how to be a juror.   Finally, he learns by the actual experience
of being in court, where his view of reality is subsumed by the
court's legal view.   Consider the situation.   People are picked
for jury service out of the blue.   They have no experience nor a
clear idea of their rights and duties.   All they know is that they
are told by the judge and the other participants in the show that
they have become most important people.   In practice they see that
this is not so.   It becomes clear that the most important figure
is the judge.   Everyone defers to him.   He is in control, even
his position in the geography of the court marks him out as the
most important personage.   He sits centrally on a raised dais and
the court looks up to him.   In this situation the over-riding
version of reality comes from his prompting.   The juror finds
himself in a contradictory situation: on the one hand he is told
that he is the most important person there but on the other hand
the evidence of his eyes belies this - it is obvious this role is
reserved for the judge.   It is the evidence of his eyes that he
believes and acts upon.   Thus Kalven and Zeisel (1966) show that
many jurors consider the verdicts that they arrive at correct
because they have decided in the way that the judge would wish.
Again, we must not think of this as due solely to the machinations
of the evil judge who forces his view upon the unsuspecting juror.
We are saying that he cannot help doing this.   The trial process
conspires against everyone alike.   This is not to say that some
judges do not try to force their version of reality down the throats
of the jury but even if they were not that objective it becomes
difficult to avoid.   And so the jury, taking its cues from the
court and from the effects of the professional socialization of
lawyers, legitimates the state's version of the world; that of
the consensus society.   The jury, as representative of the common
people and the reasonable man accept and celebrate the law's view
of the world.

Class is also important because as long as the jury learns at

home the same things that it learns in court then the cracks in the
consensus do not so often appear.   Thus, until the implementation
of the report of the Morris Committee (1965), which advocated the
extension of jury service to virtually everyone on the electoral
roll, the jury was confined to those holding property qualifications.
This tended to make it, in the words of Lord Devlin (1956) 'middle
class and middle minded', and so far more likely to reflect a
bourgeois view of the world.   When there has been a dissonance
between home knowledge and court knowledge, it has mainly shown
itself in high-minded moral protest - something that is deeply
reassuring to the social order.   Thus the jury, by refusing to
convict, drastically reduced the amount of crimes that were punish-
able by death penalty in the late nineteenth century.   It also
helped the introduction of the crime of infanticide.   This meant
that mothers suffering post-natal depression, who killed their new
born infants, no longer faced a charge of murder (see Cornish,
1971, pp.128-33).

Recently, however, this dissonance has reasserted itself in more
political vein, especially in the Mangrove and Angry Brigade trials.
The attempt by the defence in these trials was to force the jury
away from the trial process, by appealing to their class loyalties
so that they bring their home knowledge to bear and actually umpire
and choose between realities.   In the Angry Brigade trial great
effort was made to get working class jurors so that there would be
more chance of this dissonance. (21)

Perhaps this explains the coincidence of the widening of the
jury franchise with the growing number of attacks on 'wilful' juries
and jurors. (22)   Now that it is no longer able to take for granted
the politics, morality and social loyalties of the 'new jurors',
the jury is seen as a less reliable instrument for bourgeois tastes
and needs to be replaced with something else.   The consequences of
this sort of attack are an assertion of the inquisitorial mode and
a consolidation of the position of the expert who will be able to
negotiate the reality 'impartially'.   Fourth: the introduction, in
increasing numbers, of psychiatrists and social scientists as expert
witnesses in order to facilitate an 'inquisitorial' mode.

Attempts to construct a 'scientific justice' has made its mark
in the USA where social scientists have been used as expert
witnesses in specific legal cases.   In this country, the juvenile
court is the forum where 'scientific' and 'humanitarian' ideologies,
sustained by the testimony of the expert witness, are most
pronounced.   Their incorporation expresses a guiding philosophy of
'help' rather than 'punishment'.   There is, through them, an
emphasis on 'rehabilitation'; the urge to punish is seen to be
sublimated beneath a desire to 'put under care and protection'.
Accordingly, the procedures, terminology and sanctions of the
juvenile court are very different from those of the adult criminal
court.   A great emphasis is placed on probation officer reports,
which are compiled prior to the 'trial'.   Lawyers are not
encouraged to appear; there is, instead, the same interest in
'informality', the same 'institutionalized-paternalism' that
operates in tribunals.

The problem with these acts of calculated kindness (the self-
conscious stress on informality), is that they succeed by other

means in furthering the cause of the expert.   The defendant has
been given new deliverers.   Yet his new benefactors behave
strangely.   On the one hand, they declare their benevolence and
their interest in helping him; on the other hand, they make
decisions which limit his freedom.   The kind of negotiated settlement that takes place between tribunal chairmen and expert witnesses,
creates two further problems.   The first concerns the problem of
how the tribunal-court makes up its mind to regard certain defendants
favourably enough to want to help more than others.   This touches
upon what Matza (1964) has termed the 'rampant discretionary' powers
of the juvenile court.   The second problem created by such a
negotiated settlement is that defendants are left none the wiser as
to their rights.   As passive objects of compassion and kindness
their sense of dependancy and helplessness may be seen to increase
rather than decrease.

The doctrine that the 'expert knows best' is apparent again if
we look at the process of psychiatric commitment - the incarceration
of the 'mentally ill'.   There is wide professional and lay recognition that it is much easier to be placed in a mental hospital
than to be released from one.   Many of those who are committed are
put away through the idea of 'rehabilitation'.   The rationale is
'it's in the patient's best interest'.   After confinement, the
'patient' surrenders the last of his sovereignty.   At this point
it is taken for granted that only the psychiatrist knows what
action will be in the individual's best interests.   What we
record here are the actions of honourable men.   We do not imply
any organized conspiracy against people.   All we point to are some
of the outcomes that are often only dimly understood by the
agencies that spawn them.   Psychiatry like law, is concerned with
norms of conduct and techniques of social control.   As such,
definitions of 'illness' by psychiatrists depend more on the social
situation in which it occurs, than on the nature of the 'object'
(the individual) being defined.   Some examples of this phenomenon
would include the labelling of dissidents in the USSR and in
Northern Ireland as 'mad' or 'sick'.   For those like Szasz (1975a,
b), the psychiatrist is a social tranquillizer, whose 'goal is to
protect the peace of deep-rooted institutions', like the family,
marriage, or the state itself (whether it recognizes this function
or not).   One example of how the psychiatrist gets caught up in
upholding institutional values, is provided by Maddison's (1973)
analysis of the role of the student counsellor in the university
(p.118):

> Farnsworth presents the following list as 'examples of behaviour
> that suggest the presence of emotionally unstable persons, viz.
> 'Library vandalism, cheating and plagiarism, stealing in the
> college and community stores or in the dormitories, unacceptable
> or antisocial sexual practices (overt homosexuality, exhibition-
> ism, promiscuity), and the unwise and unregulated use of harmful
> drugs'.

> Psychiatrists are seen by other authors as particularly
> helpful in dealing with phenomena such as vandalism, for 'it is
> an especially trying problem for any academic community and
> helping some students to develop respectful attitudes toward
> property is a very difficult task.'

Seen from this perspective much psychiatric commitment and diagnosis
is a style of social control masquerading under a humanitarian
ideology.   The dominant idea behind this kind of thinking is one
which insists that 'the only decent way to treat a criminal is to
label him as sick'.   The 'sick' label is a denial of the authenticity of the person and his acts; it is a denial of freedom
itself.   The last word here must belong to Cohen (1973a, p.126):
    We should be wary of the increasing permeation of psychiatric
    ideologies into everyday understandings of the world.   This
    permeation is not necessarily liberal or progressive.
Again this assumes a scientism where there are impartial arbiters
of truth.   They are introduced as non-controversial figures, as
those who can produce the real facts.   But science is always
'official' science.   It is the expert as state employee that is
important and it is his view of the world that is important.
'Experts' who are appearing for the defence and who are not official
are ridiculed.   Thus, in the 'Oz' trial, the defence expert
witnesses were subjected to a systematic attack - especially upon
their credentials and impartiality. (23)   For they were not the
true representatives of scientism: they did not support the world
that the court wanted to make real for everybody.   Here we can
see how scientism is co-opted to help the existing social order.
One of the solutions that liberals see to questions of the censorship of obscene material, is to say that legislation is only
necessary when the materials can be proved to 'harm'. (24)   But
harm is not an immutable, value free concept and, as can be seen
from the 'Oz' and other trials, it is the state's conception of it
that wins the day.   In the Angry Brigade trial the prosecution
'experts' themselves received this sort of attack.   Their evidence
was attacked, root and branch, as coming from those working for
government departments and so being a part of the state machine.
This was so successful that at the end the prosecution virtually
gave up science and told the jury to rely on 'common sense'
instead. (25)

MAKING THE TRIAL POLITICAL

So far we have looked at how the 'fight' becomes choreographed, and
thus fixed and depoliticized.   The tendency of our analysis so
far, is to claim that any attack on the consensus reality in the
trial makes that trial political.   This implies a glorification
of the deviant: the claim that the 'criminal' activities of the
lumpenproletariat are in themselves self-conscious political
activity against the establishment.   The kicking and screaming of
the lumpenproletariat, however it might expose police brutality
and corruption is proto-political activity in that it is merely
the unseeing reaction of someone caught in a repressive society.
Here then a new vision of the world is not shown but questions are
raised concerning the problems of living in a capitalist society.
(26)   These actions then can politicize the trial in so far as by
breaking its consensus, they raise the questions of men's real
interests even if these questions are not self-consciously articulated by the participants.   Thus trials like those involving

members of the Welsh Language Society (27) raise, by the actions of the participants, the question of the consensus. In trying to break the ordered image of the trial they force the existence of this society to be considered as a political question. (28)

When we talk of the 'political trial' our position is not some plea for the return to the 'Queensbury rules' where all realities have an equal chance of establishing themselves. This would imply an ideological laissez faire, it being irrelevant which reality wins. What is important is not just to break the orderly consensus to show that there is a fight, but also to show a vision of the world that, by corresponding to men's real interests as free and creative beings, will establish a world that will free them instead of dominating and enslaving them. Man has a real interest in setting up a socialist society because only within it will he be able to live as truly human, not the passive-adaptive creature of capitalist society. And so though our analysis has centred upon behaviour in the trial, the objective of that behaviour is important. The objective must be such that the society as a whole can be questioned and questions of men's real interests raised. (29)

With this in mind, we go forward to give a typology and examples of trials that we consider political. Here we are looking not just for the use of the trial to fight legal battles but one where a particular vision of the world is put forward. Though this makes a crucial distinction between being tried for political acts and making the trial political, we do not want to forget the object for, as we have said, not every version of 'political' will do. We are interested in a self-conscious transcending of the trial in terms of men's real interests.

We start then, with a situation where the legal reality was transcended, where legal victory became secondary to showing the decadence of our society and the desirability of another. In doing this the defendants triumphantly accepted their guilt and used it to make political points. In the Chicago conspiracy trial Abbie Hoffman, one of the co-defendants, wrote (Epstein, 1970, pp. 120-1):

> I want to be tried not because I support the National Liberation Front - which I do - but because I have long hair. Not because I support the Black Liberation Movement, but because I smoke dope. Not because I am against a capitalist system, but because I think property eats shit. Not because I believe in student power, but that the schools should be destroyed. Not because I'm against corporate liberalism, but because I think people should do whatever the fuck they want and not because I am trying to organize the working class but because I think kids should kill their parents. I'm guilty of a conspiracy all right. Guilty of creating liberated land in which we can do whatever the fuck we decide. Guilty of helping to bring the Woodstock Nation to the whole earth.

This sort of anarcl > view was repeated in the actual trial. Here the trial was turne i into what can only be described as popular theatre. In taking on the elements of farce that the defendants gave it, it can best be compared with the trial scene in 'Alice in Wonderland'. The following scraps of the transcript give something of the flavour of the courtroom as popular theatre (Levine, 1971, pp.149-50):

Q. Did you see some people urinate on the Pentagon?
A. On the Pentagon itself?
Q. Or at the Pentagon?
A. In that general area in Washington?
Q. Yes.
A. There were in all over 100,000 people. That is, people have that biological habit.
Q. And did you?
A. Yes.
Q. Did you symbolically -
A. Did I go and look?
Q. Did you symbolically and did you - did you symbolically urinate on the Pentagon, Mr. Hoffman?
A. I symbolically urinate on the Pentagon?
Q. Yes.
A. Nearby yes, in the bushes, there, maybe 3,000 feet away from the Pentagon. I didn't get that close. Pee on the walls of the Pentagon?
     You are getting to be out of sight actually. You think there is a law against it?
Q. Are you done, Mr. Hoffman?
A. I am done when you are.
Q. Did you ever on a prior occasion state that a sense of integration possesses you and comes from pissing on the Pentagon?
A. I said from combining political attitudes with biological necessity, there is a sense of integration, yes. I think I said it that way, not the way you said it, but -
Q. You had a good time at the Pentagon, didn't you, Mr. Hoffman?
A. Yes, I did, I am having a good time now.
     Could I - I feel that biological necessity now. Could I be excused for a slight recess?
The Court: We will take a brief recess, ladies and gentlemen of the jury.

But this sort of approach is not without its problem for it seems to present defendants who want to define their trial as political with a critical dilemma. Which is more important: to concentrate on transcending the trial itself or to concentrate on more short term goals as winning legal victories. For the latter will prevent incarceration and enable the fight to be carried on outside the court. In 'We Are Everywhere', Rubin's (1971) book on the Chicago trial, this is clearly shown, by cataloguing the splits among the co-defendants. Their positions ranged from those who wanted to fight a purely legal battle, through those who wanted a mixture of both to those, like Rubin and Hoffman, who don't care and who wanted to transform the whole thing into an anarchistic farce.

It was in this final form that the trial was fought and in this form it was a celebration of a kind of anarchistic politics; the court was not so much transcended as totally ignored. If we just ignore the court then it will fall away. This mirrors the statements of hippies at the time when asked how could American society be defeated; their answer was, 'we are older than they' - implying that if they waited long enough the society would collapse of its

own accord.   This then starts to resemble those who refuse to
recognize the court and have nothing to do with it.   For by
refusing to do this they are denying the material facts of the
world;   they are refusing to fight on 'enemy territory'.   The
problem is that this is all the territory that exists and that this
stand simply means abdicating the fight and losing.
   This also mirrors an anarchist politics in the world.   For
though their actions in the trial portray the vision of a new and
free world, they make the epistemological claim that there is no
external reality unchangeable by men now.   Thus the world can be
changed simply by recognizing this and living in a new way.   This
then becomes an anarchist view of the state;   if you ignore it,
it will go away.   But you cannot ignore the material facts of the
world, just as you cannot ignore the fact that you are being tried.
Capitalist reality will not vanish by simply wishing it away;   the
world fashioned by capitalism is no mere chimera.   Thus, though
drama as represented in the Chicago trial, has an ideological role
to play it is not the means of changing the world.   This struggle
must come about through the political practise of the organized
working class.   Capitalism has 'fixed' the world in a certain way
and the world that it created needs to be fought long and hard;
the ravages that capitalism has wrought will not disappear merely
by people's seeing a new reality.   The world we have is the world
that we have to work on.   Thus scarcity, though it has a lot to
do with the operation of the International Commodity Exchange
Market and so capitalist social formations, is also a material fact
about the world and will play a part in determining the way that
the struggle is to be carried out, and determining its outcome.
The politics that we are advocating must be such as will be able to
cope with the harsh realities of a world made in the image of
capitalism.   For the world of capitalism is the stage on which the
struggle will be fought and this stage must be transcended, it
therefore must not be ignored. (30)
   To return to our analogy of the trial: we can see this point
clearly put by Morrow in his analysis of Albert Goldman's (1944)
defence of members of the Socialist Workers' Party of America
charged with sedition in Minneapolis in 1941 (pp.iv-v):
   For the first time in this country revolutionarists systematically defended their revolutionary doctrines in a courtroom, using
   it as a forum from which to proclaim their ideas.... The false
   distinction made by bourgeois liberals - 'either persuade the
   jury or make propaganda for the outside' - did not exist for
   Albert Goldman.   He did both together.... But the essential case
   for socialism is so impregnable, so persuasive, that he could
   address his revolutionary message also to the jury, as the best
   possible means of winning at least partial concessions from the
   jury.
Here then, we have the acceptance of the stage on which the battle
is to be fought, followed by its triumphant transcending.   There
is here a recognition of the facts of life in a capitalist society
and, in accepting that, still making the trial political.   To
illustrate this further, we again take an example from Jerry Rubin
(1970).   In the hearing on the Poole Bill - an anti-radical

measure - the House Un-American Activities Committee subpoenaed
Rubin.   Rather than play this strictly legally, he dressed up in
confederate costume, treated the whole thing as a farce and so
helped get the measure ridiculed (pp.64-5):

When it came time for us crazies to testify, the theater switched
to high comedy.   Anatole Anton identified himself as James Bond.
He called Poole 'Jo-Jo' and the lawyer asking the questions 'Mr.
Lackey'.   Steve Cherkoss took the oath with what 'The New York
Times' described as a 'raised fist with the middle finger up-
lifted'.   Stuart McCrae gave the Nazi salute when he came to
the stand.   He began by saying that the hearing made him so
sick, 'I might vomit all over the table'.   Jeff Gordon shouted
at Poole: 'We are the comrades of the Amerikan soldiers.   You
and Johnson are their enemies because you have sentenced them
to die'.   Asked when he was born, Steve Hamilton called them
'yellow-bellied, racist cowards' and started giving the history
of racist-fascist Amerika.   He began a Congressional Fillibuster.
He wouldn't shut up.   He finally had to be dragged away from
the witness stand.   I awaited my turn, blowing giant bubbles
with my bubble gum, whistling patriotic songs, making sarcastic
remarks, umping up and down.
   Poole banged his gavel every two minutes.   It was a circus,
and he was barker.
   After four days of hell-raising my turn came.   I stood up.
Started to take the stand.   Poole stopped me.   He called the
hearings off.   Federal marshals grabbed me by my arms and legs
and started to carry me out of the hearing room.   'I wanna
testify!   I wanna testify!' I yelled.   I lost my tricornered
hat in the scuffle and was charged with disorderly conduct.
Joe McCarthy turned over in his grave.   The poor liberals were
so embarrassed.   The hearings embarrassed the 'dignity of
Congress'.   The Poole Bill died in committee.

In same style can be seen the activities of some of the claimants'
unions that we discussed in chapter 1 (Rose, 1973, p.412):

Another form of CU appeal activity mixes anger with a sense of
mockery, so that the sedate proceedings of a tribunal become a
carnival.   For example, where bedding and new clothing claims
have been refused by the local office, as part of the appeal,
evidence is brought forward.   While many resourceful advocates
have brought photographs, the CU style is to bring a slice of
real life into the artificiality of the proceedings.   The
bumpy spring-broken mattresses, the worn-out sheets, the
children and their too-small vests are brought to the appeal as
evidence to challenge the social security decisions.   The
individual humiliation of the home visit is turned into an
offensive weapon to expose and ridicule the meanness of the
social security system.
   The representative becomes compere and produces exhibit after
exhibit while the witnesses - whose role is audience as well as
evidence givers - switch mood from laughter to anger to pain as
the charade is played out.   The moods of the tribunal members
change too, shifting from amusement at the presenting officer's
discomfort to ill-concealed and sometimes open anger at the
mockery.   As when the silent speak, these sorts of appeals

enter into the mythology as occasions when 'we showed them'!
The difficulties overcome - of getting a free van to take the
mattresses, the active part played becomes a source of shared
warmth and inspiration.
Here then we see examples in which not only remarkable short term
victories are won, but also in which, in transcending the legal,
actions and victories are successfully defined contrary to the
meanings that the law chooses to give.   This is because they do
not make what Goldman calls the 'bourgeois' distinction between
fighting for a legal victory or fighting a political battle. (31)
     We have seen how, in the Chicago trial, the tendency was to take
the 'political' alternative and what the ideological consequences
of that were.   But by and large defendants prefer to take the legal
way out.   A good case in point is that of the Rev. Daniel Berrigan
(32) who, in 1969, was one of those Americans in the anti-war movement who destroyed draft files.   His action was obviously political;
this is not in question - but by his conventional behaviour in the
courtroom he lent legitimacy to the very thing that he opposed.
In other words, he left his politics outside of the court, electing
instead to play the part of the traditional criminal defendant while
in court.   Similarly, in this country, John Jenkins, self-styled
leader of MAC (Movement for Protecting Wales) adopted the same
position at his trial when he was accused of blowing up water pipe
lines.   His action, like Berrigan's, was obviously political in
inspiration, but also like Berrigan he chose to employ a lawyer to
defend him 'legally'.   This meant in effect, that Jenkins abandoned
any political stance accepting, whether he realized it or not, the
legitimacy of the court.   And as we saw before, the consequence,
for· the defendant, of the courts being able to sustain in such
cases a distinction between the 'political' and the 'criminal', is
to minimize the ideological basis of the defendant's act.   In this
way, the defendant's behaviour comes to lose its meaning, other, of
course, than any legal significance lawyers may care to attribute
to it.
     Often too, both alternatives are used but separately: a strictly
legal defence is fought and the political message confined to a
principled statement from the dock when all is lost.   This was
especially the case of the Irish trials (33) in Britain, though
sometimes the message did extrude from the actual legal defence.
Another instance was the trials of the Scottish Workers' Party
for bank robberies in aid of party funds in Glasgow in which the
political nature of the trial was proclaimed only after sentencing,
when the defendants made various political statements. (34)   A
recent example of this was the trial of the so-called 'Army of the
Provisional Government'. (35)
     Apart from the attitude of the defendants themselves what is
crucial in escaping the 'bourgeois distinction' is the attitude of
the lawyers when there are any, who are to do some of the defending.
Despite such lawyers' sincere espousal of radicalism, as lawyers,
they will usually favour the legal mode, supporting the movement by
fighting its legal battles in a legal way. (36)   The Chicago trial
was significant in the stance taken by the defence attorneys who in
the words of Macdonald 'shared the alienation of their clients'
(Levine, 1971, pp.152-3):

Continued cross-examination of Defendant A. Hoffman by Government
Attorney Schultz.

Q.	In fact you thought it was a great boon to you that your case (requesting a permit to use city park - ed.) had been assigned to Judge Lynch because you could make a lot of hay out of it, isn't that right, Mr. Hoffman?
A.	No, no, I had learned at that time that they had turned down the McCarthy people's request for a permit, and I thought if they weren't going to get it, we sure as hell weren't either, and that was one of the decisions.
The Court:	Mr. Witness, we don't allow profanity from the witness stand.
The Witness:	Well, I wouldn't want - all right.
By Mr. Schultz:	
Q.	When did you prepare, Mr. Hoffman, your -
The Court:	And I don't like being laughed at by the Witness - by a Witness in this court, sir.
The Witness:	I know that laughing is a crime. I already -
The Court:	I direct you not to laugh at an observation by the Court. I don't laugh at you.
The Witness:	Are you sure?
The Court:	I should?
The Witness:	I said, 'Are you sure?'
The Court:	I haven't laughed at you during all of the many weeks and months of this trial.
The Witness:	Well -
Mr. Schultz:	May I proceed, your Honor?
The Court:	Yes, you may.
Mr. Kunstler:	I am not sure, your Honor, 'hell' is classified as profanity, and I think from what has been circulated in this courtroom it's hardly profane language.
The Court:	Oh, I will concede that it is a lesser degree of -
Mr. Kunstler:	I am not even sure it is classified as profanity.
The Court:	You don't think so?
Mr. Kunstler:	I don't think -
The Court:	Well, probably not among your clients, but I -
Mr. Kunstler:	I take it among your friends, too, Judge, and I would say you have used it and everyone else has used it.
The Court:	I don't allow a witness to testify that way on the witness stand, if you don't mind sir.
Mr. Kunstler:	I object to the dictionary -
The Court:	We strive here to conduct this Court in the traditional -
Mr. Kunstler:	You say my clients are habituated to using 'hell', you know, which is a categorization of my clients. My clients use lots of words, and your friends use lots of words -
The Court:	I don't think you know any of my friends.
Mr. Kunstler:	You'd be surprised, your Honor.
The Court:	Please don't -

Mr. Kunstler: The father of one of our staff men is a close
                friend of yours.
The Court: If they know you, they haven't told me about it.
Mr. Schultz: Your Honor, may we proceed?

The tactic that emerges from this is that of the 'mixed defence'
which uses both self-representation and professional advocates.
In this way the Goldman dichotomy is avoided and a front presented
which enables the lawyers to be kept from transforming the question
into a legal one.   The trial of Purdue and Prescott (37) shows us
how trials conducted by professional QCs can run ('Anarchy', 7,
p.30):

   The defence was not, in fact, the most impressive part of the
   trial.   After the arrest of Jake and Ian a defence group had
   been set up.   It had been thought that at least one of them
   would defend himself and, in fact, right up to the beginning of
   the defence Jake was thinking of defending himself.   But both
   of them were defended in a gentlemanly fashion by Q.Cs. who
   treated the whole trial in an apologetic embarrassment at having
   to even attempt a defence.   Ian's barrister hardly opened his
   mouth until his summing up.   He did not call Ian.   Jake's
   barrister contented himself with very mild, though occasionally
   not bad, cross-examinations.   It has been suggested that he
   followed a deliberate policy of not incurring Melford Stevenson's wrath.   But one had the feeling that he would not know
   how to incur it even if he had wanted to, and if, by some
   horrible misfortune had incurred it, he would be the first to
   apologise.   He never attacked when attack would have been
   worthwhile.   Duncan's defence was mainly a plea of mitigation,
   explaining Jake's deprived childhood in an orphanage, how he
   had spent so much time in prison and other institutions, his
   unhappy association with drugs and so on.   Because he was a
   bourgeois lawyer, Duncan was completely unable to see Jake as
   a person and so had to define him in bourgeois terms - as a
   'poor unfortunate', someone we should feel sorry for.   He could
   not understand his politics or feel any sympathy for them for
   the same reason and so was unable to examine Jake on them.

In the Angry Brigade trial, though the defence team, which consisted
of self-representors, professional advocates and McKenzie-men,
found it difficult, they worked hard at challenging the reality of
the court and in particular, appealing to the jury.   They put
forward the case that the jury had more in common with the defendants
than with the court and the judge.   They tried to separate the jury
from the court and convince them that they shared, with the defendants, a particular vision of the world. (38)   The jury was treated
as a (Blake, 1975, p.7):

   double edged weapon for bourgeois legality; they are needed to
   fulfil the mythical role in the notion of judgment by the people,
   but at the same time they are a collection of living subjects
   including workers and oppressed people alike.   With proper use
   of the challenges, with a long trial, with the increasing publicity about state corruption, with the raising of the theoretical tone of the urban public generally, with nebulous charges
   and a political approach to prosecution, the jury's role in the

battle against the state can be a real and decisive one.   Of
course revolutionary consciousness is created by experience not
by propaganda alone;   juries won't be convinced by simply a
'political' final speech from counsel or defendant, the trial has
to be presented to them, the jury has to experience the politics
of the situation for themselves, if this is done political
speeches by the defendant etc. can be instrumental in getting the
right decision.   Otherwise, of course, juries will always take
a reasonable view as to what is reasonable doubt.

Again contrast this with the defence produced at the trial of the
Shrewsbury three.   Here the trial was conducted in a more or less
legal manner with the political element added in a speech from the
dock by the defendants. (39)   But as 'Up Against the Law' (UPAL 4,
p.30) said of the defence:

it also has to be said that most of the defence lawyers in the
case did not, and could not, represent the class interests of
the workers.   Lawyers are mostly a sheepish middle   class lot
who care sod all for the strikers in the dock.   The class war
was not continued in the courtroom because the judge was determined to stop and none of the lawyers had the legal knowledge
to beat the judge.

It is essential that at least one of the 24 defendants themselves, give the jury the full story.   Lawyers will always be
intimidated by judges, but you can't gag us in the same way.

The Angry Brigade trial was partly successful.   It did not make
the 'bourgeois' distinction. (40)   What was won was not won by the
law;   it was won by wrenching the law away from the ruling class.

This mode of defence must be seen in the context of the general
political consciousness of the society.   For these tactics work
more readily if the society itself is on the boil.   Thus the Angry
Brigade trial, (41) while trying to take on some of the features
of the Chicago trial, did not have the same impact, because of the
relatively greater stability of British society at the time.   Thus
the IRA can refuse to recognize the court in Ulster because their
fight is already going on outside;   consensus in any case is
shattered.

Their actions in turning their backs on the court are not the
actions of anarchists, refusing to recognize the realities of the
world.   In doing this symbolically they transfer their struggle
outside into the courtroom and those actions make the trial, for
them, political.   Compare here some of the Welsh Language trials,
where the refusal to recognize the court takes the form of speaking
only in Welsh.   This cannot be subjected to the same analysis as
the IRA in Ulster, because not only is there a great deal of
sympathy for nationalism among the establishment but the country is
not polarized.   The consensus is maintained and that rules out the
activities of the more 'extreme' elements.   In any case the protest
is often defused by providing Welsh speaking judges and police.
Again in 1924 with the labour movement in the ascendant, the editor
of the 'Worker's Weekly' was charged under the Disaffection Act,
but a storm of protest from the Labour movement caused the case to
be dropped. (42)

Returning to the quotation from UPAL, this mode leads to attacks
on those involved.   Thus lawyers involved in these defences have a

hard time if they break out of the rules of the game.   Their acts
are defined as discourteous, demeaning the dignity of the court,
contrary to professional etiquette, and their professional associations move to discipline them.   This is because lawyers are expected
to help to preserve the consensus ideology of the trial and are
attacked when they step out of line. (43)

It is not just the defendants however who can make the trial
political.   Over-aggressive reactions on the part of the state can
also help.   Thus the Chicago trial was undoubtedly helped by the
stupidity of the judge.   And the over-reaction of judges like
Stevenson and Argyle (44) have helped to transform trials, not
particularly political in themselves, into ones which begin to show
these characteristics.

In this section we sought to show some of the ways that people
respond to the law and lawyers by evolving new styles of representation and by treating the law as political.   The starting point
for those who have tried to resist is an attack upon the reification
of the law, legal institutions, legal processes, and the role of the
lawyer in our society.   Thus the reactions to law that we have
described, represent attempts by people either to establish a
measure of control over law - to construct a law which protects
their interest and does not repress them - or to build alternative
institutions and develop alternative ways of acting upon the world
for themselves.   The trial, in this light, can be viewed as a
vision of the recreated world.   Our final words in this book
concern the political defendant in the political trial.   Law is an
imperial code.   Its very claim to universality, as Rock (1974)
points out, implies that law represents a reified world.   By contrast new styles of representation and courtroom conduct, the new
model trial, offer men one escape route from dehumanization.

SEIZE THE TIME

NOTES

CHAPTER 1 IMAGES OF LAW

1 In 1970 a group of staff and students at Warwick University
   working under the editorship of E.P. Thompson, produced a book
   called 'Warwick University Ltd'.   The book dealt with the
   consequences for the university of the attempts of its founders
   to make their institution 'useful' to 'business interests'.
   Some of the results of this striving for 'relevance' and the
   eagerness to serve, were seen by Thompson in the following
   way (1970, p.163):
   > what is wrong...is the whole system of values - the entire
   > ordering of human priorities - of this insistent managerial
   > propaganda.   It is sad to see even the scholars themselves
   > hesitate in their work and wonder about the use of what
   > they are doing...they capitulate without a struggle before
   > the intellectually specious proposal that a university can
   > train young men and women, who have no industrial experience,
   > in a 'managerial science' in which they master no single
   > academic skill...but which will miraculously equip them to
   > 'manage' the affairs of (others)...step by step the defensive
   > scholar resigns his wider allegiances - to a national or
   > international discourse of ideas - and retreats within the
   > limited area of manoeuvre alloted to him within the managerial
   > structure.
2 Although no national figures are presently available, one of the
   authors has some evidence, taken from his study of a Law Society
   in a large provincial city, that changes in the economic terms
   of work of solicitors have generated some structural unemployment
   among them.   Solicitors who have suffered in this way are those
   whose practice depended heavily upon conveyancing, where a drop
   in the number of houses being built and sold has seriously
   undermined their market situation.   The rise in consumerism
   (e.g. 'do-it-yourself' divorces) has also contributed to the
   downturn in traditional areas of legal activity for a number of
   solicitors.   Our second kind of market situation is a potent
   factor in the move by law teachers into new research areas.

With the traditional subjects being to a degree 'over-researched' (by this we mean the difficulty of thinking of something distinctive to write in fields like land law, contract and trusts), advancement to the academic ladder becomes difficult.   Hence the establishment of new fields of research such as poverty law and socio-legal studies, and the spectacular career rises of some of those who have made the move into these new fields.

For an important discussion of some of the facts that tend to force a redefinition of both the organization and content of professional education, see Kuhn (1962).   Kuhn, although writing about the education and socialization of scientists, has much to say that is of interest to those concerned with legal education.   In particular, Kuhn has a great deal to say about the relationship between professional education on the one hand, and the market situation of practitioners on the other.   Thus when 'suitable' (i.e. remunerative) work is plentiful, students and practitioners seldom question the relevance of their professional education.   However, in times of crisis, when such work becomes scarce, more critical attention is paid to the quality of professional education.   The fossilization of English legal education has undoubtedly been linked to the abundant living which lawyers could, until very recently, make by working over traditional territory.

3 One of the points made by Simons and Smith (1972), was that one way of encouraging redeployment would be to pay those who worked in 'radical' areas more money.

4 There is an assumption, commonly met among traditional lawyers, that 'socio-legal' studies is something that everyone will understand, while trusts, etc. will only be understood by the 'expert'.   This is one of the reasons why the claims of the 'new law' are sometimes resisted.

5 Renner (1949), in one of the few analyses that took Marx seriously, examined the changing functions of the institution of private property, and showed how it came to play an increasing role as capitalism developed.   It is the examination, in the materialist mode, of such institutions, that we have in mind here.   These are conspicuous by their absence in socio-legal studies.

6 The Court of Appeal decision in McKenzie v. McKenzie (1970) 3 AER 1034 CA, concerned divorce proceedings in which the husband petitioner was refused legal aid by the trial court. As an alternative he brought a barrister friend who was acting in an unofficial capacity into court to assist him with the legal technicalities.   The judge ruled that the husband could not have such an adviser, whereupon the latter left the court. On appeal the Court of Appeal held unanimously that 'every person has the right to have a friend present in court beside him, to assist by prompting, taking notes and quietly giving advice.'   A wide range of people might act as advisers, not just friends but also social workers, lawyers and law students. Hence the significance of the McKenzie ruling for clinical legal education programmes.

7 From 'Praxis 2', published by staff and students at the University of Kent Law School.   This particular edition of their

magazine carried no date or page numbers.
8   See, for example, the proposals for the reform of English legal
    education made in the Ormrod Report (i.e. Report of the
    Committee on Legal Education, Cmnd 4595, HMSO, London, 1971).
    One of the Committee's recommendations was that the possibility
    of running legal aid clinics 'should be explored'(para.185(17);
    see also para.135).
9   For empirical data in this connection see Miliband (1973),
    Abel-Smith and Stevens (1968) and Paterson (1974).
10 In this way the expanding market for law mirrors the way in
    which aid to the third world, though altruistic in a sense,
    actually aids the western capitalist powers by creating new
    markets where they can expand their trade and so their pros-
    perity. See Hayter (1969).
11 See Robson (1947, p.410):
    Society demands that its judges be biased in certain
    directions no less insistently than it demands that they
    shall be unbiased in others.   A man who had not a standard
    of moral values which approximated broadly to the accepted
    opinions of the day, who had no beliefs as to what is harm-
    ful to society and what beneficial, who had no bias in
    favour of marriage as aga'   . promiscuous sexual relations,
    honesty as against dece'., truthfulness as against lying;
    who did not think wealth better than poverty, orthodox
    religion preferable to atheism, courage better than coward-
    ice, constitutional government more desirable than anarchy
    would not be tolerated as a judge on the bench of any
    Western country.
    The following quotation from the judgment in Gee v. Freeman
    (1959) 16 Dominion Law Reports, p.74 illustrates the point
    well.
    A judge who tries a theft charge may be safely assumed to
    be against thefts.
12 McCrystal, Chester, Aris and Shawcross (1973) give this descrip-
    tion of him (pp.253-5):
    Ervin is not a cloakroom politician.   He is of Scots-
    Presbyterian stock and, like his father, spent most of his
    life practicing law in the little town of Morganton, a
    textile-mill and furniture-making community in the Blue
    Ridge foothills of the Appalachian mountains.   It is Bible-
    belt country, where religion and politics are unclouded by
    doubt and uncertainty.   But he is not quite the simple
    country lawyer he likes to pretend.   He graduated with
    honours from the Harvard Law School and became a member of
    North Carolina's Supreme Court.   But throughout his career,
    which now spans more than fifty years, he has clung fast to
    two guiding principles: a belief in the sanctity of
    individual rights and an abiding love of the Constitution
    of the United States, which he describes as 'the most
    precious possession of the American people.'
        He also has a rare eloquence derived from much reading
    and rereading of his three basic texts, the Constitution,
    the Authorized Version of the Bible, and the works of
    William Shakespeare....

He is a man for old verities rather than 'new guidelines'.
Films like 'Anatomy of a Murder' and 'The Klansman' and
programmes like 'Perry Mason' and 'Sutherland's Law' also
portray this image well.

13 Jackson (1975) makes similar points with respect to early law
and its relationship to religicus 'law'. See also here Dowrick
(1961).

14 The media's treatment of the final collapse of Cambodia and
Vietnam mirrored this exactly.

15 Madzimbamuto v. Lardner Burke (1966) General Division High
Court, Rhodesia.

16 See the Report of Enquiry into Allegations against the Security
Forces of physical brutality in Northern Ireland arising out of
events on 9 August 1971, Cmnd 4823, 1971.

17 See also the essays by Eckelaar and Finnis in Simpson (1973).

18 See also Kinoy (1971) and Black (1971).

19 For this sort of ideological view see Vile (1967), Hayek (1975)
and Friedrich (1968).

20 See Friedrich (1963, pp.200-6) for confusions in the notions of
authority, legitimacy and legality.

21 See Joseph (1975). In this pamphlet he exemplifies the ideas
that we have been describing. He says that law has become too
much of a 'political football' and argues for a bill of rights
standing outside of this arena and for less law.

22 Thus one might understand the degeneration of a 'workers' state'
in Russia because of the external pressures which made more
capitalistic arrangements necessary for survival. See Cliff
(1970).

23 See Tictin (1973).

24 See Cox (1975).

25 See also the speeches of various Conservatives about the
necessity of upholding the rule of law. In particular,
Hailsham, in a speech to the Devon Magistrates reported in
'The Times', 12 April 1972 and a speech to the Junior Carlton
Club, made shortly afterwards. Also Joseph (1975).

26 See also Tay and Kamenka (1971, 1973) for a description of this
move, which they see as a move to a bureaucratic-administrative
mode of law. Though this political and ideological move is
well catalogued, they, in common with Weber, see this as the
end point of legal development - new and more 'socialist' forms
being impossible.

27 See Tompkins and Anderson (1971) for an explanation of the
events at Kent State, where National Guardsmen shot students
demonstrating about the invasion of Cambodia, in terms of
'lack of communication'.

In the context of industry see the Labour government's plans
for 'industrial democracy'. See Winkler (1975) for an explanation of the political economy of these plans.

28 For a summary of the extent of these studies see Kutchinsky
(1973). There is also a world wide association for these
studies.

29 This ideological move from 'high' legality to the 'liberal'
form that we are documenting in this chapter has taken place
much earlier in eastern Europe. Here law has been much earlier
put into low profile. There are nationalized professions,

workers' courts, and informality.   They mark the movement in
those societies to forms of participation.   But, as analysis
of them shows, control is not given up by those who run the
society and official social science is, like here, concerned
with how to keep these fragile social systems going.   A leading
example in law is Podgorecki et al. (1973).   They manifest
then, an earlier stage of what is going on here.   The results
in law have been so bad as to force some to cry for a return of
the old style legality.   See also Tay and Kamenka (1971, 1973).

30   The point is here that this sort of activity is akin to 'expose'
criminology and other similar liberal manifestations.   For a
discussion of the use and limitations of such a criminology see
Taylor, Walton and Young (1975).   The problem is that for all
their attack on such expose criminology it is very difficult to
distinguish, at times, the political practice and the epistemological foundations of their own 'critical criminology'.   For
a fuller statement of this see Bankowski, Mungham and Young
(1975).

31   According to one study, 'In the short period since Claimants'
Unions began to come into existence, they have shown that poor
people, acting together in support of each others' claims can
win payments from the Social Security which would be refused
to individuals acting on their own behalf' (Jordan, 1973, p.20).
Chapter 2 of his book gives a detailed account of the origins
and genesis of one Claimants' Union.

32   See here: Illich (1975), Friedson (1972), Cannon (1972), Dennis
(1970).

33   See Linden (1971).   An example of this is in Hirwaun, where
the people of this village in Wales stopped, by force, the
installation of natural gas containers by the Gas Board.
Contrast this with the oil refinery at Canvey Island, where
the nuisance continues unabated.

34   See Churchman v. The Joint Shop Stewards' Committee of the Port
of London, 1972 2 AER 603, Midland Cold Storage v. Turner, 1972
2 AER 773, Midland Cold Storage v. Steen, 1972 2 AER 941.

35   Here again the strictures of expose criminology must be borne
in mind.   For a statement of what not to do see Hirst (1975).

36   See Anderson (1964) and Solidarity (1972).

37   See O'Neill (1972) for a discussion of the 'public' and 'private'
under capitalism.

38   See Taylor, Walton and Young (1975), and the critical comment
on them in Currie (1974).

CHAPTER 2   LEGAL PROBLEMS AND SOCIAL PROBLEMS

1   See Clairborne (1971).   His article is a critique of Alvin
Toffler's 'Future Shock', a book in the futurological mode which
attracted a lot of largely favourable reviews in the late 1960s.
Clairborne gives as an example of 'schlock' what he calls
'Rampant Reification', whereby 'conceptual abstractions are
transformed into causal realities'.   Thus Toffler (1971) speaks
of the 'moving current of change' as 'an elemental force' and of

'that great, growling engine of change - technology'.   Which
of course completely begs the question of what fuels the
engine and whose hand is on the throttle.

2 The texts reviewed are: Sir C.K. Allen (1958); Cross and
Hand (1971); P.S. James (1972); A.K.R. Kiralfy (1954);
O. Hood Phillips (1970); G. Williams (1969); G. Wilson (1973),
and M. Zander (1973).   Each of these texts is fully referenced
in the bibliography at the end of the book.

3 Mills (1963) asked this question in his seminal essay 'The
Professional Ideology of Social Pathologists', where he did a
content analysis of American textbooks on 'social problems' and
'social pathology'.   We have borrowed freely from his analytic-
al model in writing this chapter.

4 Midgley writes (1975):

It is possible to find in almost every secondary work on
Bentham(excepting certain 'specialisations') and every legal
history that attempts to account for legal developments
throughout the nineteenth century references to the
influences of Bentham.

While the near-deification ofBentham proceeded apace in legal
histories, there were others who approached his work in a more
sceptical spirit (Marx, 1928, p.671):

Bentham is a purely English phenomenon.   I do not even
except the German philosopher, Christian Wolfe, when I
declare that at no time and in no country has the most
trivial commonplace ever before strutted about with such
appalling self-satisfaction.   The principle of utility was
not discovered by Bentham.   He merely reproduced in a dull
and spiritliess fashion what Helvetius and other French
writers of the eighteenth century had said before him so
brilliantly.   To know what is useful to a dog we must study
dog nature.   This nature cannot be excogitated from the
principle of utility.   Applying the same considerations to
man, he that would pass judgement on all human activities,
movements, relations, etc., in accordance with the principle
of utility, must first become acquainted with human nature
in general, and then with human nature as modified in each
specific historical epoch.   But Bentham makes short work of
it.   In his arid and simple way, he assumes the modern
petty bourgeois, and above all the modern English petty
bourgeois, to be normal man.   Whatever seems useful to this
queer sort of normal man and to his world, is regarded as
useful in and by itself.   By this yardstick, Bentham
proceeds to measure everything past, present and to come.
For instance, the Christian religion is 'useful' because it
forbids that which the penal law condemns;   art criticism is
'harmful' because it disturbs worthy folk in their enjoyment
of Martin Tupper (a bad poet) and so on.... The good Bentham
has filled piles upon piles of books with rubbish of this
sort, his motto being 'no day without writing a few lines at
least.'   Had I the pluck of my friend, Heinrich Heine, I
should call Mr. Jeremy a genius in the way of bourgeois
stupidity.

5   As Weber himself acknowledged elsewhere, this is a somewhat
    over-simplified account of the factors that have determined the
    character of the English legal system.   Thus the particular
    constituents of English law were never entirely governed by
    structural changes in the economy, a powerful countervailing
    influence being the English legal profession itself.   In Weber's
    words:
       In England, the reason for the failure of all efforts at a
       rational codification of law, as well as the failure to borrow
       Roman law, was due to the successful resistance against such
       rationalisation offered by the great and centrally organised
       lawyers' guilds.... They retained in their hands juristic
       training as an empirical and highly developed technology, and
       they successfully fought all moves towards rational law that
       threatened their social and material position.... The pre-
       dominant reasons for the differences, which still exist, in
       the development of substantive law in England (and the
       Continent) do not rest upon this economic factor...these
       differences have sprung from the lawfully autonomous develop-
       ment of the respective structures of domination (Gerth and
       Mills, 1948, pp.217-18).
6   See, for example, the list of recommended 'general reading' for
    law students in Glanville Williams's book (1973), where social
    science is defined almost exclusively in terms of criminology
    and penology.
7   We can, perhaps, add a third assumption to the list.   Namely,
    the assumption of those who are committed to the idea that
    legal problems need to be multiplied, especially among the poor.
    According to this view, the eradication of poverty is reducible
    to having the problems of the poor defined as legal ones, and
    hence open to a final solution in courts of law.   Typical of
    the proponents of this view are Carlin and Howard, who have
    proposed
       that a distinctive characteristic of the poor, and an
       essential condition of their predicament, is their lack of
       participation in the legal and governmental process.   Thus
       the answer to the question of whether the poor have legal
       problems and need lawyers turns ultimately on the strength
       of our commitment to the extension of citizenship, for
       enfranchisement necessarily rests on the capacity to
       participate in and make effective use of the legal order -
       in our legal system, this means access to competent legal
       representation (1969, p.342).
    The trouble with this view - which is one especially popular
    among 'liberal' lawyers and any legal professional anxious to
    push law to the people - is (i) it implies that the balm of law
    is an effective antidote for the inequalities generated by
    basic structural cleavages in society, and (ii) that the 'law
    strategy' for conflict resolution and dispute settlement is the
    best.   Against the first inference we can cite the work of
    Kincaid (1973) on poverty and equality in Britain.   For him,
    and it is a view we share
       Poverty cannot be considered as a residual, historically
       determined defect of an otherwise fair society, but as

integral element that helps support a competitive social order.   It follows therefore that proposals to reduce poverty often involve very much more than technical and administrative problems.   They tend rather to raise issues of principle about the whole structure of society (p.24). And against the second inference we can cite the works of Morris and Lewis which are discussed in the main text of this chapter.

8   A good account of the complexity of such exchanges, viewed historically, is to be found in Samaha (1974); see especially the prologue and chapter 3.

9   The keen concern with material interest and monopolistic devices for protecting it, is nothing new among lawyers.   We find, for example, the following passage in Thomas's major study of types of religious belief and practice in sixteenth and seventeenth century England (1973):

> The parish clergyman did not merely preside over the formal occasion of religious worship.   He was also expected to be a guide and mentor to his parishioners.   When disputes broke out between the laity it was to him they were ideally referred.   It was often claimed that there were fewer law-suits in Catholic countries because their priests acted as arbiters for their flocks.   But the same ideal of clerical counselling was to be found in a Protestant environment. George Herbert expected the model parson to be a lawyer as well as a pastor: 'He endures not that any of his flock should go to law; but in any controversy that they should resort to him as their judge.'   Bishop Williams of Lincoln was praised by his biographer for arbitrating in contentious matters so as to avoid litigation; while Samuel Fairclough was only one of many Puritan ministers who were famous for making up quarrels between their parishioners.   Peace-making was a duty incumbent upon all brands of clergy. During the Civil War the lawyers in Parliament were said to have fallen out with their Presbyterian allies, 'not so much upon conscience, as upon fear that the Presbytery spoil their market, and take up most of the country pleas without law' (pp.182-3).

10   See chapter 8 of Becker's book for an elaboration of the distinction he makes between 'rule creators' and 'rule enforcers'. We should note that Becker's approach gives only a partial account of how rules are made and applied.   As Taylor (1973) has pointed out, Becker does not answer the fundamental question of why anyone wanted to introduce the Tax Act in the first place.

11   Consider, for example, some of the contemporary 'crusades' in Britain and North America against the pollution of the environ-ment by industrial effluent.   Such campaigns are invariably initiated by small groups of local activists (the 'moral crusaders') who may later be supported by some of the manufac-turers whose factories were the cause of the crusade in the first place.   But their primary interest in joining is not in a clean environment, but in the elimination of business competi-tors.   Thus, if anti-pollution measures become law, some firms may be better able to afford to implement them than others. This puts the non-complying company at risk, and thereby

strengthens the market position of its 'moral' competitor.   The
mosaic of a crusade is often a convenient blend of moral force
and personal advantage.   See also Paulus (1975) on this point.

12 We should note that the changing designation of drinking which
Gusfield describes reflects only a struggle for power and
influence among different groups of 'experts'.   What the
drinkers themselves thought is not recorded.

13 An excellent example of this phenomenon was the passing of the
1971 Industrial Relations Act.   For an account of the kind of
group values being restated in legal terms and enshrined in the
late Act, see E.P. Thompson's famous essay 'Sir, Writing by
Candlelight...' (1970).   Thompson describes there the reaction
of one influential segment of the 'community' to the strike of
the electricity power station workers in the winter of 1970.
It was a study, in Thompson's own words, of 'the epistolary
levée en masse of the readers of "The Times"' (p.1135).

14 The committee may well have been 'large and powerful', but it
is difficult to see how it could pass as a representative
sample of that 'growing public anxiety' Longford was so concerned to satisfy.   The committee had 53 members;   while the
House of Lords (7), churchmen (8), the education professions
(9) and senior executives in industry and commerce (10) were
well represented, delegates from the 'other public' were
conspicuous only by their absence.   There were, for example,
no manual or ordinary (i.e. non-professional) white-collar
workers on the committee, of either sex.

15 For a somewhat different view on the genesis and maintenance
of rules and laws in British and American society, see Rock
(1974).

CHAPTER 3   UP AGAINST THE LAW

1 Exactly how 'recent' are these innovations in legal servicing
is open to question.   For example Egerton (1945), in his
historical study of legal aid provision and reform, describes
what might be regarded as prototypes of the 'new' legal advice
and aid schemes, in operation well before the First World War.
It is clear from reading Egerton's book, that there has long
existed a caucus inside the legal profession who have favoured
projects designed to take the law and lawyers to the people.
Bearing this in mind we are left with the question - why is it
that only now has the old idea begun to attract much more
general support from among lawyers?   The leadership of the
legal profession - at both the national and the local level -
claim evidence of 'new attitudes' held by lawyers, of a new
sense of service and giving.   In this we try, on the basis of
our own empirical work on lawyers, to explain the genesis of
the 'new concern' in rather different terms, looking principally at changes in the work and market situation of segments
of the English legal profession.

2 The present Lord Chancellor has talked about increasing the
spread of legal services, in this way:
   (We must) extend legal services and, in particular, law

centres, as fast as funds will permit.... A further possible development in this field would be the greater use of duty solicitor schemes. These have the great merit of needing no further legislation, for their use is already envisaged in the Legal Advice and Assistance Act of 1972.... A number of local law societies have started such schemes outside London, and I hope that many more will be initiated as soon as possible (Hansard, pp.381-2, Thursday 21 March 1974, Parliamentary Debates, House of Lords).

3 The fieldwork for this study was completed in 1974. During that time we interviewed nearly all of the solicitors on the duty rota, magistrates' clerks, the stipendiary magistrate and policemen who worked regularly in and around the magistrates' courts, including the charge office and the cells. In addition, each duty solicitor was asked to fill in a report for detailing the number and type of cases he obtained through the scheme. Only a fragment of our findings are presented here. Again we would like to thank Phil Thomas for the major role he played at this stage of the work. The bulk of the material is currently being prepared by him and one of the authors for publication elsewhere.

4 The Law Society was founded in 1825. Since 1877 no person can be admitted as a solicitor unless they have passed exams held under the auspices of the Society. The Council of the Law Society has the power to make rules regarding professional conduct and to discipline erring solicitors. Provincial law societies work on somewhat similar lines, but will sometimes appeal to the Council for adjudication in local disputes. For a fuller account of the institutional links between the two, see Earl Jowitt, 'The Dictionary of English Law', London, Sweet & Maxwell, 1959.

5 It should not be thought that lawyers are the sole crusaders on behalf of the 'new law'. Social workers have also interested themselves in this area; hence the current climate of opinion in that profession which is highly favourable to courses and training in welfare rights and lay advocacy. Some of the reasons for, and implications of their participation, are described later in this chapter.

6 Lawyers are members of a segmental profession. This term, borrowed from the work of Bucher and Strauss, refers to the way in which:

In actuality, the assumption of relative homogeneity within the profession is not entirely useful: there are many identities, many values and many interests. These amount not merely to differentiation or simple variation. They tend to become patterned and shared; coalitions develop and flourish - and in opposition to some others.... We shall develop the idea of professions as loose amalgamations of segments pursuing different objectives in different manners and more or less delicately held together under a common name at a particular period in history (Bucher and Strauss, 1961, pp.325-6).

For an account of some of the factors which have helped to produce a segmental legal profession, with special reference to

the USA, see Rueschemeyer (1964). An abridged version of his
essay appears in Aubert (1971).

7   The use of the term 'hustler' is quite appropriate in this
context. We can illustrate two distinct facets of it through
the following example. The example refers to the particular
demands placed upon the lawyer who is engaged in hustling
work. In many ways his competence is connected with his legal
knowledge only indirectly and sometimes not at all. Instead,
interpersonal skills assume great importance, plus all the
energy that is required to set up contacts, to do the glad-
handing, to be accessible, to be known, to be thought of as
'a good bloke'. Because of this, many lawyers see this kind
of legal work as best done by younger men.

8   We can make this point another way by paraphrasing something
Veblen once said. Thus advocacy, as it is most commonly
demonstrated every day in magistrates' courts, bears about as
much relationship to the art of the great legal advocates as
bull-fighting does to agriculture.

9   Some support for our point about the undemanding character of
much advocacy work in the lower courts can be found in an
article by Platt and Pollock (1974) on the styles of work and
legal careers of public defenders in the American court system.
Many of the issues we raise in this chapter and later, in
chapter 4 -the reasons for the growth of legal services, the
implications for the relationship between the law, lawyers and
the state, etc. - are also discussed by them, and there emerges
a broad area of agreement between us.

10   Lawyers quite unconsciously - but very revealingly - will often
talk about 'ordinary people' and the law; a species apparently
quite distinct from that other branch of mankind, the lawyers.
The ordinary, in this context, is implicitly set against the
expert; the unknowing against those who know. And it is
further implied that it is both only sensible and possible for
the 'ordinary' to go on being 'ordinary', and for those who
'know' to administer on their behalf. This attitude was
captured perfectly in a television programme on 3 July 1975
on the workings of the jury system in England and Wales, where
eminent members of the legal profession, among them a former
Lord Chancellor and Louis Blom-Cooper QC, articulated these
sentiments exactly. For them the only good juror was a person
who was able to transcend his ordinariness, in order to become
like a lawyer.

11   This tendency has been observed elsewhere. See, for example,
Ferrari (1974).

12   See, for example, the work of Winkler and Pahl (1974), Winkler
(1975), Miller (1972) and Harris (1972).

13   The Narodniks were members of the non-Marxist intelligentsia
who originally hoped to accomplish the regeneration of Czarist
Russia by 'going to the people' ('narod'). According to one
account, the Narodniks saw 'the mission of (gifted) minorities
to lead the people towards higher ways of living...the duty of
the intellectual is to devote his life to giving back to the
people some part of the debt he owed them for his superior

opportunities' (Berdyaev, 1937, p.64).   Russian Narodniks of
all shades 'did not feel themselves an organic part of the
people; the people was to be found outside them.   Intellect
was not a function of the life of the people, it was broken
off from that life, and felt guilty in relation to people'
(Cole, 1954, p.55).

14   For a development of these points, but with reference to a
different substantive field, see Woolley (n.d.).

15   Wolfe coined this neologism to describe certain types of career
bureaucrats.   In a celebrated essay, 'Mau-Mauing the Flak
Catchers', he gives an account of a particular bureaucrat who
worked for the Office of Economic Opportunity in San Francisco.
An organizational lifer: a No.2 man whose job it was to keep
the hot issues and the dirty work away from the No.1 man.   As
Wolfe put in (1971, pp.132-3):

> This man is the flak catcher.   His job is to catch the flak
> for the No.1 man.   He's like the professional mourners you
> can hire in Chinatown.   They have certified wailers,
> professional mourners, in Chinatown, and when your loved one
> dies, you can hire the professional mourners to wail at the
> funeral and show what a great loss to the community the
> departed is.   In the same way this lifer is ready to catch
> whatever flak you're sending up.   It doesn't matter what
> bureau they put him in.   It's all the same.   Poverty,
> Japanese imports, valley fever, tomato-crop parity, partial
> disability, home loans, second-probate accounting, the
> Inter-state 90 detour change order, lockouts, secondary
> boycotts, G.I. alimony, the Pakistani quota, cinch mites,
> Tularemic Loa loa, veterans' dental benefits, workmen's
> compensation, suspended exercise rebates - whatever you're
> angry about, it doesn't matter, he's there to catch the
> flak.   He's a lifer.

The analogy we are pursuing here should not blind us to the fact
that in many magistrates' courts - especially ones where lay
magistrates are on the bench - the clerk is more often than not
the 'No.1 man', and any flak catching that might be done is not
done by him.

16   We examine courtroom encounters in more detail in the next
chapter.   We close discussion on this point, for the moment,
with this illustration of our thesis, taken from our fieldwork
notes.   A defendant was brought before the stipendiary magistrate on a charge of causing a death by dangerous driving.   He
was represented, on legal aid, by a solicitor.   On being brought
into court, the defendant sat in the dock, head bowed.   While
he was being ushered to the dock, his solicitor, the prosecuting
solicitor, the charge officer and the stipendiary went in to a
huddle, whispering the facts of the case among themselves.
After this had gone on for three or four minutes the defendant,
clearly under great strain, leapt to his feet shouting, 'I can't
hear!   I can't hear!'   The stipendiary, breaking from the
huddle to deal with the interruption, smiled at the man and
said, 'Don't worry Mr -, this needn't concern you - it's only
legal stuff.'

17   We are grateful, in what follows, to Tony Balmer who kindly let
us see his unpublished dissertation. See Balmer (1974).

CHAPTER 4 A POWER ELITE: THE LEGAL PROFESSION IN PROCESS

1 The relevance of Marshall et al. lies in the way in which their
   ideas appear today in the guise of the reformist rhetoric of
   the liberal and radical lawyer. Both of these are similarly
   committed to making the world a better place through the
   instrument of the caring profession.
2 The processes of selection for pupillage and articles are of
   crucial importance here. Students who wish to practise as a
   barrister will first have to read in the chambers of a junior
   barrister. This is known as pupillage and a year's pupillage
   is obligatory for those who intend to practise in England.
   For a fuller discussion of the formal mechanisms involved, see
   Williams (1973, pp.164-80). Williams also provides a useful
   account of the formal steps involved in getting articles,
   which are a pre-requisite for students who want to enter the
   solicitors' branch of the legal profession. The point about
   articles and pupillage is that it is not at all clear as to
   why some applicants are preferred to others. Some clues are
   offered by Williams (1973, p.183): 'Finding a suitable firm
   for articles is not easy if you have no friends or relatives
   who are in a position to help.' What we lack at present is
   any research on the details of these processes of selection.
   For example, what criteria of 'suitability-unsuitability' are
   employed? Who is deemed to be good 'lawyer material' and
   why? What part is played by nepotism and patronage?
3 Yet another example of the effect rendered by this particular
   form of social distancing is given in Wincott's (1974) book.
   His book is a personal memoir of the 1931 Invergordon naval
   mutiny. One of the problems faced by the rebellious sailors
   was in getting information about what tactics their officers
   were likely to use in trying to contain or suppress the rising.
   Wincott, in the passage below, describes some of the useful -
   for the sailors - unintended consequences of naval officers
   viewing certain types of sailors as servants, as non-persons:
       But we had our sources of information too, and they enabled
       us to counter any manoeuvre of the officers throughout the
       strike. Officers' servants and messengers were lower deck
       men like us, and every meeting of officers a servant or
       messenger was nearby. Nobody taught them to creep around
       in cinema spy style - they were simply overlooked. It was
       the old story that the officers did not count them for
       anything and talked quite freely in their presence (p.96).
   The main point here, of course, as with the examples we cited
   in the text, is that the practice of social distance is not
   based upon personal prejudice or idiosyncracy (though these may
   produce special effects in specific instances), but flows
   instead from inequalities of power, status and resources
   between men.
4 The importance of language, etiquette and form is no new
   discovery, in this context. Ross writes (1969, p.112):
       trial and sentence should...enjoy...ceremonial backing,
       because court procedure may be made a powerful means of
       intimidating both accused and onlookers. 'Our magistrates,'

observes Pascal, 'are well aware of this mystery. Their
scarlet robes, the ermine in which they wrap themselves like
furred cats, the halls in which they administer justice, the
fleurs-de-lis, and all their august apparatus, are most
necessary.'

5 According to Blumberg (1969, p.322):

The institutional setting of the court defines a role for
the defense counsel in a criminal case radically different
from the one traditionally depicted. Sociologists and
others have focused their attention on the deprivations and
social disabilities of such variables as race, ethnicity,
and social class as being the source of an accused person's
defeat in a criminal court. Largely over-looked is the
variable of the court organisation itself, which possesses
a thrust, purpose, and direction of its own. It is grounded
in pragmatic values, bureaucratic priorities, and administrative instruments. These exalt maximum production and the
particularistic career designs of organisational incumbents,
whose occupational and career commitments tend to generate
a set of priorities. These priorities exert a higher claim
than the stated ideological goals of 'due process of law',
and are often inconsistent with them.

6 The interview with the policeman concerned was part of a research
programme we undertook into innovations in legal servicing. The
organization of the programme, and some of the findings, are
explained in chapter 3; see note 2.

7 For another application of the 'market-model', this time with
reference to the genesis of the 'radical sociologist', see
Mungham and Pearson (1972). It should be understood that we
are not arguing a reductionist thesis here; we are not suggesting that lawyer radicalization can be simply reduced to changes
in the market situation of lawyers.

8 The Socio-Legal Group of the Society of Public Teachers of Law
is one such structure. Some of the debates in this group are
cast in the terms that we have described. The alternatives are
seen as either to liberalize, by staying within the law, or to
radicalize, by dropping out of it. Radicalizing as a law
teacher is not mentioned. The issue is further complicated by
the same rhetoric being used in a debate as to what the sociology of law means. Here 'radical' means merely the adoption of
a social science perspective.

9 See Bankowski, Mungham and Young (1975) where this analysis is
applied to criminologists.

CHAPTER 5 EPISTEMOLOGY AND OPPRESSION

1 This is well portrayed in the prevailing vision of the future
as the same as the present but bigger. 'Bigger is better' is
the ideological message of this sort of technological society.
Thus the film '2001: A Space Odyssey' shows a radical future
as consisting of Hilton Hotels in space. In politics, this
progression to scientific rationality is shown in the idea
that politics is really the slow but steady progression to Roy

Jenkins, Jeremy Thorpe, Willie Whitelaw and men of that ilk.
2 For elaboration of these points see Habermas (1972) and (1974).
3 This is the cultural form in which debates in our society take place. A vivid example of this occurred on the Robin Day phone-in programme about the Common Market (BBC radio, 20 May 1975). On this particular programme Callaghan was answering questions. He was asked by one 'phoner' about when householders could expect to be sent pamphlets setting out the pros and cons of entry. Callaghan replied that soon the government would be distributing to every household three such pamphlets; one from the pro-market lobby telling us to say 'Yes', an anti-lobby one saying 'No' and one from the government recommending that we stay in the market. The 'phoner' then said that this wasn't really fair - since it meant that the case for staying in was presented twice, whereas the case for coming out was carried only in a single publication. Not so, says Callaghan. The government is neutral in the matter. It has decided, on the facts available, to recommend to the British people that Britain stay in the market. Unlike the two lobbies referred to, the government, Callaghan continued, seeks only to be fair and to give good advice. There is apolitical debate about the issue, and there exists, over and above that, the authoritative declaration of government, made after 'careful consideration of the best facts available'.

   This shows how 'facts' and 'science' are used to give the state a neutral stance - when it manifestly is not neutral - as an independent arbiter of decisions. For an elaboration of this form of debate in the media see Williams (1974).
4 For an extended discussion of the epistemological issues raised here see Bankowski, Mungham and Young (1975).
5 Quoted by Taylor (1973, p.18).
6 See Sachs (1973).
7 For a description of the inquisitorial system see Merryman (1969). Briefly, in the French criminal law, it is a system whereby the police enquiry is directed by an examining magistrate, (the juge d'instuction) - a neutral official who then goes on to see if there are to be further proceedings.
8 For this point of view see Wootton (1959).
9 Here see the work of the 'liberal empiricists', especially Cornish (1971) and Zander (1973).
10 See Kuhn (1962), Barnes (1972) and (1974) and Eccleshall (1975).
11 Jay (1973) gives a good account of this point as developed in the 'critical theory' of the Frankfurt School.
12 See the manifesto of the European Group for the Study of Deviance and Social Control, paragraph 1 of which states:
   The dominant mode of analysis of crime, deviance and social control, as represented in research literature and policy practice, consists of variants of positivism: a concentration on the collection of criminal statistics and the attempt to characterise criminal and deviant acts as the products of psychologically defective and 'abnormal' personalities. Agencies of social control are studied in an uncritical way or from the point of view of how to make them more effective. The control perspective dominates comparative criminological

research;   in individual countries and in international
organisations such as the Council of Europe, official and
governmental agencies are funding research and expecting
academics to provide findings which will help to improve
methods and techniques of social control.

13   See Dashwood (1972) for a liberal's eye-view of this trial.

14   Lambert (1971) and Banton (1964) show well how the police can
create expectations of violence in this way.

15   See Rose and Rose (1970), and Dickson (1974). See also the
'Radical Science Journal', 1 and 2.

16   There are also conservative attacks on Mark and the CLRC which
basically say that everything is all right and nothing needs to
be changed. This can only be explained by supposing that these
critics are so insulated by a legal reality that they do not
realize that the world as they know it is, is suffering from
attacks. For this sort of view see MacKenna (1972).

17   This again is seen in Mark (1973) and in various interviews
given by him to the press, especially the 'Observer', 23 March
1975. He claims that 'some lawyers put defences into the mouths
of their clients' and thus subvert the 'natural reality' of the
trial. The plea here is to let those who know - in this case
the police - get on with the job.

> I do not really understand that question. The police
> probably have more experience of crime, criminals and
> criminal trials than anyone else. They alone, for example,
> see the 60 per cent of crime which is not cleared up. Of
> course, their views are not necessarily to be given undue
> weight. But should they not be heard? Is the suggestion
> that the ability to think about their problems and to
> express themselves publicly is in some way a threat to civil
> rights? They do not, after all, play any part in enacting
> the laws, in assessing guilt, or determining punishment.
> They seem to me to have not only the right but a duty to say
> whether the system they are required to operate is, in their
> view, fair to all concerned and reasonably satisfactory as a
> protection for society.

The links with scientism are also shown for:

> .... The more effective the system of investigation and
> trial in determining the truth (rather than technical guilt
> in criminal issues), the fewer police would be required.
> A simple example of this can be seen in the present employ-
> ment of traffic wardens and the fixed penalty system. If
> it were possible to introduce a really effective fixed
> penalty system, with severe punishment for those who defied
> it, the number of traffic wardens and the amount of the
> fixed penalty could both be reduced.
>   A number of police will always be required for preventive
> purposes and for the many social tasks only indirectly
> related to the criminal law. But the number required for
> enforcement purposes will always be determined to some
> extent by the acceptability and effectiveness of the laws
> they enforce.

Of course, such systems, involving highly sophisticated surveillance techniques of 'suspects' very loosely defined, mark a massive diminution in civil liberties.

18 See Arnison (1974). Here building workers were charged with conspiracy to intimidate within the terms of s.7 of the Conspiracy and Protection of Property Act (1875).

19 See Bankowski (1973a) for an elaboration of this argument. This point is further supported by the Prevention of Terrorism (Temporary Provisions) Act 1974. Section 2(1) of which comes close to saying that a member of a prescribed organization is to be defined by the material and literature that he has in his possession.

20 See Garfinkel (1967, pp.104-15).

21 'Up Against the Law', a radical magazine published irregularly for defendants, said of the jury in this and the Mangrove trial:

Obviously you've got to fight for a working class jury. The court is an arena of class conflict....

For example, in the Mangrove trial, which had a mixed middle and working class jury, the middle class ones were the ones who stood out for conviction all the way down the line, and had to be fought tooth and nail inside the jury room before agreeing to acquittals in all riot charges.

With a working class jury you stand a very much better chance, although you have to expect and will have to deal with the fact that within the ranks of the jury, both individually and collectively, there is both hostility to the system and at the same time, a certain deference to authority, which is reinforced by the court structure and the judge.

In the Stoke Newington 8 trial, the first major defence application which was successful was to have the judge ask the jury if they felt prejudiced beforehand, and to dis-qualify themselves if they belonged to the Tory party, had relatives in the police, army or had interests in any of the companies or places that had been bombed....

Meanwhile, the jury has to be coaxed, encouraged and cajoled into understanding the use of law in the class war. Tell them that justice comes first - what they feel is right is what counts. The judge will hate this. Fine! Let the judge hate it. And let the judge show whose side he's on. That way it's much easier for the jury to acquit, once they appreciate how much the judge is leaning on them to arrive at an impartial verdict of guilty (no.4, p.34).

Note especially how the law attacks the jurors that step out of line and thus prevents the interjection of the political into the case. Thus it is no longer possible to ask of the jury the sort of questions that were asked in the Stoke Newington Trial. Lord Widgery has ruled that questions may only be put to jurors to find if they have a fairly direct interest in the case, as opposed to general political prejudice. This was also shown by Hailsham who, when Lord Chancellor, abolished the right to know the occupation of the jurors. 'Coincidentally' this was done just before the Shrewsbury trial.

22 See the Northern Ireland (Emergency Provisions) Act 1973. One
    of its provisions abolished trial by jury for scheduled offences,
    the reason being that it was unsafe to try terrorists in front
    of jurors. For an analysis of this Act see Tansey (1975).
        The BBC TV programme, 'Man Alive' (3 July 1975), did a
    documentary which reflected the great unease felt by lawyers,
    and others, about the jury system.
23 See Palmer (1971) for an account of this trial. The accused
    were charged with publishing obscene material, the magazine
    'Oz'.
24 See Bankowski (1973b) for an elaboration of this argument.
25 This is also shown by Platts-Mills in his attack on expert
    witnesses and expert evidence in the trial of the Uxbridge
    Eight - eight Irishmen who were charged with causing various
    explosions in Uxbridge and London. In his examination of
    Smith, a civilian fingerprint officer from New Scotland Yard,
    he forced to be made known publicly what previously had only
    been made known, in confidence, to selected members of the
    legal profession. This was the fact that a new technique of
    lifting fingerprints could also be used to 'plant' them as
    incriminating evidence. One of the accused, Cornelius McFadden,
    used this as a defence. In court this was brought out by
    counsel for the defence, Platts-Mills, in his cross-examination
    of Smith, the 'official' fingerprint expert. The following
    extract shows his, and the judge's (Melford-Stevenson's)
    reluctance to accept this line of questioning.
        Platts-Mills: This has been done only with a powdered
        finger. I want to show that you can lift an unpowdered
        fingerprint and that it will light up and become perfectly
        visible.... Do you think that we can do it together, only
        powdering it when we have got the planted one? [no answer]
        Are you willing to try?
        Judge: Try what?
        Platts-Mills: Putting a fingerprint, or whatever you choose
        to put, but not powdering it at all but simply making the
        perspiration mark.
        Smith: My Lord, do you think this is in the best interests
        of justice, to demonstrate this to a court full of people?
        Judge: No, I don't think it is. Nor do I think it is very
        relevant but I am not going to stop it.
        Platts-Mills: What you are saying is that you think that
        with knowledge that fingerprints could be lifted and then
        planted somewhere else, undermines the confidence reposed
        in fingerprints and therefore it is not in the best interests
        of justice that it should be done. Is that what you are
        saying?
        Smith: I feel that any sort of demonstration of this nature
    could encourage criminals to indulge in this sort of thing.
        Mr. Platts-Mills made the point to the jury that the
    prosecution had brought no evidence to show that it would
    have been impossible to plant the timing device with its
    fingerprint in the van because the police had the van under
    observation at all times. He argued that, first, it was
    scientifically possible to lift and plant a fingerprint, and

secondly there had been ample opportunity for someone to
have placed the timing device with its planted print in his
client's van.

   He never suggested who this 'someone' might be, and he
resisted accusations from the judge that he was, in effect
if not in fact, accusing the police of this. The police
certainly see it this way. They argue that it would be
difficult, if not impossible, for someone without finger-
printing experience to find the print he wanted, lift it
without damaging it, and plant it so as to fool an expert.
Therefore, they say, the main candidate would be a fingerprint officer.

   But, the police say, to prevent such an occurrence, the
fingerprint branch has such a system of checks and counter
checks that for any such plant to take place there would
have to be a conspiracy involving nearly all the senior
officers. The branch is made up of 350 civilians and only
11 police officers - who are being phased out. Chief
Superintendent Lambourne says: 'I would put the odds against
a fingerprint officer getting away with planting a fingerprint at ten million to one' ('Sunday Times', 23 March 1975).
The vindicating of fingerprint evidence is, of course, important
to the prosecution because of the important part they play in
securing convictions in British trials.

26 For an analysis of the dangers of the notion of the deviant as
   authentic see Young (1975). He also shows what the political
   consequences of the conception of the deviant as analytically
   central to 'the new deviancy' were.

27 See Beresford Ellis (1968) and 'Planet 12' (1972).

28 Thus such actions can actually politicize the debate by showing
   it in terms of class war and not in terms of a consensus. It
   is in this way that the election of Thatcher as leader of the
   Conservative party will re-politicize British politics. It
   will force the divides and not, as Heath did latterly, the
   agreement of 'reasonable' men, to be emphasized.

29 See Habermas (1972).

30 This can best be seen in the rise and fall of the 'underground'
   and the 'politics of bohemia'. These politics were predicated
   upon a world of abundance - capitalism continuing to be able
   to deliver the goods. As the political economy declined so did
   these politics. The reality of the world had caught up and led
   either to a liberal stance which said: 'How can I survive in a
   world that is basically unliveable in' or to political practices
   which moved from the quasi-anarchist politics of the day to
   organizations which could more realistically cope with the
   declining political economy of western capitalism and the
   dangers and challenges that that would bring.

31 This tension is also exhibited by the 'conservative' radical
   lawyers as Pritt (1973, p.39):

      the primary object of a good political defence is not to win
      the case - although victory, if it should perchance come, is
      very welcome and useful - but to maintain and propagate the
      client's political point of view. One must never sacrifice
      or compromise principles for the sake of winning (or even

securing a shorter sentence). Such a defence as: 'My
client is a young man who was carried away by his enthusiasm;
he now knows better and will not do such a thing again', is
quite inadmissible. It is vital to justify the accused's
action politically....

32 See Berrigan (1971).

33 Thus, the trial of the nine IRA bombers was brought to chaos
after the process was over and sentencing due:
> Shouts, jeers and handclapping greeted the sentences, which
> totalled to 117 years. The uproar came from the dock and
> the crowded public gallery. And the trial was halted on
> the judge's orders while the police escorted wives and girl-
> friends of the accused men out of the Birmingham Crown
> Court. Meanwhile the men in the cells were taken back to
> the docks amid shouts of 'Up the Peoples' Army'. The
> protest began when Donegal born Stephen Blake told the
> court: 'We are here to free our country from the plague
> that has haunted us for the past eight hundred years'.
> Others in the dock applauded backed by a chorus of cheers
> and handclapping from the public gallery ('Sun', 3 May 1975).

34 In the trial of members of the Scottish Workers' Party one of
the accused, just before the end of the trial, dismissed his
counsel and made a statement after sentencing.
> He said that what had brought him to the court was violence
> against the working class, the same violence that had put
> 150,000 persons out of work in Scotland and led to children
> again suffering from rickets.... Lord Dunpark again inter-
> rupted, You must not make a political speech. Lygate then
> said that people could not get work so that their only alter-
> native was to join the army and fight in Ulster and murder
> Irishmen and women. Lord Dunpark said that violence in
> Ireland had nothing to do with the sentence to be passed on
> Lygate. Lygate went on to talk about the oppression of the
> working class and said that a day would come when those who
> judged him and his fellow accused would themselves be judged.
> Lygate and McPherson raised their arms in a clenched fist
> salute and shouted - Long live the Workers of Scotland
> ('Glasgow Herald', 21 March 1972).

35 Here the accused were charged with criminally conspiring to
further the aims of the Army of the Provisional Government of
Scotland - the defence took the line that this was the laughable
antics of idiots. It was only after sentencing that it became
clear that they were deadly serious.
> Yesterday, Mr. Lionel Daiches, QC, summing up for William
> Anderson, one of the accused still charged with conspiracy,
> poured ridicule on the charge, and brought smiles around the
> court as he conjured up a spectacle of co-accused Major
> Frederick Boothby and General Amin of Uganda 'marching side
> by side at the head of a piebald army of ebony Highlanders
> in tartan tiger skins, to the sound of jungle drums and
> bagpipes to capture Achnashellach.'
> Mr. Daiches had already been told by Lord Keith that one
> charge against his client of conspiring to blow up labour
> exchanges had lacked corroboration.... 'Or', he added amid

renewed laughter, 'they may have taken the view that these documents being fed to them by Boyd indicated a sort of Crazy Gang who regularly attend a Mad Hatter's tea party, or purely were the result of fantasy and rubbish.'

'What is the APG?' he asked. 'Nobody has the slightest idea as to what this organisation is, whether it exists any more or if it exists at all. What is its strength? Wherein does it operate? Who are its troops? Where are its offices? Who is its librarian? Who is its Chancellor of the Exchequer?'

A similar line had been taken earlier by Mr. Herbert Kerrigan, defence counsel for William Murray. He said that from the indictment the jury might have believed that the whole nation was personally threatened....

'As the evidence has come out there have been some sinister aspects,' he said, 'but there have also been aspects which rival any farce which has been presented in the Citizens' theatre here in Glasgow or any theatre throughout the country.'.... In a long statement issued through his solicitor after he was sentenced, Anderson said that the APG had been wounded but 'when the time does come the people of Scotland need never doubt its readiness and ability to answer the nation's call.'

The Establishment had attempted to abort the birth of an emergent people but 'the poignant cry of life has been heard the world over. Those imprisoned have sacrificed their families and perhaps face the end of their free lives, but the nation begins its hope for freedom and justice' ('Scotsman', 23 and 24 May 1975).

36 This happened in 1945 when some anarchists were charged under the defence regulations ('Wildcat', 1, no date).

None of the accused liked the way their case was presented. Marie Louise in particular wanted to defend herself and did not want to rely on the technicalities of the law for an acquittal. On the other hand, if the object of the whole proceedings was to silence the Freedom Press it would have been foolish to strike intransigent attitudes and get, in consequence, far longer sentences. In the event, she and George Woodcock were able to carry on the work of the paper during the period when their comrades were in jail.... The defence solicitor was a man named Rutledge, who was over-shadowed by his clerk, the genial and flamboyant Ernest Silverman, a tragic character most of whose life was spent in prison for innumerable cases of petty embezzlement (he later died in Parkhurst serving a long sentence of preventive detention). The Freedom Press trial was probably his finest hour. He was certainly a good and honest friend to the defendants, and they in later years made great efforts to alleviate his lot. Ernest briefed some very eminent barristers: John Maude (later a Tory MP and a judge) to defend Hewetson and Richards, Derek Curtis Bennett for Marie Louise, and James Burge for Philip Sansom. Here of course were the tactical dilemmas for anarchists. Having engaged an expensive defence you put yourselves in their hands, and the defence line was that here were four upright citizens

(Richards was working as a civil engineer at the time and
Hewetson was casualty officer at Paddington Hospital)
putting forward their idealistic point of view with no
intention of causing disaffection....

For such lawyers being a communist is something that does not
impinge on the way that they act legally, though it influences
the people for whom they fight. In court they are lawyers to
a man. See Blake's (1975) attack on Platts-Mills. The writer
goes on to ask if the tactics were correct. In so doing he
brings out the dilemma of revolutionaries. Are they individuals
'prepared to face martyrdom for a cause, or for its propaganda
effect' or are they 'a group of people with a functional task
to perform'? In this case he sides with the latter view,
concluding that it is better to have 'Freedom Press' published.

37 They were charged with conspiracy to cause explosions and were
one of the run-ups to the Angry Brigade Trial.

38 We quote snatches of the dialogue:

Here D.C. Doyle, one of the prosecution witnesses, was being
cross-examined as to the true nature of some of the 'incriminating' documents that the defendants were alleged to have in
their possession. The cross-examination was wide-ranging and
covered police functions, police corruption and police relations
with the private security industry.

M: Macdonald (Defence Counsel)
D: D.C. Doyle

   M So that is something else that might be found out about
isn't it? What the relation is between the police force
and Securicor?

   D Yes.

   M And if you were investigating Securicor - because that's
one of the matters in these documents - you would want,
would you not, to find out who runs the firm and how it
was organised; if you were looking at Securicor's social
functions?

   D That's not necessarily so....

   M Well, if you were only concerned with robbery with
Securicor, it wouldn't really concern you who was a
director of it, would it?

   D No.

   M On the other hand, if you were concerned with who runs the
organisation, what sort of people they are, what other
interests they have, whether they are directors of other
companies, if and whether they are ex-police officers,
that is the sort of thing you would want to find out?

   D Again, that depends....

   M Yes, if your interests are that you want to see the
function which Securicor firms play, and what kind of
people they are who run them, then you would want to find
out who the directors are, what connections they had with
industry, whether they were managing directors of other
firms, whether they are ex-police officers; wouldn't you?

John Barker (B) x Doyle (D)

   B This morning you were asked a lot of questions about the

names and addresses of police officers being written down.

D   Yes.

B   And I think you said that you couldn't think of any good reason why people should want to do that.

D   Yes.

B   Well, for example, if you suspected that a detective sergeant at West End Central, earning £2,000 a year, owned a £30,000 house in the outer suburbs of London, if you thought that, that might prompt you to find out the address and go and look at it.

D   No.

B   No? You wouldn't think there was anything suspicious about that?

D   No...he might have money of his own.

B   So you would in fact assume that he would have money of his own, you wouldn't be curious or interested at all?

D   I would assume he was honest like all police officers are....
                          (laughter)

B   Would you include the police officers in the recent Saor Eire trial in that definition?

Justice James: You needn't answer that question; it has nothing to do with this case at all.

B   Well I think that it is a relevant question since the reply has just been given that all police officers are honest.

James: I've told you that it is not a proper question, Mr. Barker.

B   So does that mean that you certainly wouldn't have the same idea - the same belief - when you are talking, say, about young people with long hair - you wouldn't say that all young people with long hair were honest, would you?
(Bulletin No.4 of the Stoke Newington Eight)

36   See Arnison (1974) here. This book shows how the defence was conducted. The lawyers for the defence are seen more as brilliant lawyers scoring legal points against overwhelming odds than part of a disaffected defence collective. Again there is a plea for 'scientism': 'facts' are presented and the jury is left with the task of deciding the truth after direction from the judge.
   Do they ever get all the facts? Do they ever get the whole truth and nothing but the truth? Are there not times when neither the prosecution nor the defence want the whole truth? Each side is trying to win a case, but, (especially in political trials), it is useless to pretend that a process is going on where a real investigation is being carried out in order to determine the truth (p.54).

40   Four out of the eight charged were acquitted. The defence was conducted so as to (a) select a working class jury, (b) attack scientific evidence, (c) provide a mixed defence strategy - the lawyers being forced to respect decisions of the defence collective, (d) invite the jury to ask questions directly - this was ruled against, but a lot of pertinent questions were asked through the judge, (e) attack police motives and psychology, (f) relate the defence to their political opposition to the state:

The defendants opened up their lives to the jury. They
carefully explained the whys and wherefores of their class
opposition to the state. They were so successful in getting
jury support on purely political matters, e.g. their
research against the notorious Freshwater property tycoons,
that Mathews made a big point of summing up for the prosecution against any 'feelings' influencing the jury's verdict.

Mathews told the jury, 'it matters not what your feelings
may be about capitalist landlords'...whilst conceding that
such companies may not be very savoury features of our
society, Mathews was saying, - stick strictly to the law,
members of the jury - even though the law protects precisely
these property tycoons. There is no hypocricy like courtroom hypocricy. Always make the jury understand the charade
that it is.

They turned the conspiracy on it's head, and told the
jury about the conspiracy of bosses, cabinet ministers,
prosecutors and judges to find scapegoats for the Angry
Brigade, and to protect their property with every ruthless
means at their disposal.

The defence prevented the prosecution from gaining the
victory the establishment expected. And with a little more
luck, all 8 would have been acquitted ('UPAL', 2, p.39).

41 The trial was forgotten by the British press until the results
were announced and could be interpreted in a consensual way.
Thus the trial was normal and the defendants were 'irrational',
'drug crazed', 'hippies', etc. For example:

Cannabis and LSD were a vital part of the scene. Money and
other possessions were considered communal property. Sex
was free and easy. Very free. Very easy. A man who
fancied a girl resident could easily have her favours. The
same went for a girl who fancied a man. Or a girl who
fancied a girl.... In these unsavoury surroundings, the
disgruntled of all nations met and chatted through the night
about revolutions of the past...and revolutions still to
come ('Sun', 7 December 1972).

42 Another example is John Maclean who in April 1918 was arrested
for sedition.

This time he defended himself. Asked whether he was guilty
or not guilty, he replied 'I refuse to plead!' and asked
whether he wished to object to any members of the jury, he
replied, 'I object to the whole lot of them!' He addressed
the jury for 75 minutes: 'I am not here as the accused; I
am here as the accuser of capitalism dripping with blood
from head to foot.' He was sentenced to five years' penal
servitude.

In July he went on hunger strike, was forcibly fed, and
his health was permanently broken. With the end of the war
and the approach of the general election, the authorities
decided to release him - in December ('Wildcat', 1, no date).

43 See here the attack on Platts-Mills and others in the Uxbridge
Eight trial. After the conviction Melford Stevenson, the judge,
praised the bomb squad officers:

He said: 'They have endured with dignity and courtesy the

wild accusations of fraud, forgery, and general dishonesty
which have been flung at them from the witness box without
any practical basis.'

Mr. Justice Melford Stevenson then turned to the defence
counsel. Their duty, he said, was not discharged by slavish
subservience, to what were called clients' instructions.
The client was entitled in addition to the judgment and
experience of members of the Bar in conducting his defence.

'Counsel are, or should be, something more than a mere
loudspeaker to a maladjusted set. One would have hoped that
that judgment and experience would have spared the police
and their witnesses the insulting suggestions made in this
case. It has been a mudslinging defence,' he said.

The judge suggested that legal aid for costs incurred in
the form of defence he had been criticising should be dis-
allowed. His remarks, welcomed by all the policemen in
court, will also be welcomed by Sir Robert Mark, Commissioner
of the Metropolitan Police, who has repeatedly criticised
defence lawyers who make allegations against the police while
defending accused persons ('Guardian', 20 March 1975).
Certainly this seems an odd attack as Platts-Mills has himself
been the subject of attack by more radical lawyers. See Blake
(1975). His conduct here was more in the nature of good cross
examination of the prosecution expert witnesses (see note 25).
He was in fact defended by the Bar Council who almost attacked
Stevenson by name and the 'Guardian' said: 'to the outside
observer the trial of the eight Irishmen has all the marks of
the Bar maintaining its exemplary tradition of defending even
the worst offenders.' On the other hand many of the lawyers
who, on our analysis, take part in more political defences have
been attacked quite severely by their professional associations.
Apparently at a recent Bar Council A.G.M. the then Attorney-
General made remarks to the effect that the Bar could not
tolerate defence lawyers treating trials politically; what
amazing impudence for a member of the capitalist Conservative
cabinet to state that it was the defendants who were bringing
politics into the courtroom; having dragged the defendant
into the dock the state now wishes to limit what he can say
there. This impertinent threat should be totally rejected
by all lawyers who see their duty as representing their
client rather than being a neutral mediator or interpreter
between the state and the defendant (Blake, 1975, p.7).
This illustrates the point we make in chapter 4 that to be
radical and be a lawyer, the pressures are tremendous to be
'really' professional.

Another example is the trial of the Baader Meinhof gang.
Here there is no bourgeois distinction at all. The trial
struggle was also clearly linked to their political activities
outside. The lawyers were so much of a problem that a bill
had to go through the Bundestag to exclude certain of them from
the court proceedings.

44 See Stevenson's attack on Platts-Mills (note 43). See also
    Palmer (1971) for the way in which Argyle's handling of the
    case prevented the work that Leary, the prosecutor, was doing
    in defusing it.

BIBLIOGRAPHY

ABEL-SMITH, B. and STEVENS, R. (1968), 'In Search of Justice',
London: Allen Lane.
ALLEN, A.F. (1963), 'Poverty and the Administration of Federal
Criminal Justice', Report of the Attorney General's Committee,
Washington DC, Government Printing Office.
ALLEN, C.K. (1958), 'Law in the Making', Oxford: Clarendon Press.
ANDERSON, A. (1964), 'Hungary 56', London: Solidarity.
ANDREWS, W. (ed.) (1963), 'Constitutions and Constitutionalism',
New Jersey: Nostrand.
ARNISON, J. (1974), 'The Shrewsbury Three', London: Lawrence &
Wishart.
AUBERT, V. (ed.) (1971), 'Sociology of Law', Harmondsworth: Penguin.
AUDEN, W.H. (1966), 'Collected Shorter Poems', London: Faber &
Faber.
BALMER, T. (1974), 'The Origin and Genesis of Neighbourhood Law
Centres in England and Wales', unpublished dissertation, Department
of Sociology, University College, Cardiff.
BANKOWSKI, Z. (1973a), What Is a Group?, Paper read to the Assoc-
iation for Legal and Social Philosophy, University of Edinburgh,
April.
BANKOWSKI, Z. (1973b), Pornocracy, 'Cambrian Law Review', pp.22-9.
BANKOWSKI, Z. and MUNGHAM, G. (1974), Warwick University Ltd.
Continued, 'British Journal of Law and Society', vol.1, no.2,
pp.179-84.
BANKOWSKI, Z., MUNGHAM, G. and YOUNG, P. (1975), Radical Criminology
or Radical Criminologists?, unpublished Ms, Universities of Cardiff
and Edinburgh.
BANTON, M. (1964), 'The Policeman in the Community', London:
Tavistock.
BARBER, B. (1972), 'Superman and Common Man', Harmondsworth: Penguin.
BARNES, B. (1974), 'Scientific Knowledge and Sociological Theory',
London: Routledge & Kegan Paul.
BARNES, B. (ed.) (1972), 'The Sociology of Science', Harmondsworth:
Penguin.
BARTHES, R. (1973), 'Mythologies', London: Paladin.
BECKER, E. (1972), 'The Birth and Death of Meaning', Harmondsworth:
Penguin.

166

BECKER, H. (1963), 'Outsiders: Studies in the Sociology of Deviance', New York: Free Press.

BERDYAEV, N. (1937), 'The Origin of Russian Communism', London: Centenary Press.

BERESFORD ELLIS, P. (1968), 'Wales, A Nation Again', London: Tandem.

BERGER, P. and LUCKMANN, T. (1969), 'The Social Construction of Reality', London: Allen Lane.

BERRIGAN, D. (1971), 'Trial of the Catonsville Nine', Boston: Beacon Press.

BETTELHEIM, B. (1970), 'The Informed Heart', London: Paladin.

BINNS,   (1973), The Marxist Theory of Truth, 'Radical Philosophy', 4, pp.3-10.

BLACK, D. (1972), Boundaries of Legal Sociology, 'Yale Law Journal', vol.81, pp.1086-100.

BLACK, J. (1971), 'Radical Lawyers', New York: Avon.

BLAKE, N. (1975), The Role of the Radical Lawyer, 'Haldane Society Bulletin', vol.2, no.2, pp.3-8.

BLOM-COOPER, L. (ed.) (1975), 'Progress in Penal Reform', Oxford University Press.

BLUMBERG, A. (1969), The Practise of Law as a Confidence Game, in Aubert (1971), pp.321-31.

BLUMBERG, A. (1970), Lawyers with Convictions, in A. Blumberg (ed.), 'The Scales of Justice', Chicago: Aldine, 1970, pp.51-68.

BLYTHE, R. (1964), 'The Age of Illusion', Harmondsworth: Penguin.

BUCHER, R. and STRAUSS, A. (1961), Professions in Process, 'American Journal of Sociology', vol.66, pp.325-34.

CANNON, C. (1972), Social Workers: Training and Professionalism, in T. Pateman (ed.), 'Counter Course', Harmondsworth: Penguin, 1972.

CARLIN, J.E. and HOWARD, J. (1971), Legal Representation and Class Justice, in Aubert (1971), pp.332-50.

CASTRO, F. (1968), 'History Will Absolve Me', London: Jonathan Cape.

CHOMSKY, N. (1969), 'American Power and the New Mandarins', Harmondsworth: Penguin.

CLAIRBORNE, R. (1971), Future Schlock, 'Nation', 25 January, pp.117-20.

CLEAVER, E. (1970), 'Soul on Ice', London: Panther.

CLIFF, T. (1970), 'Russia: A Marxist Analysis', London: Pluto Press.

COATES, K. and SILBURN, R. (1970), 'Poverty: The Forgotten Englishmen', Harmondsworth: Penguin.

COGLEY, J. (ed.) (1963), 'Natural Law and Modern Society', New York: World Publishing.

COHEN, S. (1973a), Protest, Unrest and Delinquency: Convergences in Labels and Behaviour, 'International Journal of Criminology and Penology', vol.1, no.2, pp.117-28.

COHEN, S. (1973b), 'Folk Devils and Moral Panics', London: Paladin.

COHEN, S. (ed.) (1971), 'Images of Deviance', Harmondsworth: Penguin.

COKE, LORD (1817), 'Institutes of the Laws of England', London: Hargrave & Butler.

COLE, G.D.H. (1954), 'Socialist Thought: Volume II - Marxism and Anarchism 1850-1890', London: Macmillan.

CORNISH, W. (1971), 'The Jury', Harmondsworth: Penguin.

COTTERELL, R. and WOODCLIFF, J. (1974), The Teaching of Jurisprudence in British Universities, 'Journal of the Society of Teachers of Public Law', vol.13, pp.73-89.

COUNCIL OF THE LAW SOCIETY (1969), 'Second Memorandum on Legal Advice and Assistance', London.

COX, A. (1975), Watergate and the U.S. Constitution, 'British Journal of Law and Society', vol.2, no.1, pp.1-13.

CRIMINAL LAW REVISION COMMITTEE (1972), 'Eleventh Report: Evidence General', London: HMSO, Cmnd 4991.

CROSS, Lord and HAND, G.J. (1971), 'Radcliffe and Cross: The English Legal System', London: Butterworth, fifth edition.

CURRIE, E. (1974), Beyond Criminology - A Review of the New Criminology, 'Issues in Criminology', vol.9, p.139.

DASHWOOD, A. (1972), Juries in a Multi-Racial Society, 'Criminal Law Review', pp.85-94.

DAVIES, J.G. (1972), The Magistrate's Dilemma, 'Planet 12', pp.46-58.

DENNIS, N. (1970), 'People and Planning', London: Faber & Faber.

D'ENTREVES, A.P. (1970), 'Natural Law', London: Hutchinson.

DEVLIN, P. (1956), 'Trial By Jury', London: Stevens.

DICKSON, D. (1974), 'Alternative Technology', London: Fontana.

DICKSON, D.T. (1968), Bureaucracy and Morality: An Organisational Perspective on a Moral Crusade, 'Social Problems', vol.16, pp.143-56.

DIMBLEBY, J. (1971), The Oz Trial, 'New Statesman', 30 July, pp.144-6.

DONALDSON, J. (1972), 'The Times', 11 November.

DOWRICK, F. (1961), 'Justice According to the English Common Lawyers', London: Butterworth.

ECCLESHALL, B. (1975), Technology and Liberation, 'Radical Philosophy', 11, pp.9-16.

EGERTON, R. (1945), 'Legal Aid', London: Routledge & Kegan Paul.

ENGELS, F. (1920), 'The Condition of the Working Class in England in 1844', London: Allen & Unwin.

EPSTEIN, J. (ed.) (1970), 'The Great Conspiracy Trial', New York: Random House.

EVERTON, A.R. (1972), 'Law as a Liberal Study', London: Butterworth.

FARNSWORTH, D.L. (1957), 'Mental Health in College and University', Cambridge, Mass.: Harvard University Press.

FARRAR, J.H. (1974), 'Law Reform and the Law Commission', London: Sweet & Maxwell.

FERRARI, V. (1974), Some Sociological Implications Concerning Legal Aid Reform in Italy, 'British Journal of Law and Society', vol.1, no.1, pp.81-3.

FEUERBACH, L. (1841), 'The Essence of Christianity', trans. G.Eliot, New York and London: Harper & Row, 1966.

FRANCIS COMMITTEE (1971), 'Report of the Committee on the Rent Acts', London: HMSO, Cmnd 4609.

FRANK, J. (1950), 'Courts on Trial', Princeton University Press.

FRIEDRICH, C. (1963), 'The Philosophy of Law in a Historical Perspective', University of Chicago Press.

FRIEDRICH, C. (1968), 'Constitutional Government and Democracy', Waltham, Mass.: Blaisdell.

FRIEDSON, E. (1972), 'The Profession of Medicine', New York: Dodd, Mead.

FULLER, L. (1969), 'The Morality of Law', New Haven: Yale University Press.

GARFINKEL, H. (1955), Conditions of Successful Degradation Ceremonies, 'American Journal of Sociology', vol.61, pp.420-4.
GARFINKEL, H. (1967), 'Studies in Ethnomethodology', Englewood Cliffs, New Jersey: Prentice-Hall.
GERTH, H.H. and MILLS, C. WRIGHT, (1948), 'From Max Weber', London: Routledge & Kegan Paul.
GIBSON, T. (1970), Toward a Libertarian Criminology, 'Catalyst', pp.55-8.
GOFFMAN, E. (1971), 'The Presentation of Self in Everyday Life', Harmondsworth: Penguin.
GOLDMAN, A. (1944), 'In Defence of Socialism', New York: Pioneer Publications.
GRIFFITH, J. (1975), Judges and a Bill of Rights, 'New Statesman', 10 January, pp.38-9.
GUSFIELD, J.R. (1967), Moral Passage: The Symbolic Process in Public Designations of Deviance, 'Social Problems', vol.15, pp.175-88.
HABERMAS, J. (1972), 'Knowledge and Human Interests', London: Heinemann.
HABERMAS, J. (1974), 'Theory and Practice', London: Heinemann.
HAKMAN, N. (1971), Old and New Left Activity in the Legal Order, 'Journal of Social Issues', vol.27, no.1, pp.105-21.
HALMOS, P. (1970), 'The Personal Service Society', London: Constable.
HARRIS, N. (1972), 'Competition and the Corporate State', London: Methuen.
HART, H.L.A. (1961), 'The Concept of Law', Oxford: Clarendon Press.
HAYDEN, T. (1970), 'Trial', New York: Holt, Rinehart & Winston.
HAYEK, F. (1975), 'Law, Liberty and Legislation', London: Routledge & Kegan Paul.
HAYTER, T. (1969), 'Aid as Imperialism', Harmondsworth: Penguin.
HELLER, J. (1964), 'Catch-22', London: Corgi.
HIRST, P.Q. (1975), Marx and Engels on Crime, Law and Morality, in Taylor, Walton and Young (1975), pp.203-32.
HONORE, A. (1967), Reflections on Revolutions, 'Irish Jurist', pp.268-78.
HOOD PHILLIPS, O. (1970), 'A First Book of English Law', London: Sweet & Maxwell, sixth edition.
HOROWITZ, I.L. and LEIBOWITZ, M. (1968), Social Deviance and Political Marginality, 'Social Problems', vol.16, pp.280-96.
HUGHES, E.C. (1971), 'The Sociological Eye: Selected Papers on Work, Self and the Study of Society', Chicago: Aldine-Atherton.
IFANS, M. (1972), The Courts and the Police, 'Planet 12', pp.9-16.
ILLICH, I. (1972), 'De-Schooling Society', New York: Harper & Row.
ILLICH, I. (1975), 'Medical Nemesis: The Expropriation of Health', London: Calder & Boyars.
JACKSON, B. (1975), From Dharma to Law, 'American Journal of Comparative Law', vol.23, pp.490-512.
JACKSON, R.M. (1967), 'The Machinery of Justice in England', Cambridge University Press, fifth edition.
JAMES, P.S. (1972), 'Introduction to English Law', London: Butterworth, eighth edition.
JAY, M. (1973), 'The Dialectical Imagination', London: Heinemann.
JENKINS, P. (1974), Portrait of a Presidency, 'New Statesman', 17 May.

JOHNSON, T. (1973), 'Professions and Power', London: Macmillan.
JONES, H.W. (1967), 'Law and the Social Role of Science', New York: Rockefeller University Press.
JORDAN, B. (1973), 'Paupers: The Making of a New Claiming Class', London: Routledge & Kegan Paul.
JOSEPH, K. (1975), 'Freedom Under the Law', London: Conservative Political Centre.
KAFKA, F. (1967), 'Metamorphosis', Harmondsworth: Penguin.
KALVEN, H. and ZEISEL, H. (1966), 'The American Jury', Boston: Little, Brown.
KAUPEN, W. (1970), The Relationship of the West German People to Law and the Institutions of Law, unpublished MS.
KAUPEN, W. (1971), Public Attitudes to Law and Legal Institutions in West Germany, 'Anwaltsblatt', no.3, March.
KAUPEN, W. (1973), Public Opinion of Law in a Democratic Society, in Podgorecki (1973), pp.43-64.
KAYE, J. (1973), Irish Prisoners, 'New Society', 6 September, pp.565-6.
KINCAID, J.C. (1973), 'Poverty and Equality in Britain', Harmondsworth: Penguin.
KING, M. (ed.) (1973), 'Guilty Until Proved Innocent?', London: Release Lawyers Group.
KINOY, A. (1971), The Role of the Radical Lawyer and Teacher of Law, in Lefcourt (1971), pp.276-99.
KIRALFY, A.K.R. (1954), 'The English Legal System', London: Sweet & Maxwell.
KOLAKOWSKI, L. (1971), 'Marxism and Beyond', London: Paladin.
KUHN, T. (1962), 'The Structure of Scientific Revolutions', University of Chicago Press.
KUTCHINSKY, B. (1973), The Legal Consciousness, in Podgorecki (1973), pp.101-38.
LAING, R.D. (1972), 'Knots', Harmondsworth: Penguin.
LAMBERT, J. (1971), 'Crime, Police and Race Relations in Birmingham', Oxford University Press.
LAW COMMISSION, (1973), 'Working Paper 1950 (Inchoate Offences)', London, HMSO.
LAW SOCIETY, (1974), Legal Aid in Tribunals: The Law Society's View, 'New Law Journal', vol.24, 2 May, pp.399-400.
LEFCOURT, R. (ed.) (1971), 'Law Against the People', New York, Vintage.
LEMERT, E. (1970), 'Social Action and Legal Change', Chicago: Aldine.
LEOVINGER, L. (1966), Law and Science as Rival Systems, 'University of Florida Law Review', vol.19, pp.530-51.
LEVINE, M. (ed.) (1971), 'The Tales of Hoffman', New York: Bantam.
LINDEN, A. (1971), Tort Law as Ombudsman, 'Canadian Bar Review', pp.154-68.
LLEWELLYN, K.N. (1960), 'The Common Law Tradition', Boston: Little, Brown.
LLEWELLYN, K.N. (1962), 'Jurisprudence', University of Chicago Press.
LONGFORD, Lord (ed.) (1972), 'Pornography: The Longford Report', London: Coronet.
LUKACS, G. (1971), 'History and Class Consciousness', London: Merlin Press.

McCABE, S. and PURVES, R. (1972), 'The Jury at Work', Oxford: Blackwell.

McCRYSTAL, C., CHESTER, L., ARIS, S. and SHAWCROSS, W. (1973), 'Watergate: The Full Inside Story', London: Deutsch.

MACDONALD, D. (1971), Introduction, in Levine (1971), pp.xviii-xix.

MacKENNA, B. (1972), Criminal Law Revision Committee's Eleventh Report: Some Comments, 'Criminal Law Review', pp.605-21.

McLELLAN, D. (1973), 'Karl Marx: His Life and Thought', London: Macmillan.

MADDISON, S. (1973), Mindless Militants? Psychiatry and the University, in Taylor and Taylor (1973), pp.111-35.

MARCUSE, H. (1969), 'Essay on Liberation', Harmondsworth: Penguin.

MARK, R. (1973), Minority Verdict, 'Listener', 8 November.

MARRIS, P. and REIN, M. (1972), 'Dilemmas of Social Reform', Harmondsworth: Penguin.

MARSHALL, T.J. (1963), 'Sociology at the Crossroads', London: Heinemann.

MARX, K. (1928), 'Capital', vol.1, Moscow: Foreign Languages Publishing House.

MARX, K. (1946 edn), 'Selected Works', vol.1, London: Lawrence & Wishart.

MARX, K. and ENGELS, F. (1848), 'Manifesto of the Communist Party', in 'Marx-Engels Selected Works', vol.1, London: Lawrence & Wishart, 1950; also Moscow: Foreign Languages Publishing House, 1951.

MATZA, D. (1964), 'Delinquency and Drift', New York: Wiley.

MERRYMAN, J. (1969), 'The Civil Law Tradition', Stanford University Press.

MESZAROS, I. (1972), 'Marx's Theory of Alienation', London: Merlin Press, third edition.

MIDGLEY, S. (1975), Some Comments on Legal History, unpublished MS, Department of Public Law, University of Edinburgh.

MILIBAND, R. (1973), 'The State in Capitalist Society', London: Quartet.

MILLER, A.S. (1972), Legal Foundations and the Corporate State, 'Journal of Economic Issues', vol.6, no.1, pp.59-79.

MILLS, C. WRIGHT (1963), The Professional Ideology of Social Pathologists, in I.L. Horowitz (ed.) 'Power, Politics and People', Oxford University Press (1963), pp.525-52.

MORRIS, P. (1973), Access to What? To Whom? And Why?, paper read at the International Sociological Association, Sociology of Law Research Committee meeting, Cambridge University, September.

MORRIS, P. and ZANDER, M. (1973), The Allocation of Criminal Legal Aid in Magistrates' Courts - a Study in London Courts, 'Law Society's Gazette', vol.70, 3 October, p.2372.

MORRIS, P., WHITE, R. and LEWIS, P. (1973), 'Social Needs and Legal Action', London: Martin Robertson.

MORRIS COMMITTEE (1965), 'Report of the Departmental Committee on Jury Service', London: HMSO, Cmnd 2627.

MUNGHAM, G. (1975), Social Workers and Political Action, in H. Jones (ed.) (1975), 'Towards a New Social Work', London: Routledge & Kegan Paul.

MUNGHAM, G. and PEARSON, G. (1972), Radical Action and Radical Scholarship, Paper read at the Eleventh National Deviancy Symposium, University of York, 18-19 September.

NAGEL, S. (1969), 'The Legal Process from a Behavioural Perspective', Homewood, Illinois: Dorsey Press.
O'NEILL, J. (1972), 'Sociology as a Skin Trade', London: Heinemann.
PALLEY, C. (1972), Decision Making in the Area of Public Order by English Courts, in R. Finnegan et al. (eds.) 'Public Order', Bletchley: Open University Press, (1972), pp.45-83.
PALMER, T. (1971), 'The Trials of Oz', Manchester: Blond & Briggs.
PARKER, H. (1974), 'Views From the Boys', Newton Abbot: David & Charles.
PARSONS, T. (1939), The Professions and the Social Structure, 'Social Forces', vol.17, pp.457-67.
PATERSON, A. (1974), Judges: A Political Elite?, 'British Journal of Law and Society', vol.1, no.2, pp.118-35.
PAULUS, I. (1975), 'The Search For Pure Food: A Sociology of Legislation in Britain', London: Martin Robertson.
PERELMAN, C. (1963), 'The Idea of Justice and the Problem of Argument', London: Routledge & Kegan Paul.
PLATT, A. and POLLOCK, R. (1974), Channeling Lawyers: The Careers of Public Defenders, 'Issues in Criminology', vol.9, no.1, pp.1-31.
PODGORECKI, A. et al. (1973), 'Knowledge and Opinion About Law', London: Martin Robertson.
POWELL, M. (1973), 'Below Stairs', London: Pan Books.
PRITT, D. (1973), 'Law in Class and Society: Volume 3', London: Lawrence & Wishart.
RADCLIFFE, Lord (1960), 'The Law and Its Compass', Cambridge University Press.
RAVETZ, J. (1973), 'Scientific Knowledge and its Social Problems', Harmondsworth: Penguin.
RENNER, KARL (1949), 'The Institutions of Private Law and Their Social Function', London: Routledge & Kegan Paul (new edn, 1976).
ROBERTSON, G. (1973), 'Whose Conspiracy?', London: National Council for Civil Liberties.
ROBSON, W. (1947), 'Justice and Administrative Law', London: Stevens.
ROCK, P. (1973), 'Deviant Behaviour', London: Hutchinson.
ROCK? P. (1974), The Sociology of Deviance and Conceptions of Moral Order, 'British Journal of Criminology', vol.14, pp.139-49.
ROSE, H. (1973), Who Can De-label the Client? Welfare Rights from the Claimants' Perspective, 'Social Work Today', vol.4, no.13, 20 September, pp.409-13.
ROSE, H. and ROSE, S. (1970), 'Science and Society', Harmondsworth: Penguin.
ROSS, E.A. (1969), 'Social Control', Cleveland: Press of Case Western Reserve University.
RUBIN, J. (1970), 'DO IT! Scenarios for the Revolution', London: Jonathan Cape.
RUBIN, J. (1971), 'We are Everywhere', New York: Harper & Row.
RUESCHEMEYER, D. (1964), Doctors and Lawyers: A Comment on the Theory of the Professions, 'Canadian Review of Sociology and Anthropology', pp.17-30.
RUMBLE, W.(1968), 'American Legal Realism: Scepticism, Reform and the Judicial Process', Ithaca: Cornell University Press.
SACHS, A. (1973), 'Justice in South Africa', London: Heinemann.
SAMAHA, J. (1974), 'Law and Order in Historical Perspective', New York and London: Academic Press.

SCARMAN, L. (1974), 'English Law - The New Dimension', London: Stevens.
SCHWENDINGER, H. and SCHWENDINGER, J. (1975), Defenders of Order or Guardians of Human Rights, in Taylor, Walton and Young (1975), pp.113-46.
SELZNICK, P. (1963), Natural Law and Sociology, in Cogley (1963).
SELZNICK, P. (1965), Sociology of Law, 'International Encyclopedia of the Social Sciences', Berkeley, California: Macmillan.
SHONFIELD, A. (1965), 'Modern Capitalism', Oxford University Press.
SIMONS, B. and SMITH, J. (1972), Prospects for a Radical Legal Profession, paper read at the Eleventh National Deviancy Symposium, University of York, 18-19 September.
SIMPSON, A. (ed.) (1973), 'Oxford Essays in Jurisprudence', Oxford: Clarendon Press, second series.
SKOLNICK, J. (1966), 'Justice without Trial', New York and London: Wiley.
SKOLNICK, J. (1967), Social Control in the Adversary System, 'Journal of Conflict Resolution', vol.II, pp.52-70.
SOLIDARITY (1972), 'Workers' Councils', London: Solidarity.
SOLZHENITSYN, A. (1974), 'The Gulag Archipelago', London: Fontana.
SPARER, E. (1971), The Right to Welfare, in N. Dorsen (ed.), 'The Rights of Americans: What They Are - What They Should Be', New York: Pantheon, 1971.
STEDMAN-JONES, G. (1971), 'Outcast London', Oxford: Clarendon Press.
STERNBERG, D. (1972), The New Radical-Criminal Trials: A Step towards a Class-for-itself in the American Proletariat?, 'Issues in Criminology', vol.8, pp.274-301.
SZASZ, T. (1975a), 'Law, Liberty and Psychiatry', London: Routledge & Kegan Paul.
SZASZ, T. (1975b) 'Ideology and Insanity', Harmondsworth: Penguin.
TANSEY, R. (1975), An Analysis of the Northern Ireland Emergency Provisions Act 1973, 'Haldane Society Bulletin', vol.2, no.2, pp.8-17.
TAY, A. and KAMENKA, E. (1971), Beyond the French Revolution: Communist Socialism and the Concept of Law, 'University of Toronto Law Review', vol.21, pp.109-40.
TAY, A. and KAMENKA, E. (1973), Beyond Bourgeois Individualism: The Contemporary Crisis in Legal Ideology, paper read at the World Congress on Philosophy of Law and Social Philosophy, Madrid, 7 September.
TAYLOR, I. and TAYLOR, L. (1973), 'Politics and Deviance', Harmondsworth: Penguin.
TAYLOR, I., WALTON, P. and YOUNG, J. (eds) (1975), 'Critical Criminology', London: Routledge & Kegan Paul.
TAYLOR, L. (1973), 'Deviance and Society', London: Nelson.
THOMAS, K. (1973), 'Religion and the Decline of Magic', Harmondsworth: Penguin.
THOMPSON, E.P. (1968), 'The Making of the English Working Class', Harmondsworth: Penguin.
THOMPSON, E.P. (1970), Sir, Writing by Candlelight..., 'New Society', 24 December, pp.1135-6.
THOMPSON, E.P. (ed.) (1970), 'Warwick University Ltd.', Harmondsworth: Penguin.

TICTIN, H. (1973), The Political Economy of the Soviet Intellectual, 'Critique', no.2, pp.5-21.
TOFFLER, A. (1971), 'Future Shock', London: Pan Books.
TOMPKINS, P.K. and ANDERSON, E.V.B. (1971), 'Communication Crisis at Kent State', New York: Gordon & Breach.
TWINING, W. (1974), Some Jobs for Jurisprudence, 'British Journal of Law and Society', vol.1, no.2, pp.149-74.
VILE, M. (1967), 'Constitutionalism and the Separation of Powers', Oxford: Clarendon Press.
VINKE, P. (1970), Attitudes to Certain Aspects of Taxation, unpublished MS, University of Leiden.
VINKE, P. and VAN HOUTTE, J. (1973), Attitudes Concerning the Acceptance of Legislation among Various Social Groups, in Podgorecki (1973), pp.13-42.
WALKER, M.G. and WALKER, R.G. (1972), 'The English Legal System', London: Butterworth, third edition.
WEBER, M. (1965), 'The Protestant Ethic and the Spirit of Capitalism', trans. T. Parsons, London: Allen & Unwin.
WESTERGAARD, J. (1972), Sociology, the Myth of Classlessness, in R. Blackburn (ed.) 'Ideology in Social Science', Harmondsworth: Penguin, 1972.
WEXLER, S. (1970), Practicing Law for Poor People, 'Yale Law Journal', vol.79, pp.1049-67.
WILLIAMS, G. (1973), 'Learning the Law', London: Stevens, ninth edition.
WILLIAMS, R. (1974), 'Technology and Cultural Form', London: Fontana.
WILSON, G. (1973), 'Cases and Materials on the English Legal System', London: Sweet & Maxwell.
WINCOTT, L. (1974), 'Invergordon Mutineer', London: Weidenfeld & Nicolson.
WINKLER, J. (1975), Corporatism, 'British Journal of Law and Society', vol.2, no.2.
WINKLER, J. and PAHL, R. (1974), The Coming Corporatism, 'New Society', 10 October, pp.72-6.
WOLFE, T. (1971), 'Radical Chic and Mau-Mauing the Flak-Catchers', New York: Bantam.
WOLFF, R. (1970), 'In Defence of Anarchism', New York: Harper & Row.
WOOD, A.K. (1971), The Marxian Critique of Justice, 'Philosophy and Public Affairs', pp.249-82.
WOOLLEY, T. (n.d.), The Politics of Community Action, 'Solidarity', vol.6, no.9, pp.5-14.
WOOTTON, B. (1959), 'Social Science and Social Pathology', London: Allen & Unwin.
YOUNG, J. (1975), Working Class Criminology, in Taylor, Walton and Young (1975), pp.63-94.
ZANDER, M. (1973), 'Cases and Materials on the English Legal System', London: Weidenfeld & Nicolson.
ZANDER, M. (ed.) (1970), 'What's Wrong With the Law?', London: BBC Publications.

INDEX

73